An Abundance of Graces

◆

Reflections on Sacrosanctum Concilium

Pamela Jackson

HillenbrandBooks

Chicago / Mundelein, Illinois

AN ABUNDANCE OF GRACES: REFLECTIONS ON SACROSANCTUM
CONCILIUM © 2004 Archdiocese of Chicago: Liturgy Training Publications,
1800 North Hermitage Avenue, Chicago IL 60622-1101; 1-800-933-1800,
fax 1-800-933-7094, e-mail orders@ltp.org. All rights reserved. See our
website at www.ltp.org.

Hillenbrand Books is an imprint of Liturgy Training Publications (LTP) and
the Liturgical Institute at the University of Saint Mary of the Lake (USML).
The imprint is focused on contemporary and classical theological thought
concerning the liturgy of the Catholic Church. Available at bookstores everywhere, or through LTP by calling 1-800-933-1800 or visiting www.ltp.org.
Further information about the **Hillenbrand Books** publishing program is
available from the University of Saint Mary of the Lake/Mundelein Seminary,
1000 East Maple Avenue, Mundelein, IL 60060 (847-837-4542), on the
web at www.usml.edu/liturgicalinstitute, or e-mail litinst@usml.edu.

Cover © The Crosiers/Gene Plaisted, OSC.

Printed in the United States of America.

Library of Congress Control Number: 2004107701

ISBN 1-59525-003-4

HABUND

"In order that the Christian people may more surely derive
an abundance of graces from the liturgy, the Church desires
to undertake with great care a general reform of the liturgy itself."
Sacrosanctum Concilium 21

Contents

Preface   vi

Part I:
Sacrosanctum Concilium's Understanding of the Liturgy   2

Part II:
The Nature of the Reforms   10

Part III:
Toward a Fuller Implementation   26

Notes
Part I   65
Part II   68
Part III   74

◆

Appendix
Sacrosanctum Concilium   86
Pius X, *Tra le sollecitudini*   116
Pius XII, *Mediator Dei*   124

Preface

In the fall of 2002, after a long conversation, a friend who is a physician and faithful Catholic told me I should write an article "about why they changed the liturgy." My experience as a seminary professor and conference speaker led me to recognize immediately that an article explaining *why* Vatican II's Constitution on the Sacred Liturgy *(Sacrosanctum Concilium)* called for liturgical reform would meet an increasing need, especially as the Constitution's fortieth anniversary drew near. But by the time most of the work on the article was done a few months later, it had become an essay too lengthy to publish in its entirety in a journal. Also, since a number of the points made were based on comparisons of quotations from original texts of Church documents, I wanted to provide the relevant Latin citations in footnotes so that readers who were interested could see what led to my conclusions, and the kind of documentation I wanted to add would make the work even longer.

As I considered the best way to make the essay available, I realized that readers could come to an even deeper understanding of *Sacrosanctum Concilium* if it were easier for them to consult the texts of some of the key documents that helped prepare the way for it, as well as the Constitution itself. In his 1903 *Motu Proprio* on Church music, *Tra le sollecitudini*, Pope Pius X spoke of the importance of active participation in the liturgy, a conviction that became central to the reform called for by *Sacrosanctum Concilium.* Yet the reader who wanted to see how this concern for active participation was part of its original context would have difficulty finding a copy of an English translation of *Tra le sollecitudini* in print. Similarly, in the course of my research I saw how much of *Sacrosanctum Concilium* was based on the theology of Pius XII's milestone encyclical on the liturgy, *Mediator Dei* (1947), and needs to be understood in light of it. While a careful reading of *Mediator Dei* would allow readers to discover for themselves the relationship between the two documents, *Mediator Dei*, also, was not easily available for purchase.

The present volume thus includes with the essay *An Abundance of Graces* the texts of *Sacrosanctum Concilium, Tra le sollecitudini,* and *Mediator Dei.* Since most of the work on the essay was completed before the promulgation of *Ecclesia de Eucharistia,* it does not cite either that encyclical or Pope John Paul II's recent Apostolic Letter on Sacred Liturgy on the Fortieth Anniversary of *Sacrosanctum Concilium.* However, in that Apostolic Letter, the pope calls for an "examination of conscience" concerning the reception of *Sacrosanctum Concilium* and how deeply it has been assimilated in the life of the Church, and it is my hope that this volume can assist in such reflection.

An Abundance of Graces has been written for all who are seeking a deeper understanding of the meaning of the liturgy and why it was reformed. In the final part of the essay, I consider which aspects of *Sacrosanctum Concilium* might still be more fully implemented so that the liturgical reform it set in motion might bear yet more of the fruit of spiritual renewal it was intended to bring. In writing that final section, I have had in mind especially my former students, now young priests, who have taken to heart the Council's admonition that in order for the desired renewal to become a reality they must be "thoroughly imbued with the spirit of the liturgy and make themselves its teachers," who are constantly seeking new insight into how to enable those they serve to meet Christ in the liturgy.

An Abundance
of Graces

Part I

Sacrosanctum Concilium's
Understanding of the Liturgy

On December 4, 1963, the Constitution on the Sacred Liturgy, *Sacrosanctum Concilium*, was approved by the Second Vatican Council in a vote of 2,147 to 4. It was the first document produced by Vatican II, and in promulgating it, Pope Paul VI noted that "the liturgy was the first subject to be examined and the first, too, in a sense, in intrinsic worth and in importance for the life of the Church."[1] In 1985 the Final Report of the Extraordinary Synod of Bishops would speak of the reforms of the liturgy that had resulted from *Sacrosanctum Concilium* as "the most visible fruit of the whole work of the Council,"[2] and for many Catholics the now-old "new liturgy" is the main thing that symbolizes for them the post–Vatican II Church.

But *why* did the Council call for changes to be made in the liturgy? Both those who lived through the transition and younger Catholics who have attended liturgy workshops can list what the major changes were and supply reasons for them. Yet a careful reading of *Sacrosanctum Concilium* reveals that the popular understandings of the reasons for the changes do not reflect the depth of the Council's vision of the liturgy, nor why that vision led it to call for liturgical reform. In hindsight, it appears that in the heady rush toward a "renewed liturgy," constructing and implementing that liturgy ended up taking priority over clearly communicating all of the Council's intentions in authorizing it, and that in the catechesis that did take place, some parts of *Sacrosanctum Concilium* were emphasized at the expense of others, while some key aspects were neglected.

The fortieth anniversary of the Constitution's promulgation rightly calls for celebration of the good that has come from the liturgical reforms it set in motion.[3] As part of this celebration, a commemoration worthy of *Sacrosanctum Concilium* also invites a close reading of the text, to consider whether yet more good could come from a more complete understanding of all that the Council had hoped would be accomplished through it. As a contribution to such commemoration, this essay will reflect on the Constitution in light of three questions: 1) What is *Sacrosanctum Concilium's* vision of what is actually "going on" in the celebration of the liturgy, of the purpose for which the liturgy was given to the Church? 2) What is the nature of the changes in the way the liturgy is celebrated that the Council Fathers call for so that the liturgy can better fulfill this purpose? 3) What aspects of *Sacrosanctum Concilium* do not appear to have yet received the attention they deserve?

The sources of Sacrosanctum Concilium

Before turning to the text of the Constitution, it is important to recall that it did not suddenly appear out of nowhere, but was the culmination of over a hundred years of research, reflection, writing, and pastoral work of the Liturgical Movement.[4] Some of the hallmark themes of *Sacrosanctum Concilium* that are immediately identified with it, and some of the very phrases that are instantly recognized as found in it, had in fact already appeared in earlier Church documents inspired by the Liturgical Movement. Leo XIII's *Mirae caritatis* (1902) spoke of the eucharistic liturgy as the "font and most important gift" of all God's gifts;[5] later, Pius XII would refer to it as the "font and center of Christian piety," the "chief action of divine worship."[6] It was Pius X who, in his *Motu Proprio* on Church music (1903), affirmed that "active participation in the most sacred mysteries and in the public and solemn prayer of the Church" was the "first and indispensable source" of the "true Christian spirit" that he wanted to see flourish among the faithful.[7] Pius XI, in *Divini Cultus* (1928), declared that in order that the faithful more actively participate in divine worship, they should sing the parts of the Mass that belong to them in Gregorian chant, because it is important that they not be "strangers and silent spectators" at Mass.[8]

In 1947, Pius XII promulgated *Mediator Dei*, the first encyclical dedicated entirely to liturgy, a theological analysis of the liturgy that incorporated the best insights of the Liturgical Movement and made use of some of the very texts just cited. Further, as a systematic theological reflection, *Mediator Dei* developed theological under-standings of certain aspects of the liturgy that would reappear in *Sacrosanctum Concilium,* including the liturgy as exercise of Christ's high-priestly office, where the faithful offer the sacrifice by the hands of the priest, and "to a certain extent in union with him," and ways Christ is present in the liturgy.[9] At the time *Sacrosanctum Concilium* was published, commentators were quick to point out how heavily it relied on *Mediator Dei,* not only for its theology but sometimes its very words, even though this is not immediately apparent from the footnotes, which provide references only to biblical, patristic, and liturgical sources, and the Council of Trent.[10]

In addition to building on earlier Church documents on the liturgy, *Sacrosanctum Concilium* reflects insights of the broader Liturgical Movement, as they had matured over the previous century. Lambert Beauduin's strong pastoral concern that laity and clergy alike understand the meaning of what is happening in the celebration of the liturgy so that they could truly experience it as source of their life as Christians finds a resonance throughout the Constitution.[11] The scholarly labors of Odo Casel in bringing attention to the Paschal Mystery as heart of the liturgy came to fruition in *Sacrosanctum Concilium's* taking as one of its guiding principles, the reenactment of the Paschal Mystery of Christ in the liturgy of the Church.[12] The Constitution's call for participation that is not only "active" (as in earlier documents), but also "conscious," calls to mind the insistence of American liturgical pioneer Virgil Michel in the 1930s that the "active" participation called for by Pius X must also be "intelligent."[13]

In 1956 an international congress on "The Renewal of the Liturgy during the Pontificate of Pope Pius XII" was held in Assisi, as a tribute to the pope in his eightieth year. Several of the principles set forth in the major addresses of liturgical scholar Joseph Jungmann and Scripture scholar (later Cardinal) Augustin Bea are found in *Sacrosanctum Concilium.*[14] In a concluding allocution, Pope Pius XII approved the work of the Congress,[15] and a substantial percentage of the bishops on the later Preparatory Commission and the Conciliar Commission responsible for the text of *Sacrosanctum Concilium,* were participants in it. Any attempt at a careful reading of the Constitution, then, must be done in mindfulness that the understanding of the liturgy articulated in prior papal documents and in the broader Liturgical Movement provides the context within which ideas expressed in *Sacrosanctum Concilium* developed, and according to which the meaning of those ideas must be interpreted.

What, then, is *Sacrosanctum Concilium's* vision of the liturgy? What does it teach is actually happening when the liturgy is celebrated? Why did God give the liturgy to the Church? These questions are addressed in the very first paragraphs of Chapter I, which provide the foundation for everything that follows, both general principles and specific reforms. While the ideas presented in these paragraphs are familiar, it is important to summarize them, because only after understanding what the Council Fathers taught the purpose of the liturgy to be, and what they taught takes place in the celebration of the liturgy, is it possible to understand why they called for reform, and what kind of reform they thought was needed.

What is the purpose of the liturgy?

After a brief introduction, the body of *Sacrosanctum Concilium* begins by explaining the purpose of the liturgy by recounting how and why it came to be, and thus by situating it in the ongoing drama of salvation history. In sum: God, who wanted all to be saved and know the truth, called a people, did mighty works to deliver them, made a covenant with them, and spoke to them by the prophets—all as preparation for the culmination of His saving work in His Son, Jesus Christ, who made it possible for human beings to be reconciled to God. The Constitution explains that Christ "achieved his task of redeeming humanity and giving glory to God, principally by the paschal mystery";[16] Christ is thus the one who—in his death and resurrection—gives perfect glory to the Father.

The reconciliation and redemption Christ won must be communicated to and received by those he won it for, so, as the Father sent Christ, Christ sent his apostles, empowered by his Spirit. The apostles preached the Gospel of Christ's redemption and brought it "into effect through the sacrifice and the sacraments, the center of the whole liturgical life."[17] In its very essence, then, the Christian liturgy is the locus where Christ in his saving death and resurrection is made present in the power of the Holy Spirit so that worshippers

may receive the redemption he won and be brought into the relationship with God for which he created them.

   Sacrosanctum Concilium thus describes Baptism as the event
where Christians are "plunged into the paschal mystery"; being united
to Christ in his dying and rising, the baptized receive the Spirit of
adoption that enables them, now reconciled, to call upon God as Father
and be true worshippers.[18] Similarly, the Church has from the beginning gathered to celebrate the Paschal Mystery in the Eucharist "in
which the victory and triumph of his death are again made present."[19]
The Constitution expands on this in its chapter on the Eucharist,
explaining that at the Last Supper,

> our savior instituted the eucharistic sacrifice of his body and blood.
> He did this in order to perpetuate the sacrifice of the cross throughout
> the centuries until he should come again and in this way to entrust to
> his beloved Bride, the Church, a memorial of his death and resurrection:
> a sacrament of love, a sign of unity, a bond of charity, a paschal banquet
> "in which Christ is eaten, the heart is filled with grace, and a pledge of
> future glory is given to us."[20]

Thus, according to *Sacrosanctum Concilium*, the purpose for which
the liturgy was given to the Church, was to provide a means through
which God's saving work in Christ could be mediated to his disciples,
until he returns at the end of ages. How, then, does it describe what
is actually happening during the celebration of the liturgy?

What is happening when the liturgy is celebrated

Sacrosanctum Concilium's understanding of what is taking place in
liturgical celebration is rooted in the vision of the Paschal Mystery—
Christ's passage through death to life, ascending to reign and pouring
out the Spirit—as heart of the liturgy; seven paragraphs of the
Constitution explicitly speak of this, and others make reference to it.[21]

   In addition to the foundational teaching on how believers
come into contact with the Paschal Mystery in Baptism and Eucharist
described above, the Constitution later adds that through the liturgy
of all the sacraments, almost every event in the lives of the faithful
can be "made holy by divine grace that flows from the paschal mystery
of Christ's passion, death, and resurrection, the fount from which all
sacraments and sacramentals draw their power."[22] Further, since time

itself has been redeemed by the Risen Lord, through the liturgical calendar's recalling of the mysteries of redemption, "the Church opens to the faithful the riches of the Lord's powers and merits, so that are in some way made present in every age in order that the faithful may lay hold on them and be filled with saving grace."[23] Thus, every Sunday, as well as every Easter, the Church celebrates the Paschal Mystery, and "unfolds the whole mystery of Christ"[24] every year. The liturgical seasons, by re-presenting the mysteries of Christ's life, make it possible for the faithful to enter into deeper union with him each year;[25] by celebrating the saints' "passage from earth to heaven, the Church proclaims the paschal mystery achieved in the saints, who have suffered and been glorified with Christ."[26]

Sacrosanctum Concilium's vision of the liturgy has several other important aspects. Since the Eucharist was instituted by Christ to perpetuate his sacrifice on the cross throughout the ages, Christ is the high priest of the new and eternal covenant who offers this sacrifice in which the covenant is renewed. Sacrosanctum Concilium speaks of the liturgy as an exercise of the priestly office of Jesus Christ, taking for granted the more extensive theological development of this traditional understanding in Mediator Dei.[27] The facts that Christ reenacts his Paschal Mystery in the liturgy, and that he is offering himself to the Father in it, make clear that Christ is present in liturgical celebrations. The Constitution describes four dimensions of this presence: 1) at Mass, both in the person of his minister, the priest, who presides in persona Christi, and above all under the eucharistic elements; 2) in the sacraments; 3) in his Word, through the proclamation of Scripture in the liturgy; 4) when the Church prays and sings, as he promised in Matthew18:20.[28] Because Christ is thus present in liturgical celebrations, Pope John Paul II explains, "the liturgy is the privileged place for the encounter of Christians with God and the one whom he has sent, Jesus Christ."[29]

For Sacrosanctum Concilium, then, the liturgy is the gathering of Christ's disciples to worship their Lord who is present in their midst, as well as, at the same time, the sacred action wherein Christ, the high priest, gives perfect worship to the Father. Further, since Christ is present, offering himself to the Father, and since the baptized are members of his Body, they are thereby joined to his gift of himself to the Father in perfect love: "in the liturgy the whole public worship is performed by the Mystical Body of Jesus Christ, that is, by the Head and his members."[30] Similarly, the Constitution's chapter on The Liturgy of the Hours describes it as "the very prayer that Christ himself, together with his Body, addresses to the Father."[31] Christ joins worshippers to himself in singing the hymn of praise that is sung eternally in heaven, and thus continues his priestly work through the Church's praise and intercession in The Liturgy of the Hours.[32]

As place where "the whole public worship is performed by the Mystical Body of Jesus Christ," the liturgy is "above all things the worship of the divine majesty."[33] Through the celebration of the Paschal Mystery, Christ is present, and through Christ the Church is given "the fullness of divine worship."[34] Since Christ in his redeeming death and resurrection gave perfect glory to God, when his Body is united to him offering his sacrifice, they are joined to his giving perfect glory to God as well. *Sacrosanctum Concilium* thus states that in the liturgy "God is perfectly glorified and the recipients made holy" and that "the liturgy is the source for achieving in the most effective way possible human sanctification and God's glorification."[35] Further, in this perfect glorification of God in the earthly liturgy, worshippers participate in a foretaste of the heavenly liturgy where Christ reigns at God's right hand, joining with the whole company of heaven in singing a hymn to His glory.[36] The Constitution's discussion of the nature of the liturgy, then, also includes the liturgy's eschatological dimension, especially in the Eucharist where worshippers "proclaim the death of the Lord until he comes," and "eagerly await the Savior, Our Lord Jesus Christ, until he, our life, shall appear and we too will appear with him in glory."[37]

Since *Sacrosanctum Concilium's* understanding of what is actually taking place when the liturgy is celebrated includes all the dimensions just described, the document affirms that "the liturgy is the summit toward which the activity of the Church is directed; at the same time it is the fount from which all the Church's power flows."[38] The liturgy is the *source* for the Church's life in the sense that, most of all in the Eucharist, it makes "the work of our redemption a present actuality" so that "grace is poured forth upon us as from a fountain."[39] Further, "the renewal in the eucharist of the covenant between the Lord and his people draws the faithful into the compelling love of Christ and sets them on fire," and participants in the Eucharist are made one in holiness.[40] The liturgy is the *summit* of the Church's activity because the ultimate goal of all preaching of the Gospel and works of mercy is that all people be reconciled to God in Baptism and celebrate this restored relationship by participating in the paschal sacrifice and feast, thus entering into communion of life with Christ.[41] Through Christ, the faithful worshipping at the Eucharist can be "formed day by day into a more perfect unity with God and with each other, so that finally God may be all in all."[42]

The first part of this essay has considered what *Sacrosanctum Concilium* teaches is the purpose of the liturgy, and how it describes what is happening in its celebration. To summarize, the Constitution states that the purpose for which God gave the liturgy to the Church was so that the salvation Christ has accomplished once and for all could be made present by the Holy Spirit in celebrations of the liturgy and communicated to the faithful. When it treats what is taking place in liturgical celebrations, the Constitution describes the liturgy as rooted in the Paschal Mystery, as an exercise of the priestly office of Jesus Christ who is present, and as locus for the public worship of his Body, where God is perfectly glorified and human beings sanctified, and a foretaste of the heavenly liturgy is given. This is the nature of the liturgy, as described in *Sacrosanctum Concilium*.

Part II

The Nature of the Reforms

Having considered *Sacrosanctum Concilium's* understanding of the liturgy and its purpose, it is now possible to turn to the second question: What was the nature of the changes in the celebration of the liturgy that it called for? Such a stunning vision of the nature of the liturgy has an inescapable consequence: the manner in which the liturgy is celebrated must be that which will best make available this theological and spiritual reality, so that worshippers can enter into it and be transformed by it, and the liturgy can thus fulfill its purpose. Since the liturgy had been instituted to enable Christians to enter into encounter with the Risen Christ, to be formed into his Body and be sent to bring his risen life to the world, everything that could be done in regard to its outward form to enable worshippers to enter into its inner reality, needed to be done. This is why the Council called for liturgical reform, and it is the key to understanding both the general principles articulated by the Constitution, and the specific reforms it called for.

The principal aim of the reforms

If Catholics know nothing else about *Sacrosanctum Concilium,* they know that its overriding concern in the reform of the liturgy was the participation of the people, as explicitly stated in paragraph 14:

> The Church earnestly desires that all the faithful be led to that full, conscious, and active participation in liturgical celebrations called for by the very nature of the liturgy. Such participation by the Christian people as "a chosen race, a royal priesthood, a holy nation, God's own people (1 Peter 2:9; cf. 2:4–5)" is their right and duty by reason of their baptism.
>
> In the reform and promotion of the liturgy, this full and active participation by all the people is the aim to be considered before all else.

For it is the primary and indispensable source from which the faithful are to derive the true Christian spirit and therefore pastors must zealously strive in all their pastoral work to achieve such participation by means of the necessary instruction.[1]

What is sometimes missed, however, is the qualifying clause—it is not just any kind of "full, conscious, and active participation" in liturgical celebrations that is mandated, but the full, conscious, and active participation *"called for by the very nature of the liturgy."* What is meant by that kind of participation, which the very nature of the liturgy calls for? Paragraphs 5 through 13 have just clearly and carefully laid out the nature of the liturgy, as summarized above. In the case of the Eucharist, this nature of the liturgy calls for those who participate in it to be attentive to and respond to their Risen Lord who is present in his minister, in the proclamation of the Word, in his sacramental body and blood, and in his Body, the Church. It calls for participants to enter reverently into this re-presentation of the Paschal Mystery, where the Risen Christ as high priest is offering himself to the Father and joining them, his Body, to himself in this act where God is perfectly glorified and they are made holy and drawn into union with God and each other. The nature of the eucharistic liturgy calls for those who participate to join together in sincerely renewing the Church's covenant with the Lord so that they may be drawn into his "compelling love" and "set on fire," grateful that they may enter into this anticipation of the heavenly liturgy. In the case of the other sacraments, the nature of the liturgy also calls for worshippers to participate in them as encounters with Christ who is present to pour out his grace upon them. It is this awe-inspiring reality that is at the heart of the kind of participation that the "very nature of the liturgy" calls for.

While this kind of full, conscious, and active participation necessarily includes external expression (as will be discussed below), it is clear that it is first of all interior: worshippers uniting their whole beings to what God is doing in the liturgy, which they understand and want to be part of. *Sacrosanctum Concilium* explicitly states that the active participation it calls for is both internal and external,[2] and when describing it, the Constitution includes along with such examples as responses and gestures, that "at the proper times all should observe a reverent silence."[3] When describing the several ways that the faithful should participate in the Eucharist, *Sacrosanctum Concilium* includes the statement (which is a conflation of two separate sections of *Mediator Dei* and a development beyond them), "by offering the immaculate Victim, not only through the hands of the priest, but also with him, they should learn to offer themselves as well."[4]

In fact, *Mediator Dei* had already provided a substantive discussion of the relationship between "exterior" and "interior" worship, teaching that the Church's worship must be both, then after giving reasons for the necessity and worth of the exterior aspect, explaining why the "chief element" must be interior.[5] In urging that all the faithful be aware that participating in the eucharistic sacrifice "is their chief duty and supreme dignity," the encyclical specifies that worshippers must not daydream, but participate "with such earnestness and concentration that they may be united as closely as possible with the High Priest, according to the Apostle: 'Let this mind be in you which was also in Christ Jesus.' "[6] When expressing approval for certain limited outward forms of congregational participation that were permitted at the time, *Mediator Dei* insists that their primary aim was to "foster and promote the people's piety and intimate union with Christ and His visible minister and to arouse those internal sentiments and dispositions" that would make their hearts like Christ's.[7] *Mediator Dei* repeatedly commends the interior aspect of lay participation in the liturgy and stresses that, whatever the manner of external participation, "constant and earnest effort must be made to unite the congregation in spirit as much as possible with the Divine Redeemer," so that they may be made more holy and greater glory may be given to God.[8]

The conviction that interior participation was the *sine qua non* of active participation in the liturgy was not confined to Roman documents. More than a decade before *Mediator Dei*, American Virgil Michel was eloquently making the same case. For Michel, the purpose of the Liturgical Movement was twofold: first, to bring the faithful into more intimate participation in the Church's liturgy, and second— just as important—thereby to empower them to bring the life of Christ imparted through liturgical participation into every aspect of their daily lives and ultimately transform society, according to a Christian order of life.[9] Michel urged that the members of Christ's Mystical Body enter "wholeheartedly and intelligently"[10] into the corporate worship of the Church; the better they understood the meaning of the liturgy in the life of the Church and thus were able to be drawn into union with Christ by actively participating in it, the greater their ability to work toward the just and compassionate society called for by Catholic social teaching. Michel critiqued those who focused on the external aspects of the liturgy rather than approaching it as "the inner worship of soul and the divine action of Christ and of God that is enacted through the visible elements of the liturgical rites," and called for "intelligent" participation, which involved both the understanding and the will.[11] He believed that what the faithful needed was understanding of the "inner action of the Mass and of the supernatural relation of the individual member to the corporate sacrifice of the Mystical Body," because "Christian participation in the Mass is the more meritorious the more it is done with an understanding of the true nature of the prayer-action of the Mass and with the willing joining of the heart and soul in that action as it unfolds itself before the senses."[12]

The "right" to "full, conscious, and active participation"

The active participation called for by the very nature of the liturgy that *Sacrosanctum Concilium* advocates, then, is first of all an active internal participation in the divine realities mediated by the liturgy. The Constitution goes on to say that this kind of participation is the "right and duty" of the Christian people "by reason of their baptism."[13] To understand what this means, it is again helpful to consider it in the context of the vision of the Liturgical Movement and of *Mediator Dei*. Virgil Michel had described the goal of the liturgical apostolate as entailing "a continuation and ever greater realization of the divine seed of life implanted in the sacrament of baptism."[14] *Mediator Dei* had taught that through Baptism "as by common right, Christians are made members of the Mystical Body of Christ the Priest, and by the 'character' which is imprinted on their souls, they are appointed to give worship to God."[15] Those who wrote *Sacrosanctum Concilium* were deeply familiar with the theology and language of *Mediator Dei*, as well as with the traditional theological understanding that at Baptism Christians receive not only justifying grace, but also an "indelible character" that empowers them to perform acts of worship in the Church through which Christ can act to bring about their salvation.

Sacrosanctum Concilium's teaching that active participation is the faithful's "right" because of their Baptism is expressing a profound theological truth. When Christians are baptized, they are plunged into Christ's dying and rising, united to him and filled with his Spirit which puts them in relationship with God as Father, and inserted into Christ's ecclesial Body. The Spirit-filled life that follows from this necessarily expresses itself in these members of Christ's Body coming together for the re-presentation of his paschal sacrifice, to be joined with Christ, their head and high priest who is present, in his giving perfect glory to the Father. It is Baptism that makes Christians capable of encountering Christ and being drawn into union with him and each other, when they gather with the members of his Body to worship him in the liturgy. To participate actively in the liturgy in all the dimensions called for by its very nature, is thus the "right" of all who have been united with Christ in Baptism and filled with his life-giving Spirit who impels them toward this—as well as, of course, their duty.

That the "active participation" *Sacrosanctum Concilium* 14 is calling for is ultimately a theological and spiritual reality becomes even more clear when it explains that the reason that this participation by all the people must be the foremost aim in the liturgical reform is that it is "the primary and indispensable source of the true Christian spirit." The "true Christian spirit" cannot, of course, come from human beings *doing* any particular thing (no matter how "actively" they do it), but only from Christ, as Christians enter into his presence and open themselves to receive his grace. Further, when Pius X had originally made the affirmation that the Constitution is using here, it was in the context of his 1903 *Motu Proprio* calling for the restoration of Church music, especially Gregorian chant.[16] Pius X thus expected that this active participation—which he called indispensable—was possible in the Tridentine Mass. Finally, if active participation is defined as performing outward actions such as standing, singing, or shaking hands, then those prevented by illness or disability from doing those things would not be able to receive the "true Christian spirit" since they would be cut off from its "indispensable source."

Clearly, it is essential to understand what the Council meant by "full, conscious, and active participation," since *Sacrosanctum Concilium* states that this is the primary aim of the reforms. Too often, in the United States, has *Sacrosanctum Concilium* 14 been less than fully understood. Some have interpreted the "right" to participate, given in Baptism, in political terms: just as becoming a U.S. citizen gives one a right to vote, etc., so becoming a member of the Church in Baptism gives one the "right" to participate in the liturgy by saying and doing things, and the more "actively" one participates (i.e., the greater the quantity of such participation), the better. Not only has the baptismal "right" to participate been misunderstood as a political right, but many have thought of participation solely in regard to its outward expressions. Some have expressed the opinion that the Mass today needs to be completely revised, because during a large percentage of it the people are just sitting there not saying or doing anything—which is thought to mean they are not participating.

The point being made by this exegesis of *Sacrosanctum Concilium* 14 is *not* that participating in external actions (e.g., joining in singing praise, prayerfully responding to the petitions of the Prayer of the Faithful, sincerely offering the peace of Christ to fellow worshippers) is unimportant. Such actions are *very* important—because they are *vehicles through which* one participates in the celebration of the Paschal Mystery as part of Christ's Body, the Church. While participating fully, consciously, and actively in the Church's liturgy today involves such actions, these actions in themselves do not constitute full, conscious, and active participation.

The need for changes in the liturgy's outward form

In the paragraphs following paragraph 14, the Constitution of course calls for many specific changes in the external form of the liturgy in order to facilitate the desired participation. This follows the logic of the Incarnation: the very fact that God has taken on human flesh, and that the Incarnate One whom we have heard, and seen with our eyes "and touched with our hands," has left those who follow him tangible ways to be united to him in the sacraments he instituted, shows that for human beings (body-persons), external, physical actions, inspire, enable, and express spiritual actions. Thirty years before *Sacrosanctum Concilium*, Odo Casel had cited the principle that "the inner life grows stronger to the extent that the external act corresponding to an interior one is consciously made: we hear a song, but the inner participation in it will be greatly heightened and made easier if we sing it ourselves,"[17] in explaining the reasons for the laity's participation in the liturgy's external form. *Mediator Dei* had affirmed the intimate link between the interior gift of self to God and its necessary exterior expressions.[18] The Constitution states that when, in the liturgy, the Church "prays or sings or acts, the faith of those taking part is nourished and their minds are raised to God, so that they may offer their worship as intelligent beings and receive his grace more abundantly."[19]

The reason that *Sacrosanctum Concilium* gives for undertaking a reform of the liturgy that includes many helpful changes in the external aspects of participation, then, is not the intrinsic value of those specific changes, but *"in order that the Christian people may more surely derive an abundance of graces from the liturgy."*[20] The purpose of the reforms was thus to make it easier for people to enter into encounter with God through the liturgy, and to participate in the divine realities mediated by it—so that the liturgy could better fulfill the purpose for which it was given to the Church.

The conviction that there needed to be outward reforms in the liturgy to enable the grace it mediated to be more accessible had informed the Liturgical Movement for many years and eventually inspired several liturgical reforms under Pius XII. At the Assisi Congress in 1956, Joseph Jungmann spoke of how originally, "the living liturgy, actively participated in, was itself for centuries the most important form of pastoral care."[21] Yet while the liturgy was supposed to lead people to conscious Christian faith and inculcate it, when the form of the liturgy had changed, "the most important means of the soul's ascent to God, the word of the liturgy itself, had become inaccessible to the people."[22] Jungmann went on to praise Pius XII for his reform of Holy Week and the Easter Vigil, which restored to the liturgy its pastoral function, by enabling the faithful "to understand and take part in the great liturgical events."[23] Augustin Bea similarly noted that the stated purpose of the Holy Week reform was "to enable the faithful to receive the richest possible fruits by an active participation in the sacred rites," and that the purpose of the liturgical reform begun by Pius X was to "render ever more accessible to the faithful" both the eucharistic body of Christ and the Word of God.[24]

At the beginning of his Apostolic Letter on the Constitution's twenty-fifth anniversary, Pope John Paul II summarized liturgical reform since the Council of Trent, including several important reforms of Pius XII. In addition to the most important reform of Holy Week and Easter, Pius XII authorized a new version of the psalter "to facilitate the understanding of the Psalms," modified the eucharistic fast "in order to facilitate access to Holy Communion," and permitted use of the vernacular in the sacramental rites.[25] The common characteristic of all these reforms is the desire to facilitate access to the grace given through the liturgy, and the specific reforms mandated not long after by *Sacrosanctum Concilium* (which explicitly stated that the experience of the recent innovations should inform those to come)[26] were inspired by the same intention. When the Constitution was promulgated, one of the *periti* of the Conciliar Commission that wrote it, Annibale Bugnini, expected that when its principles were implemented, "the Church will have a renewed liturgy that will give God's people once again a sense of the sacred mystery and help them to enter into it."[27]

The desire to do everything humanly possible to enable the grace mediated by the liturgy to be more accessible, led to a concern for greater intelligibility in the liturgy's outward form. As *Eucharisticum Mysterium* would explain in 1967, the Eucharist, "in common with the other sacraments, is the symbol of a sacred reality and the visible form of an invisible grace. *Consequently, the more intelligible the signs by which it is celebrated and worshipped, the more firmly and effectively it will enter into the minds and lives of the faithful.*"[28] The concern for greater intelligibility in the outward forms of the liturgy was inspired by several concerns. At the most basic level, if God acts in the liturgy today through word and ritual action, then the faithful should be able consciously to encounter him there. Worshippers need to understand the meaning of those words and rites, so they can function as actual medium of expression of worshippers' relationship to God—i.e., so the faithful can know what God is saying to them through those words and rites, and have a natural way of responding to Him through them. This concern for intelligibility, in turn, prompted the Council to authorize greater use of the vernacular.

It is reported that John XXIII, after celebrating the liturgy in Rome on one occasion, commented, "How sad I feel when I think of those beautiful prayers which I have just said, and which you do not understand . . . Some day these treasures must become accessible to all."[29] Greater intelligibility of the liturgy's outward form was thus important not only so that worshippers could more easily converse with

God through the words and rites, but also, on a further level, because of the liturgy's teaching function. Since the liturgy "contains rich instruction" that nourishes worshippers' faith, in addition to permitting greater use of the vernacular in its texts, the Constitution decreed that "the rites should be marked by a noble simplicity; they should be short, clear, and unencumbered by useless repetitions; they should be within the people's powers of comprehension and as a rule not require much explanation."[30] The principle of "noble simplicity" was thus aimed not at "dumbing down" the rites or making them simplistic, but at opening up the liturgy's riches for worshippers so that their faith could be strengthened and deepened.

It was not only the language of the liturgy's prayers and the structures of its ceremonies that needed to be more intelligible, but also, on an even deeper level, its symbols and ritual actions. As Romano Guardini pointed out, "the 'symbol' is in itself something corporal-spiritual, an expression of the inward through the outward," and worshippers must be able to see "the inner sense in the outward sign."[31] If an outward symbol or action requires a great deal of verbal explanation about what it signifies and why, the worshippers' attention is taken up with processing that explanation and is unable to pass through what the symbol presents, to engaging what it re-presents. While the divine reality mediated by a sacrament can never be fully grasped short of the beatific vision, the outward symbols need to be translucent rather than opaque so that the worshippers can "see" the reality, in the sense Guardini described. It was then, again, because of the desire that the liturgy be better able to fulfill its purpose as a vehicle of grace that the Council decreed that "both texts and rites should be so drawn up that they express more clearly the holy things they signify, so that the Christian people, as far as possible, are able to understand them with ease and to take part in the rites fully, actively, and as befits a community."[32]

The communal nature of the liturgy

A major aspect of the liturgy's sign-character that *Sacrosanctum Concilium* sought to make clear was its communal nature. The celebration of the Eucharist constitutes the Church and is therefore a corporate action.[33] While this reality had been expressed in various ways in the liturgical celebrations of the early centuries, historical evolution in the outward form of the liturgy had obscured it. For many, Sunday Mass was something that the priest did, while individuals in the congregation performed whatever private devotions each preferred, not necessarily related to the specific rites of the Mass as they unfolded. The Liturgical Movement had emphasized the Church as Mystical Body, and encouraged congregational singing (in Gregorian chant) of the parts of the Mass that had originally been sung by the people to help restore awareness and experience of the liturgy as corporate act. *Mediator Dei* commended such efforts that showed "in outward manner that the very nature of the Sacrifice, as offered by the Mediator between God and man, must be regarded as the act of the whole Mystical Body of Christ," though it added that such actions were not required to make the liturgy a public act or give it a social character.[34]

In order to make clear that the liturgy is by nature an action of the whole Church, *Sacrosanctum Concilium* affirmed that whenever rites could be celebrated with the presence and active participation of the faithful, this way of celebrating them was to be preferred.[35] Further, when the faithful were present, they needed to be able to engage in the liturgical action not as isolated individuals, but as members of what Guardini called "a body in which the Church is present."[36] In trying to bring this about, it would help if there were more outward actions that the faithful could perform together; this would clarify the sign that the liturgy is a corporate action, and would simultaneously provide a means through which the faithful could enact this reality.

The Constitution thus decreed that the rites should be revised to facilitate the faithful's active participation "as befits a community," by such means as "acclamations, responses, psalmody, antiphons and songs . . . actions, gestures and bearing," as well as reverent silence at the appropriate times.[37] As is fitting for a body, in which each member makes its own vital contribution, working together with the others for the good of the whole body, members are to perform the parts of the liturgy that belong to them, according to their orders, offices, or functions in the liturgy.[38] Parishes are to encourage a sense of community, especially in their celebration of Sunday Mass (a theme developed further in *Dies Domini* in 1998).[39]

The Constitution's emphasis on the liturgy as communal celebration, has sometimes been construed in political terms. Giving the people "things to do" has been understood as a long-overdue admission that the laity do have importance, and the liturgy is portrayed as centered on the action of the assembly (rather than on God). *Sacrosanctum Concilium,* however, in providing for more external means through which the laity can participate in the liturgy "as befits a community," is speaking in the broader context of its desire that the rites' outward forms should express more clearly their inward meaning.[40] Since *Sacrosanctum Concilium* understands the liturgy as an act of the whole Mystical Body of Christ, head and members, and since "the liturgy as the self-manifestation of the Church" is one of its guiding principles,[41] the Constitution is seeking to make the liturgy's external form a clearer sign of this reality by providing means through which all members of the Church may be able to express outwardly the communal nature of the liturgy.

Specific reforms

The desire that the liturgy best enable worshippers to be drawn into ever-deeper union with Christ, which led to the general concerns for accessibility and intelligibility, also informed the specific changes called for by *Sacrosanctum Concilium.* The reforms specified for the eucharistic liturgy are prefaced by the statement, "The Council makes the following decrees in order that the sacrifice of the Mass, even in its ritual forms, may become pastorally effective to the utmost degree."[42] To this end, things that might obscure the inner nature of the liturgy may be changed, and elements from the earlier tradition may be restored if they will help the liturgy better fulfill its purpose.[43]

In keeping with *Sacrosanctum Concilium*'s emphasis on the importance of the Word, that "in the liturgy God is speaking to his people and Christ is still proclaiming his Gospel," even that Christ is "present" in his Word, there is to be more reading from Scripture, taken from a "more representative portion of holy Scripture," and the one-year cycle of readings may be expanded to a multi-year cycle.[44] From this proclamation of the sacred text, "the mysteries of the faith and the guiding principles of the Christian life" are to be set forth in a homily which, at Sunday Mass, can only be omitted for a serious reason, and is strongly recommended at other times.[45] The Constitution describes preaching as "a proclamation of God's wonderful works in the history of salvation, the mystery of Christ, ever present and active within us, especially in the celebration of the liturgy."[46] Providing worshippers with a greater abundance of the Word is thus intended to open up the nature of the liturgy for them so they are reminded how salvation history culminated in the Paschal Mystery and are aware that they are participating in its re-presentation.

The Constitution also calls for the restoration of the Prayer of the Faithful, which had been the first privilege of the newly baptized in the second-century liturgy at Rome.[47] As Christ's Body, the faithful are joined to his high-priestly act of interceding with the Father for the salvation of the world, and praying aloud together for the intercessions allows them to give outward expression to this. So that worshippers can "hear" God speak through the richer share of the Word and also fulfill their intercessory role, the readings and the Prayer of the Faithful are named as parts suitable for the use of the vernacular.[48] *Sacrosanctum Concilium* also repeats *Mediator Dei's* urging that the faithful, "after the priest's communion, receive the Lord's body from the sacrifice."[49] This clarifies that the reception of communion is not a discrete act of private devotion, but rather the consummation of a sacrifice that the faithful have shared in offering. All of these specific changes in the eucharistic liturgy are intended to help worshippers understand the theological reality of what is going on so they can enter into it.

Similarly, the specific changes authorized for the rites of the other sacraments are prompted by the desire to enable them to better fulfill their purpose "to make people holy, to build up the Body of Christ," "to give worship to God," and to help them better fulfill their teaching function as signs.[50] The Constitution states that it is "of the highest importance that the faithful should readily understand the sacramental signs" and participate in the sacraments Christ instituted so that they can be nourished.[51] Here again, the underlying inspiration for the reforms is that since sacraments effect what they signify, the more clearly the grace they impart is expressed in their liturgical rite, the easier it will be for the faithful to open themselves to receive that grace. Therefore, elements that have made the nature and purpose of the rites less clear need to be changed, and the vernacular may be used in administering the sacraments.[52]

The rites for the catechumenate for adults are to be restored so that grace may be given through liturgical rites to help converts in their conversion and instruction.[53] The rites of Baptism should be revised so that they are appropriate for those who receive them, whether adults, infants, or those being baptized in danger of death when no priest or deacon is available; a new rite is to be created for those already baptized who are being received into the communion of the Church.[54] Confirmation is to be revised to make more clear its relationship with both Baptism and Eucharist.[55]

The rite for the sacrament of Penance should be revised to "more clearly express both the nature and the effect of the sacrament."[56] The marriage rite is to be "revised and enriched in such a way that it more clearly signifies the grace of the sacrament and imparts a knowledge of the obligations of the spouses."[57] Specific changes are also prescribed for the rites for the anointing of the sick and for ordination, which will make their meaning more clear.[58] The rite for funerals "should express more clearly the paschal character of Christian death"; like the marriage rite, it may make use of appropriate local traditions.[59] Every specific change called for in the rites of both the Eucharist and the other sacraments, then, was motivated by the conviction that because of the crucial importance of what the sacraments accomplish to bring people into union with Christ, the meaning of what God is offering the faithful in the sacramental encounter must be as clear as possible, so that they can knowingly and willingly respond and receive the grace the sacraments were instituted to bestow. A similar desire inspired the specific reforms of the liturgical year and The Liturgy of the Hours.[60]

What is necessary for the reforms to accomplish their purpose

While the Council Fathers prescribed specific reforms in the liturgy to accomplish general goals of accessibility and intelligibility so that people could "more surely derive an abundance of graces" from it, they knew that these reforms would not automatically bring about the participation "called for by the very nature of the liturgy." Both catechesis on the nature of the liturgy and the new rites, and worshippers' proper dispositions, would be needed in order for the reforms to accomplish their purpose.

Immediately following the statement that the full and active participation of the people in the liturgy is the aim to be considered before all else because it is "the primary and indispensable source from which the faithful are to derive the true Christian spirit," *Sacrosanctum Concilium* 14 continues, "and therefore pastors must zealously strive in all their pastoral work to achieve such participation by means of the necessary instruction." The Constitution later adds, "With zeal and patience pastors must promote the liturgical instruction of the faithful and also their active participation, both internally and externally, taking into account their age and condition, their way of life, and their stage of religious development," explaining that this is "one of their chief duties."[61] *Sacrosanctum Concilium* also gives clear directives concerning the liturgical education and formation of clergy and those who teach them so that priests will be able to provide this instruction.[62]

In addition to being instructed on the meaning of the reformed rites, the faithful are also to be taught how to prepare themselves to encounter God through them. *Mediator Dei* had emphasized that although the sacraments, as Christ's own actions, give grace to his Body, in order for them "to produce their proper effect, it is absolutely necessary that our hearts be rightly disposed to receive them," and discussed how this was to be done.[63] Virgil Michel had asserted that all the faithful should apply to their participation in the Mass at least the degree of intelligence and will they employed in their other serious activities.[64]

Sacrosanctum Concilium affirms that in order for the liturgy to "possess its full effectiveness, it is necessary that the faithful come to it with proper dispositions, that their minds be attuned to their voices, and that they co-operate with divine grace, lest they receive it in vain."[65] It therefore instructs pastors that it is their duty "to ensure that the faithful take part fully aware of what they are doing, actively engaged in the rite, and enriched by its effects."[66] The Constitution also describes ways of prayer outside the liturgy that help form in the faithful the dispositions necessary for fruitful liturgical participation.[67]

Immediately after the explanation of the Eucharist as Christ's perpetuation of the sacrifice of the cross in paragraph 47 (cited above), *Sacrosanctum Concilium* summarizes the dispositions the faithful should bring to the eucharistic sacrifice, and how they should participate in it:

> The Church, therefore, earnestly desires that Christ's faithful, when present at this mystery of faith, should not be there as strangers or silent spectators; on the contrary, through a good understanding of the rites and prayers

they should take part in the sacred service conscious of what they are doing, with devotion and full involvement. They should be instructed by God's word and nourished at the table of the Lord's body; they should give thanks to God; by offering the immaculate Victim, not only through the hands of the priest but also with him, they should learn to offer themselves as well; through Christ the Mediator, they should be formed day by day into an ever more perfect unity with God and with each other, so that finally God may be all in all.[68]

In regard to the other sacraments, *Sacrosanctum Concilium* states that when the faithful approach them with the proper dispositions (i.e., knowingly and reverently entering into the encounter with God), almost every event in their lives will be made holy by the power of Christ's death and resurrection working through the sacraments.[69] While the Constitution did seek changes in the liturgy's outward form to enable the faithful better to participate in it "fully, consciously, and actively" in all its dimensions, the Council Fathers were aware that proper dispositions were necessary in order for the changes to have their intended effect. Ultimately, conversion to faith in Jesus Christ, committing oneself to be his disciple, is the condition for the liturgical participation which the very nature of the liturgy calls for, and the deeper the faithful's conversion, the deeper their capacity for this participation.

The second part of this essay has explored the nature of the changes in the way the liturgy is celebrated that the Council Fathers called for so that the liturgy could better fulfill the purpose for which God gave it to the Church. In order to enable the faithful to participate more easily in the theological and spiritual realities mediated by the liturgy, *Sacrosanctum Concilium* provided general principles for the reform of the liturgy and authorized specific changes. In doing this, the Council was not advocating change for change's sake. The principles provided by the Constitution—whether "noble simplicity," or making the communal nature of the liturgy more apparent, or even openness to the possibility of adapting the liturgy to various cultures[70]—were not ends in themselves. All of the general principles, as well as the specific reforms approved, were intended to increase access to the spiritual reality present in the liturgy, so that the liturgy could better function as a vehicle of grace.

In his *Motu Proprio, Sacram Liturgiam* (promulgated in the month after *Sacrosanctum Concilium*), Pope Paul VI explained that several prescriptions of the Constitution, such as reforming the rites according to its decrees, and preparing liturgical books, would take time to accomplish, and that he had appointed a commission (which became known as the Consilium) for this task.[71] However, he urged bishops to begin immediately "teaching their people the power and the interior worth of the sacred liturgy."[72] Further, he specified certain prescriptions of *Sacrosanctum Concilium* that could be implemented at once, adding, "It is Our wish that these come into force without delay, *so that the faithful will no longer be deprived of the spiritual benefits which are expected from them.*"[73]

Perhaps the best summary of why the Council called for changes in the liturgy, and what it hoped these changes would accomplish, can be found in the words with which Pope Paul VI promulgated *Sacrosanctum Concilium:*

> If, at this junction, we have set out to simplify the external expression of worship, in an effort to make it more comprehensible to our people and closer to current speech, this does not mean that we wish to reduce the importance of prayer, or to put it on a lower plane than the other obligations of sacred ministry or of the apostolate. Neither does it mean that we want to make worship less expressive or less aesthetically satisfying. It is rather that we want to make it purer, more genuine, closer to the sources of truth and grace, better fitted to be the spiritual patrimony of the people.[74]

Part III

Toward a Fuller Implementation

The first part of this essay considered how *Sacrosanctum Concilium* describes the purpose of the liturgy and what is actually taking place when it is celebrated. The second part then reflected on the nature of the changes the Constitution calls for so that the liturgy can better fulfill its purpose, and summarized the specific changes it authorized. As the Consilium created to implement *Sacrosanctum Concilium* was beginning its work, its first president referred to the Constitution as "this great masterpiece which seeks to promote spiritual progress in souls and in the Church," but also as being so "full of meaning" that it "required study and reflection."[1] Having considered *Sacrosanctum Concilium's* vision of "promoting spiritual progress" in the first two parts of this essay, it is possible, in this final part, to offer some reflections on aspects of the Constitution that do not appear to have yet received the attention they deserve.

There are a number of areas where a fuller implementation of *Sacrosanctum Concilium's* vision could allow the reforms it instituted to bear more abundantly their intended fruit of spiritual renewal. Among these, four stand out as necessary foundation for the rest: 1) catechesis leading to understanding of "what is going on" in the Church's liturgy and how to participate in it; 2) appreciation of and attention to the importance of the Word of God in the liturgy; 3) liturgical formation of seminarians according to the norms of the Constitution; 4) seeking to inspire the dispositions necessary for fruitful liturgical participation. To focus on these four areas is not to imply that others (e.g., the quality of music, art, or liturgical translation) do not also need attention, but simply to hold that a fuller implementation of these four is necessary in order for work in other areas to have the effect it should. While most of what follows refers specifically to celebrations of the Eucharist, many of the same kinds of observations could be made concerning liturgical celebrations of the other sacraments and The Liturgy of the Hours, as well.

1. Catechesis on What Is Taking Place in the Liturgy

Sacrosanctum Concilium is clear that in order for the changes in the liturgy's outward form it prescribes to have their intended effect, clergy and laity alike must understand how to make use of them. It tells pastors that "with zeal and patience" they "must promote the liturgical instruction of the faithful, and also their active participation in the liturgy both internally and externally,"[2] and that, in addition to observing the laws necessary for valid and licit celebration, it is pastors' "duty to ensure that the faithful take part fully aware of what they are doing, actively engaged in the rite, and enriched by its effects."[3] Priests are to be "aided to live the liturgical life and to share it with the faithful entrusted to their care."[4]

In recounting the operational principles guiding the Consilium as it began its work, its secretary wrote that the liturgical renewal the Constitution expects could not be achieved simply by observance of rubrics, but "it requires a spirit, a mentality, a soul. It requires an 'initiation' or education in the liturgy."[5] *Sacrosanctum Concilium* itself calls for the "pastoral promotion of the liturgy" as well as its "reform." Twenty-five years after its promulgation, John Paul II wrote,

> While the reform of the liturgy desired by the Second Vatican Council can be considered already in progress, *the pastoral promotion of the liturgy constitutes a permanent commitment* to draw ever more abundantly from the riches of the liturgy that vital force which spreads from Christ to the members of his Body which is the Church.[6]

Living out this ongoing commitment depends on keeping in mind that the "full, conscious, and active participation in liturgical celebrations called for by the very nature of the liturgy" requires knowledge both of the nature of the liturgy and of what is involved in participating in it. In seeking to understand how the Council's desire for spiritual renewal through the liturgy could be more fully realized

in the United States today, it can be helpful to consider how well contemporary Catholics understand what *Sacrosanctum Concilium* teaches
about what is going on in the liturgy and their participation in it. How
many Catholics understand that the purpose of the liturgy is so that
the salvation accomplished in Christ can be made present by the Holy
Spirit in its celebration and communicated to the faithful worshipping
there? How many parishioners walk through the Church doors on
Sunday knowing they are entering into the re-presentation of the
Paschal Mystery, where the Risen Christ as high priest is offering
himself to the Father and joining them, his Body, to himself in this
sacrifice where God is perfectly glorified, and they are made holy and
drawn into union with God and each other? How many of those at
Mass are seeking to be attentive to and to respond to the Risen Lord
present in his minister, in the proclamation of the Word, and when his
Church prays and sings, as well as uniquely present in his sacramental
body and blood? How many worshippers know that they are joining
with each other in sincerely renewing the Church's covenant with
the Lord, so that they may be drawn into his "compelling love" and
"set on fire," that they are entering into the celebration of the heavenly
liturgy? If there are some who do not know that this is what they
are participating in, can it be said that the Constitution's "aim to be
considered before all else" of "full, conscious, and active participation"
has been completely fulfilled?

Catechesis on the nature of the liturgy

A good place to begin the kind of catechesis necessary to enable
Sacrosanctum Concilium's vision of the liturgy to be assimilated by
all the faithful is with the insight so central to those who wrote it:
"The liturgy is the 'performance of the Paschal Mystery.' It is the
Risen Christ continuing the work of salvation in the world today."[7]
In describing the "re-enactment of the paschal mystery" as one of the
Constitution's guiding principles, Pope John Paul II later added,

> When the faithful participate in the Eucharist, they must understand
> that truly "each time we offer this memorial sacrifice, the work of our
> redemption is accomplished," and to this end Bishops must carefully train
> the faithful to celebrate every Sunday the marvelous work that Christ has
> wrought in the mystery of his Passover, in order that they likewise may
> proclaim it to the world.[8]

This leads to the explanation that "in order to re-enact his paschal mystery, Christ is ever present in his Church, especially in liturgical celebrations," demonstrating how a solid catechesis on the centrality of the Paschal Mystery in the life of the Church and its liturgy can naturally lead to an opening up of the ways Christ is present in the liturgy.[9]

Another area where clear catechesis is needed for Catholics to participate in the liturgy as envisioned by *Sacrosanctum Concilium* is understanding of how, in the celebration of the Eucharist, Christ the High Priest is offering himself to the Father and joining his Body the Church, with him in offering his perfect sacrifice. The sacrificial character of the Mass, which was clearly articulated as early as Augustine and solemnly affirmed by the Council of Trent,[10] was reaffirmed in *Lumen Gentium* as well as *Sacrosanctum Concilium,* yet many contemporary Catholics have never had it explained to them. In discussing how only the ordained "effect the eucharistic sacrifice and offer it to God in the name of the whole people," *Dies Domini* adds,

> Yet the faithful must realize because of the common priesthood received in baptism, "they participate in the offering of the Eucharist." Although there is a distinction of roles, they still "offer to God the divine victim and themselves with him. Offering the sacrifice and receiving holy communion, they take part in the liturgy," finding in it light and strength to live their baptismal priesthood and the witness of a holy life.[11]

Further, there is also need for catechesis on how, when the faithful join in offering the sacrifice and receiving communion in it, in receiving the sacramental body of Christ, they are formed into his ecclesial Body. The Eucharist makes the Church and draws its members into unity with each other even as it draws each of them into deeper union with Christ. The celebration of the Eucharist is thus a profound self-manifestation of the Church, the community of the redeemed worshipping their Lord, renewing their covenant with him and being sent by him to bring his life to the world. While the past 40 years have heard much talk about "being community," there is still a great need for understanding the Eucharist as corporate action, where worshippers offer the sacrifice as a body and are made into Christ's Body, the Church, in receiving it.

Catechesis that will lead people to understand the "very nature of the liturgy" is needed, then, especially in the areas of how the liturgy re-presents the Paschal Mystery, the ways Christ is present in it, the sacrificial character of the Mass, and how the liturgy is corporate act. But in order for spiritual renewal to take place, worshippers need to know not only what is going on in the act they are participating in, but also what is meant by "participation."

Catechesis on what active participation involves

Sacrosanctum Concilium itself summarizes what is involved in participation in paragraph 48.[12] Rather than being strangers and silent spectators at Mass, the faithful are to participate in it "conscious of what they are doing." This conscious participation is made possible by a "good understanding of the rites and prayers"; catechesis is needed on the rites and prayers to show how the theological and spiritual realities of the liturgy's very nature are what the prayers and rites are talking about, what they *mean*. The faithful are thus invited to participate in entering into the re-presentation of the Paschal Mystery and offering the sacrifice as a community, conscious that this is what they are doing, "with devotion and full involvement." This involvement means that the statement "they should be instructed by God's Word" does not describe the fact that someone is speaking and therefore "instructing" those present, but rather that the faithful, since they are participating actively, are actually *being instructed*, learning the wisdom from God's Word that will enable them to be more faithful disciples. That the worshippers should be "nourished at the table of the Lord's body" is not simply a statement that they should receive communion; participating *conscie, pie,* and *actuose* with a good understanding of what they are doing means communicants are actually *being nourished*, actively assimilating spiritual strength that makes the life of discipleship possible just as really as ordinary food gives physical strength.[13] Similarly, "they should give thanks to God" does not refer to, e.g., members of the congregation responding, "It is right to give him thanks and praise" in rote recitation, but rather anticipates their making this response as a sincere expression of the gratitude to God that is at the center of the life of the redeemed in difficult circumstances as well as good, and as their affirmation of the intention that that gratitude be at the center of their own lives as well. The final section of paragraph 48, stating that the faithful must offer themselves to God along with the immaculate Victim, and give themselves to be formed each day into more perfect unity with God and each other, is also an existential description of what it means to participate, not simply an abstract theological statement.

Learning to participate

As Catholic congregations were exhorted to "participate" in the liturgy in the years following the Council, this vision of participation in *Sacrosanctum Concilium* 48, and the understanding of internal participation expressed through outward forms was not adequately explained.[14] The difficulty was not that the faithful consciously rejected what *Sacrosanctum Concilium* taught about the divine realities mediated by the liturgy and internal participation in them; nor was the problem that everyone was overly zealous about external participation (there are still those today who do not make all the responses, etc.). The difficulty was that the connection between internal and external participation was not explained, and people did not understand the many new forms of outward participation they were now expected to perform as having been introduced in order to facilitate the desired internal participation.

The need for catechesis on participation today, then, requires more than explaining to the faithful what active participation in the liturgy is meant to be, as described above. In order for the outward forms of participation to accomplish the purpose for which they were intended, the faithful need to *learn* internal participation so that their external participation enables it and leads to and from it. Worshippers need to know *how* to participate this way, how to enter into the liturgy as a conversation with God, where God speaks and they respond by song and prayer, and in physical actions that embody reverence or honor, etc.[15] Worshippers need to learn how to "connect to" God through the rites, prayers, and proclamation of the Word, how to express internal participation through external participation. In his letter on the Constitution's twenty-fifth anniversary, Pope John Paul II wrote of the need for "an ever-deeper grasp of the liturgy of the Church, celebrated according to the current books and *lived above all as a reality in the spiritual order.*"[16]

It is important to emphasize that this kind of active internal participation is not at all the same as what is criticized as the passive private experience of the congregation in the pre–Vatican II liturgy. Before the reforms of *Sacrosanctum Concilium,* many Catholics were instructed that they should "devoutly assist" at Mass by engaging in pious exercises such as praying the rosary or other devotional prayers, etc. In the centuries when the congregation often did not hear what the priest was saying, and what they did hear was not in their language, they were often not aware of what was going on theologically and spiritually at a given point in the liturgy, and so were unable to unite themselves interiorly to the ritual action. It was this set of circumstances that inspired the insistence of the Liturgical Movement that "Catholics should not pray at Mass—they should pray *the Mass!*"[17] Further, since those present at the same Mass were silently performing the particular acts of piety each personally found most helpful, and since many did not receive communion, the congregation was participating in the Church's "sacrament of unity" more in the manner of an aggregate of individuals present in the same room at the same time, rather than as the one Body of Christ engaged in its solemn corporate ritual.[18]

What *Sacrosanctum Concilium* sought to change was not that worshippers were praying in their minds; rather, it sought to restore to members of the congregation means through which their prayers could be connected to the liturgical action and what God was doing through it, and thereby to the prayer of other members. In order to facilitate this, the Council urged that priests should teach the faithful "to participate in the celebrations of the sacred liturgy in such a way that they can rise to sincere prayer during them." [19]

Recovering "the liturgical act"

The classic statement of what would be involved in fulfilling *Sacrosanctum Concilium*'s vision for reform of the liturgy to bring out the "full, conscious, and active participation" of the faithful, "called for by the very nature of the liturgy," was made by liturgical scholar Romano Guardini in his open letter to the Mainz liturgical Congress in 1964. Guardini described the situation in the months immediately following *Sacrosanctum Concilium*'s promulgation:

> The Council has laid the foundations for the future—and the way this came to pass and truth became manifest will remain a classic example of the way the Holy Spirit guides the Church. But now the question arises how we are to set about our task, so that truth may become a reality.[20]

As discussions were going on as to which outward forms of participation should be restored so that the truth of the faithful's active corporate participation called for by the very nature of the liturgy could become a tangible and lived reality, Guardini believed that the main problem would not be ritual or textual, but recovering what he called "the liturgical act." He explained that people in the nineteenth century were no longer capable of performing that act, and were not even aware that such a thing existed. For them religious conduct was "an individual inward matter" and liturgy had the character of an "official, public ceremonial. But the sense of the liturgical action was thereby lost. The faithful did not perform a proper liturgical act at all; it was simply a private and inward act, surrounded by ceremonial and not infrequently accompanied by a feeling that the ceremonial was really a disturbing factor."[21]

Guardini described the uniqueness and importance of the liturgical act as lying in the fact that it had been "performed by individuals who did, however, insofar as they were a sociological entity, form a *corpus:* the congregation, or rather the Church present therein. The act embraced not only a spiritual inwardness, but the whole man, body as well as spirit. Therefore the external action was in itself a 'prayer,' a religious act. . . ."[22] For Guardini, it was crucial that consideration of the best way for *Sacrosanctum Concilium's* reforms to be implemented not be confined to discussions of the external means provided for the congregation's participation and of the use of the vernacular:

> The question is whether the wonderful opportunities now open to the liturgy will achieve their full realization: whether we shall be satisfied with just removing anomalies, taking new situations into account, giving better instruction on the meaning of ceremonies and liturgical vessels or *whether we shall relearn a forgotten way of doing things and recapture lost attitudes.*[23]

After providing clear descriptions of how the "liturgical act" is realized both in doing (as in a procession) and in looking (as in "reading" a symbol), Guardini emphasized the importance of the corporate nature of the active and full participation of the congregation in this act: "The act is done by every individual, not as an isolated individual, but as a member of a body in which the Church is present."[24] He stressed that in order for the Council's intentions to be fulfilled, the faithful would need not only instruction about outward changes, but would also have to *learn* the liturgical act, because if this does not happen, "reforms of rites and texts will not help much."[25] Guardini believed that *Sacrosanctum Concilium* had ushered in a new phase for the Liturgical Movement, the purpose of which was "infusing new life in the liturgy" by seeking to understand and recover the liturgical act.

To advocate, 40 years later, that the full, conscious, and active participation the Council sought involved worshippers consciously entering into encounter with God through the rites and texts of the liturgy as part of a corporate assembly, is essentially to agree with Guardini that what is needed in order for *Sacrosanctum Concilium* to accomplish its purpose is for the faithful to learn to perform the "liturgical act." It is sometimes assumed that speaking of entering into union with God through the rites and prayers of the liturgy is *pro forma* pious rhetoric, but only if this describes a reality—something that actually happens—is it possible to make sense of *Sacrosanctum Concilium* 10's speaking of the liturgy as "fount from which all the Church's power flows" and "source for achieving in the most effective way possible human sanctification and God's glorification." The energy generated by participation that is not aware of the very nature of the liturgy and is primarily external, does not last much longer than well-intentioned human enthusiasm;[26] only by giving themselves to God through the rites and prayers of the liturgy do worshippers open themselves up to the transforming grace that enables them to bring Christ's life to the world.[27] As early as 1980, Pope John Paul II exhorted, "It is therefore necessary and urgent to activate a new and *intensive education* in order to discover all the richness contained in the liturgy."[28]

Toward developing a liturgical spirituality

Catechesis on the nature of the liturgy and what participation is, and helping people learn how to "perform the liturgical act," would also contribute to the realization of one of the Liturgical Movement's cherished desires, which *Sacrosanctum Concilium* envisions as part of the spiritual renewal its implementation will lead to: that all the prayer of the Church's members be rooted in the Church's prayer in the liturgy.[29] This is not to say that only prayer made during a liturgical celebration has value, but rather that the prayer-life of individual members of the faithful should flow from the prayer of the whole Church in its public encounter with God in worship, and be shaped by it. *Sacrosanctum Concilium* 17 states that seminarians "shall be given a liturgical formation in their spiritual life" and calls for seminaries and religious houses to be "thoroughly permeated by the spirit of the liturgy"; the next paragraph adds that priests are to be aided "to live the liturgical life and to share it with the faithful entrusted to their care."[30] The underlying vision here is that the Church, as community of prayer, lives out each day centered on the reality of God's revelation of Himself in His Son Jesus Christ in the power of the Holy Spirit focused in the re-presentation of Christ's Paschal Mystery in the eucharistic liturgy, and within the unfolding of Christ's life through the liturgical year and commemorations of the saints, embodied both in the daily Mass and The Liturgy of the Hours. Each individual member of the Church community who prays outside the liturgical assembly does so inspired by and within the embrace of this prayer of the whole community, rather than engaging in private meditations that ignore this reality.

As Joseph Jungmann explained, "The spiritual world, to which we as redeemed belong, should come alive whenever the Church gathers in prayer. In this manner the faithful should be led to a conscious faith, and be sustained in it."[31] In the liturgy the faithful are presented with a view of reality as God sees it so that they can assimilate that perception and allow their lives to be guided by it. Further, Jungmann affirmed that the liturgy was also intended to lead the people to Christian prayer,[32] describing how in the early Church, the liturgy with its Trinitarian and Christological language was a guide to Christian prayer, and how, in fact, it was through the liturgy that people learned to relate to God.[33] Patristic preaching (especially mystagogical homilies) bears eloquent witness to the way that the rites and prayers of the liturgy were a privileged source for understanding and explaining what it means for the redeemed to live their lives in relationship with God. To grasp how greatly the situation had changed by the twentieth century, it is only necessary to read Lambert Beauduin's frank description of his spiritual life in his early years as a dedicated priest, concluding,

> The liturgical acts properly speaking were for me a formality of worship that had no appreciable influence on the direction of my piety. The same is true of the yearly retreats: meditation, examen, recollection alone

mattered—a whole spirituality on the border of the liturgy and separated by an air-tight partition.[34]

In his promulgation of *Sacrosanctum Concilium,* Pope Paul VI spoke of the liturgy as both "the first source of the divine life which is given to us" and as "the first school of the spiritual life,"[35] thus bringing into focus two main characteristics of a liturgical spirituality. First, a liturgical spirituality understands God's actions through the liturgy as central source for the spiritual life—the prayer life—of the faithful. Second, since the liturgy is "the school of the prayer of the Church,"[36] it is from the richness of language, images, and grammar of the liturgy that the faithful learn to enter into conversation with God outside the liturgy.

This understanding of the liturgy as privileged source for the spiritual life and school of prayer is the context within which *Sacrosanctum Concilium* stated that popular devotions in accord with Church norms "are to be endorsed," but they "should be so fashioned that they harmonize with the liturgical seasons, accord with the sacred liturgy, are in some way derived from it, and lead the people to it, since, in fact, the liturgy, by its very nature, surpasses all of them."[37] The postconciliar rite for eucharistic adoration thus describes the purpose of worship shown to the Blessed Sacrament outside of Mass as being the celebration of the eucharistic sacrifice, and as extending the grace of that sacrifice, and adds that those who participate in eucharistic adoration foster the proper dispositions to participate frequently in Mass and communion.[38] A true liturgical spirituality does not discourage prayer outside the eucharistic assembly, but seeks to root it in the eucharistic celebration, rather than being in competition with the Church's liturgy or existing in a separate realm.

Catechesis on what is taking place in the liturgy would make it possible for the faithful to experience the liturgy as "source and summit" of the Christian life and thus enable them to develop this kind of spirituality flowing from the liturgy and leading back to it. The development of a liturgical spirituality could also be fostered by more examples of Catholics living as though the liturgy were "source and summit" of their own lives as Christians. *Sacrosanctum Concilium* calls for pastors to be "imbued with the spirit of the liturgy" and to lead their flock not only by word but also by example.[39] Not only priests, but those who serve in liturgical ministries, such as servers and readers,

> also exercise a genuine liturgical function. They ought to discharge their office, therefore, with the sincere devotion and decorum demanded by so exalted a ministry and rightly expected of them by God's people.
>
> Consequently they must all be deeply imbued with the spirit of the liturgy, in the measure proper to each one, and they must be trained to perform their functions in a correct and orderly manner.[40]

If those in the sanctuary perform the ministries entrusted to them as if they were serving in the Church community's solemn encounter with God in Christ in the Holy Spirit, it would help those in the congregation enter into the celebration as "source and summit" of their lives. Further, since the prayer-texts of the liturgy communicate the theological and spiritual realities made present as the liturgy unfolds, it would be helpful to have translations that more fully convey the richness of these realities as found in the Latin originals, in language that is fittingly beautiful.

In calling for the "pastoral promotion of the liturgy" and instruction, *Sacrosanctum Concilium* envisions that the faithful will receive catechesis on the nature of the liturgy and participation in it, and be enabled to learn participation. Yet after 40 years, it seems as true as it was after 25 that

> much still remains to be done to help priests and the faithful to grasp the meaning of the liturgical rites and texts, to develop the dignity and beauty of celebrations and the places where they are held, and to promote, as the Fathers did, a "mystagogic catechesis" of the sacraments.[41]

2. The Importance of the Word in the Liturgy

Another aspect of *Sacrosanctum Concilium* that has yet to be fully explored and assimilated is its understanding of the importance of the Word of God in the liturgy. *Mediator Dei* had affirmed that Christ was present in the liturgy: "in the person of his minister and above all under the eucharistic species";[42] in the sacraments; and in the Church's prayer of praise and petition. *Sacrosanctum Concilium* 7 repeats these ways Christ is present with the significant addition that he "is present in his Word, since it is he himself who speaks when the holy Scriptures are read in the Church." *Sacrosanctum Concilium* 24 states that "Sacred Scripture is of the greatest importance in the celebration of the liturgy," and Pope John Paul II has referred to "the presence of the Word of God" as being one of the three guiding principles of the Constitution.[43] While many of the implications of *Sacrosanctum Concilium's* statements about the Word of God were developed in postconciliar documents, especially the *Introduction to the Lectionary for Mass* (1981), much of the richness of its understanding of the role of the Word has yet to be appropriated in the way parish liturgies are celebrated.

God speaks through the proclamation of the Word

Sacrosanctum Concilium 33 affirms that "in the liturgy God is speaking to his people and Christ is still proclaiming his gospel." This echoes the conviction expressed, implicitly and explicitly, in much Patristic preaching, that when the Word of God is proclaimed in the liturgical assembly, God actually speaks through that proclamation to those who listen.[44] For the Fathers this was not a pious figure of speech, but a description of how the Holy Spirit works through the reading of God's inspired Word to enable worshippers to "hear" God speak to them in a living and life-changing way. The *Introduction to the Lectionary for Mass* provides contemporary reflection on what it means that God speaks to His people in the liturgy. The Holy Spirit, it explains, "brings home to each person individually everything that in the proclamation of the Word is spoken for the good of the whole gathering of the faithful" and makes "what we hear outwardly have its effect inwardly."[45]

Sacrosanctum Concilium 33 continues, "And the people are responding to God by both song and prayer." The *Introduction to the Lectionary* reflects that

> when God communicates his Word, he expects a response, one, that is, of listening and adoring "in Spirit and in truth" (Jeremiah 4:23). The Holy Spirit makes that response effective, so that what is heard in the celebration of the liturgy may be carried out in a way of life: "Be doers of the word and not hearers only." (James 1:22)[46]

Dies Domini (1998) develops this further, speaking of the proclamation of the Word in the liturgy as "a dialogue between God and his people, a dialogue in which the wonders of salvation are proclaimed and the demands of the covenant are continually re-stated."[47] God's people "are drawn to respond to this dialogue of love by giving thanks and praise, also by demonstrating their fidelity to the task of continual 'conversion.'" Thus,

> The proclamation of the Word in the Sunday Eucharistic celebration takes on the solemn tone found in the Old Testament at moments when the covenant was renewed, when the law was proclaimed and the community of Israel was called—like the people in the desert at the foot of Sinai (cf. Exodus 19:7–8; 24:3–7)—to repeat its *yes*, renewing its decision to be faithful to God and to obey his commandments. In speaking his Word, God awaits our response: a response which Christ has already made for us with his *amen* (cf. 2 Corinthians 1:20–22) and which echoes in us through the Holy Spirit so that what we hear may involve us at the deepest level.[48]

When the Word is proclaimed, then, "the congregation of Christ's faithful even today receives from God the word of his covenant through the faith that comes by hearing, and must respond to that word in faith, so that they may become more and more truly the people of the New Covenant."[49]

The conviction that "in the liturgy God is speaking to his people and Christ is still proclaiming his gospel" helped inspire the permission for the Scripture lessons to be read in the vernacular, so that the faithful could know what God was saying as His Word was being proclaimed, without having to consult a printed translation. But how many Catholics are aware that they can "hear" God speak to them "individually" through the proclamation of the Word, that it can "involve them at the deepest level"? How many are aware that in listening to the Word proclaimed, they are entering into an occasion of covenant renewal, where they respond by committing themselves to "continual conversion"? To foster this awareness, both congregation and readers need to be encouraged to approach the Liturgy of the Word in a manner that indicates that God speaking through His Word is a reality, rather than a rhetorical convention.

The training of readers must go beyond instructing them to speak loudly and master difficult pronunciations beforehand. In the very least, the basic meaning of the text must be clear. This means that the proper words within each sentence must be emphasized, and that there not be a break in the middle of a phrase, followed by the

remainder of the phrase being run together with the beginning of the
next sentence so that the inspired author's train of thought is unin-
telligible.[50] Readers need to be encouraged not only to practice the
readings aloud in advance, but to pray through them, and to be aware
that when they approach the lectern to read, they are "loaning" their
lungs and vocal chords to the Holy Spirit so that God may speak
His Word through them. When a reading is over, "the dialogue
between God and his people taking place through the Holy Spirit
demands short intervals of silence, suited to the assembled congregation, as an opportunity to take the Word of God to heart and to
prepare a response to it in prayer."[51]

Faith is nourished through the proclamation of the Word

Another facet of *Sacrosanctum Concilium's* teaching on the Word of God
in the liturgy that deserves further attention is its description of the
Word proclaimed as nourishment. When the Scriptures are proclaimed,
as well as when the Church "prays or sings or acts, the faith of those
taking part is nourished and their minds are raised to God, so that
they may offer him their worship as intelligent beings and receive his
grace more abundantly."[52] *Dei Verbum* also speaks of Scripture as
nourishment, and affirms that "The Church has always venerated the
divine Scriptures just as she venerates the body of the Lord, since from
the table of both the Word of God and of the body of Christ she
unceasingly receives and offers to the faithful the bread of life, especially
in the sacred liturgy."[53]

The groundwork for the Constitution's understanding of the
Word proclaimed as nourishment was laid in such preconciliar work as
Augustin Bea's address to the Assisi Congress in 1956. In discussing
the pastoral function, importance, and efficacy of the Word of God in
the liturgy, Bea describes the role of the liturgical proclamation of the
Word and preaching in forming the faith of Christians in the early
centuries. After recounting how this nourishment of the Word helped
strengthen the faithful, fortified them against persecution and heresy,
and formed many lay apologists, Bea concludes,

> There is perhaps no more convincing experimental proof of the pastoral
> value of the Word of God in the liturgy than this constant practice of the
> first centuries of Christianity and its abundant fruit manifested in the holy

life of so many of the faithful, in the heroic death of so many martyrs, in the testimony of so many defenders of the faith.[54]

Bea goes on to describe the theological aspects of the great power of God's Word proclaimed, especially when united to the eucharistic sacrifice, and also the severe challenges of handing on the faith in an age increasingly darkened by materialism and atheism. He explains how this had led to a desire that the lectionary should be expanded to include more "preachable pericopes," perhaps in a three- or four-year cycle, because "this would be a great advantage in our day for the cure of souls."[55] In the conclusion of his address, Bea refers to the image of the "two tables in the treasure house of the Church," the table of the Word and the table of the body of Christ, and affirms, "It is the great purpose of the liturgical reform to render ever more accessible to the faithful these two tables given us by God himself."[56]

Sacrosanctum Concilium, after describing the Word proclaimed as nourishment that enables the faithful to receive grace more abundantly, goes on to state that "in sacred celebrations there is to be more reading from holy Scripture and it is to be more varied and apposite."[57] In prescribing specific reforms for the Mass, the Constitution calls for the treasures of the Bible to be opened up more lavishly so that a richer table of God's Word may be prepared for the faithful; "in this way a more representative portion of holy Scripture will be read to the people in the course of a prescribed number of years."[58] Scholars like Bea had hoped for the richer fare of pericopes drawn from a greater range of biblical books, as well as a greater number of pericopes, in order to provide a more nourishing diet to strengthen the faithful. The Apostolic Constitution *Missale Romanum* promulgating the new missal, explains how the new Lectionary meets both needs. First, preceding the Epistle and Gospel for Sunday Mass, there is now an additional reading normally taken from the Old Testament: "In this way the continuity of the development of the history of salvation will become more clearly apparent and be expressed in the very words of divine revelation."[59] Second, the new Lectionary contains a three-year cycle of readings for Sundays, as well as a two-year cycle for weekdays, and other sets of readings for saints' days, ritual Masses, etc. After explaining how the faithful can now hear, Sunday after Sunday, a much richer and more comprehensive account of how God works with his people, Pope Paul VI adds,

> We cherish the firm hope that, through the influence of these new arrange-
> ments, both priests and people will together prepare themselves more
> effectively for the celebration of the Lord's Supper and, at the same time,
> will daily receive increasing nourishment from the Word of God through
> more intensive reflection on holy Scripture.[60]

Thus, understanding the Word proclaimed as nourishment and source of grace, *Sacrosanctum Concilium* called for it to be more available to the faithful in much more abundant measure through the new Lectionary, and made it accessible to them through authorizing vernacular translation. Twenty-five years later Pope John Paul II would give thanks "that the table of the Word of God is now more abundantly furnished for all."[61] Yet being nourished requires more than being in the presence of food. After affirming that the liturgical proclamation of the Word is source of life and power, the *Introduction to the Lectionary* adds, "The Word of God reverently received moves the heart and its desires toward conversion and toward a life resplendent with both individual and community faith, since God's Word is the food of the Christian life and the source of the prayer of the whole Church."[62] How many Catholics today have been taught how to "reverently receive" the Word of God proclaimed in the liturgy, how to be fed and strengthened by it as Christians of early centuries were, how to "more intensively reflect on it" each day, and know it as spiritual sustenance in their lives? In order for the lectionary reform authorized by the Constitution to have its intended effect as source of grace, the faithful need to know how to avail themselves of that grace.

"Christ is present in his Word"

Sacrosanctum Concilium goes beyond affirming that God speaks through the proclamation of the Word in the liturgy and nourishes His people through that proclamation, by teaching that Christ "is present in his Word, since it is he himself who speaks when the holy Scriptures are read in the Church."[63] The *Introduction to the Lectionary* explains that "Christ's word gathers the people of God as one and increases and sustains them,"[64] and urges that "the faithful should be keenly aware of the one presence of Christ" in the Word of God as well as, above all, under the eucharistic species.[65] The Pontifical Biblical Commission affirms that since the new liturgy places the proclamation of the Word "in the midst of the community of believers, gathered around Christ so as to draw near to God," it "brings about the most perfect actualization of the biblical texts."[66] It is Christ's presence in the Word, where he is "still proclaiming his gospel"[67] that enables the syllables of the text spoken by the reader to become life-giving words, bearers of Christ's saving action.

As already noted, *Sacrosanctum Concilium* added Christ's presence in his Word to the ways Christ is present in the liturgy already given in *Mediator Dei;* this calls for theological explicitation of the sense in which Christ is present in his Word. At the most basic level, as one commentator explains,

> The liturgy, because it is the activation of the mystery of Christ, is a sacramental celebration of the Scriptures. The word of the liturgy is the word of the Scriptures; and in the liturgy the Scriptures acquire new saving effectiveness because Christ is present and acting in a special way in these Church actions.[68]

While further theological reflection on the full significance of Christ's presence in his Word in the liturgy must be ongoing, on a practical level, worshippers need to approach the proclamation of the Word mindful that Christ is present there. Pope John Paul II has urged that since Christ is present in his Word proclaimed, it is to be "listened to in faith and assimilated in prayer,"[69] adding that the dignity of the book and place of proclamation, and the reader's awareness that he or she is the "spokesman of God," enable this to happen. Since Christ is present in his Word and still proclaiming his Gospel, deacons and priests should proclaim the Gospel reading with a carefulness that conveys Christ's presence to the hearers, and bring that carefulness and reverence to the preparation of homilies.

The purpose of preaching

Sacrosanctum Concilium affirms that since the homily is part of the liturgy, it is not to be omitted at Sunday and holy day Masses with a congregation "except for a serious reason."[70] While this norm is generally followed, less attention has been given to what the Constitution says about the *content* of preaching: "Preaching should draw its content

mainly from scriptural and liturgical sources, being a proclamation
of God's wonderful works in the history of salvation, the mystery of
Christ, ever present and active within us, especially in the celebration
of the liturgy."[71] "By means of the homily the mysteries of the faith
and the guiding principles of the Christian life are expounded from
the sacred text during the course of the liturgical year."[72] "The ministry of preaching is to be fulfilled with exactitude and fidelity."[73]

In order to understand what this kind of preaching would be
like, it is necessary first to consider what effect the proclamation of
the Word in the liturgy is intended to have. When the Scriptures are
proclaimed, the story of how God in His merciful love has consistently
acted to save His people is unfolded week by week, and the Holy
Spirit works through that proclamation to invite all in the assembly to
understand their own lives in terms of that story, to open themselves
more fully to the working of God's saving grace set forth there. In
the liturgy, "God's wonderful past works in the history of salvation are
presented anew as mysterious realities,"[74] and the proclamation of
God's Word not only presents God's saving deeds, "when this Word is
proclaimed in the Church and put into living practice, it enlightens
the faithful through the working of the Holy Spirit and draws them
into the entire mystery of the Lord as a reality to be lived."[75] Further,
the proclamation of the Word is addressed to the community as
a whole as well as individually: "Whenever, therefore, the Church,
gathered by the Holy Spirit for liturgical celebration, announces and
proclaims the Word of God, she is aware of being a new people in
whom the covenant made in the past is perfected and fulfilled."[76]

God's acting to bring His people to Himself through the
proclamation of the Word culminates in the Liturgy of the Eucharist:

> In the Word of God the divine covenant is announced; in the Eucharist
> the new and everlasting covenant is renewed. . . . It can never be forgotten,
> therefore, that the divine word read and proclaimed by the Church in the
> liturgy has as its purpose the sacrifice of the New Covenant and the
> banquet of grace, that is, the Eucharist.[77]

The very way the readings have been selected and arranged is to allow
the assembly to see how what all of salvation history has been leading
up to is their union with God in Christ at this Eucharist:

. . . the Order of Readings for Mass aptly presents from Sacred Scripture
the principal deeds and words belonging to the history of salvation. As
its many places and events are recalled in the liturgy of the word, it will
become clear to the faithful that the history of salvation is continued here
and now in the representation of Christ's paschal mystery celebrated
through the Eucharist.[78]

The kind of preaching envisioned by the Constitution is
preaching that enables the Scripture readings proclaimed to have the
effects just described. The "spiritual world," which Jungmann speaks
of as "coming alive" in the liturgy, is a world centered on God, with all
persons and things seen in relationship to Him. The ultimate paradigm
and icon of this spiritual world is found in Scripture. When the Word
is proclaimed, the world of the Scripture is opened up and made present
to the assembly through that proclamation. The task of the preacher
is to enable the worshippers to see how this has happened and allow
themselves to be drawn into that scriptural world so that they can
experience themselves and the rest of the liturgy from that vantage
point—as connected to salvation history and steeped in and formed
by scriptural language. Preaching opens up what God is doing through
the proclamation of *these* readings to *this* congregation at *this* time,
functioning as a bridge between the Scripture proclaimed and the faithful. It shows how the story of God's works in the history of salvation
that was read, has extended outward to draw the worshippers in and
incorporate them into the story of God's people, where their lives, too,
are understood in relationship to God, and it shows how the spiritual
realities spoken about in the readings are mediated by them—made
present to the faithful to transform them. [79]

Preaching that is "a proclamation of God's wonderful works
in the history of salvation" calls attention to what God has done in the
Scripture proclaimed and asks, "What does this mean for us at this
liturgy?" If there is a connection between an Old Testament lesson and
the Gospel, it asks, "What does this tell us about the consistency with
which God works, the faithfulness of His love?" Preaching that explains
"the guiding principles of the Christian life" asks, "What is the wisdom
about how to live given by Christ in this Gospel, or by the other
inspired authors?" Preaching that is a proclamation of "the mystery
of Christ ever present and active within us, especially in the celebration
of the liturgy," asks, "What are these readings telling us about God

in Christ pouring out his life for us to give us new life in union with Christ in the Holy Spirit? What does this new life in Christ empowered by his Spirit look like, how does it manifest itself, and how can we enter into it?" This preaching opens up the Scriptures so that God can work through them to form the worshippers in their redeemed identity as disciples of Christ and as the people of God, and teach them how to be more faithful disciples.

Learning to hear what God is saying to the Church week by week through the proclamation of the Word, is much easier for worshippers if they know the logic of how the Order of Readings in the Lectionary is arranged and how specific readings are selected; a preacher whose preaching is rooted in the way the Church uses Scripture in the Lectionary can gradually impart this knowledge to the faithful even as he focuses on expounding the readings themselves. Further, if preachers are earnestly "listening to the Word"[80] as part of their homily preparation, this will be communicated through their preaching on any text, even if they are not aware of it, and the faithful who listen will be simultaneously learning to pray from Scripture. It has been pointed out above that in order for *Sacrosanctum Concilium's* lectionary reform to bear its intended fruit, the faithful need to know how to hear God speak through the Word proclaimed and how to be nourished by it. If these things are a preacher's lived experience, then every time he preaches he will be leading the faithful toward them by his example, regardless of the readings he is preaching on, or whether he is consciously trying to. The Introduction to the Lectionary describes the homilist as leading the faithful "to an affective knowledge of Scripture," adding, "He opens their minds to thanksgiving for the wonderful works of God."[81]

Sacrosanctum Concilium's call for a mandatory homily is one of the means toward its goal to make the Mass "pastorally effective to the utmost degree."[82] In order for this goal to be fulfilled, there needs to be greater attention to the kind of preaching described in the Constitution and later documents, preaching that serves as a bridge between the rich scriptural world opened up in the proclamation of the Word and the lives of the worshippers, which enables them to recognize and accept all God wants to do for them through His Word proclaimed.

The scriptural character of the entire liturgy

In explaining the crucial importance of Scripture in the celebration of the liturgy, *Sacrosanctum Concilium* states, "It is from Scripture that the readings are given and explained in the homily and that psalms are sung; the prayers, collects, and liturgical songs are Scriptural in their inspiration; it is from the Scriptures that actions and prayers derive their meaning." [83] The *Introduction to the Lectionary* refers to the Word of God as the "foundation of the liturgical celebration," [84] and Pope John Paul II describes the liturgy as "totally permeated by the Word of God." [85] The faithful's participation in the liturgy is expressed in gestures, actions, and words that "derive their full meaning not simply from their origin in human experience but from the Word of God and the economy of salvation, to which they refer." [86]

A few months after the Constitution was promulgated, liturgical scholar Louis Bouyer wrote,

> Not only because the Bible provides us with the readings given in the liturgy, but because it has directly inspired the whole of it, the liturgy will never again become the familiar prayer of Christians if the Bible remains for them a sealed book, which it still is, unfortunately, not only for the majority of them, but for too many priests. [87]

Bouyer understands *Sacrosanctum Concilium's* call for more readings from Scripture in liturgical celebrations as a way of providing the faithful with the initiation into the Bible which is the necessary basis for understanding the liturgy. [88] How many Catholics at Mass each Sunday are aware of the scriptural source of almost every part of the liturgy they are worshipping in, and of the meaning the scriptural context adds to what they are hearing, saying, or doing? Sometimes it is not possible to recognize the scriptural origin of a prayer because the English translation has so paraphrased the Latin that the direct reference or allusion to a scriptural text is no longer apparent, but this is not always the case. Problematic translations of specific texts aside, the fact remains that ultimately, the language of the liturgy is the language of Scripture, and in order for the faithful to appreciate the full richness of what is going on in the liturgy they are participating in, they must be as at home in the language of Scripture as they are in their native tongue.

Promoting a warm and living love for Scripture

After describing how the entire liturgy is scripturally based, *Sacrosanctum Concilium* 24 concludes, "Thus to achieve the reform, progress, and adaptation of the liturgy, it is essential to promote that warm and living love for Scripture to which the venerable tradition of both Eastern and Western rites gives testimony." Twenty-five years later, Pope John Paul II affirmed that "growth in the liturgical life and consequently progress in Christian life cannot be achieved except by continually promoting among the faithful, and above all among priests, "that warm and living knowledge." [89] True renewal," he explained, "sets further and ever new requirements," including: "fidelity to the authoritative meaning of the Scriptures"; appropriate "interior dispositions of the ministers of the Word"; proclaiming the Word in such a manner that "it may be perceived for what it is"; careful homily preparation; the faithful's effort "to participate at the table of the Word"; "a taste for prayer with the psalms"; and "a desire to discover Christ—like the disciples at Emmaus—at the table of the Word and the bread." [90]

In *Dies Domini,* the pope reflects at greater length on how love for Scripture is required in order for the reformed liturgy to accomplish its purpose: "In considering the Sunday Eucharist more than thirty years after the Council, we need to assess how well the Word of God is being proclaimed and how effectively the people of God have grown in knowledge and love of Sacred Scripture." [91] Stating that the two aspects of this, celebration and personal appropriation, are closely related, he explains that, in regard to celebration, the permission for proclamation of Scripture in the vernacular "must awaken a new sense of responsibility toward the Word, allowing 'the distinctive character of the sacred text' to shine forth 'even in the mode of reading or singing.'" [92]

In regard to personal appropriation, the pope urges that the faithful prepare themselves well for the hearing of the Word proclaimed through "an apt knowledge of Scripture," and, if possible, through "special initiatives designed to deepen understanding of the biblical readings, particularly those used on Sundays and holy days." [93] In fact,

> if Christian individuals and families are not regularly drawing new life
> from the readings of the sacred text in a spirit of prayer and docility to the

Church's interpretation, then it is difficult for the liturgical proclamation of the Word of God alone to produce the fruit we might expect.[94]

The pope therefore points out the value of meetings where priests, ministers, and faithful prepare the Sunday liturgy, "reflecting beforehand on the Word of God which will be proclaimed," so that through the praying, singing, listening, and preaching working together, all the assembly may be penetrated more powerfully by that Word.[95] The *Introduction to the Lectionary* notes that in order to prepare themselves to hear the Word, in addition to learning more about Scripture, the faithful should also desire an understanding of how the texts proclaimed are used in the liturgy.[96] Further, all the faithful should "always be ready to listen gladly to God's Word," since love of the Scripture is "a force reinvigorating and renewing the entire people of God."[97] While the Constitution itself foresaw that a "warm and living love for Scripture" was one of the conditions for a fruitful reform of the liturgy, how many contemporary Catholics have ever heard this or learned how to cultivate that love?

Fostering a genuine love for Scripture in the faithful would contribute to the Word proclaimed bearing more fruit both in the liturgical celebration and outside it. A living love for Scripture inspires worshippers to "listen to the Word of God with an inward and outward reverence that will bring them continuous growth in the spiritual life and draw them more deeply into the mystery which is celebrated."[98] This love also helps the faithful, when they hear the Word proclaimed "and reflect deeply on it . . . to respond to it actively with full faith, hope and charity through prayer and self-giving, and not only during Mass but in their entire Christian life."[99] The *Introduction to the Lectionary* explains that the faithful's participation in the liturgy increases to the degree that, as they listen to the Word proclaimed, they "strive harder" to commit themselves to the Word made flesh in Christ. "Thus they endeavor to conform their way of life to what they celebrate in the liturgy, and thus in turn to bring to the celebration of the liturgy all that they do in life."[100]

Sacrosanctum Concilium 24 affirms that "Sacred Scripture is of the greatest importance in the celebration of the liturgy." More attention to what the Constitution said about the Word in the liturgy has a crucial role in enabling the reforms it authorized to bear more abundantly their intended fruit. "The more profound our understanding of the importance of the celebration of the liturgy, the higher our appreciation of the importance of God's Word. Whatever we say of the one, we can say in turn of the other, because each recalls the mystery of Christ and each in its own way causes the mystery to be carried forward."[101] The Word proclaimed

> unceasingly calls to mind and extends the economy of salvation, which achieves its fullest expression in the liturgy. The liturgical celebration becomes therefore the continuing, complete, and effective presentation of God's Word.
>
> The Word of God constantly proclaimed in the liturgy is always, then, a living and effective Word through the power of the Holy Spirit. It expresses the Father's love that never fails in its effectiveness towards us.[102]

3. Liturgical Formation of Seminarians

So far it has been stated that in order for the Mass reformed by Vatican II to have its intended effect, worshippers need to know what is going on in the liturgy, that they need catechesis, especially concerning the following: the re-presentation of the Paschal Mystery in the liturgy and the ways Christ is present, the Mass as sacrifice, the corporate nature of the Eucharist, and what participation is, and that they need formation in how to participate. Also, worshippers need to learn how to listen to God speaking through the proclamation of the Word, experience that Word as nourishment, recognize Christ present in it, love Scripture and know it as native language, and allow the Word proclaimed in the liturgy to be incarnated in their lives. This immediately raises the question, how are good, faithful Catholics to know these things or experience them as part of their lives as Christians unless they are made aware of them? That, of course, raises the question, how are priests to communicate these things to their congregations unless they themselves have been taught about them in depth, or learned to live them, themselves?

Those who wrote the Constitution understood that priests who were well-trained and formed in its vision of the liturgy were a necessary condition for that vision to become a reality. Immediately after stating that full, conscious, and active participation was the primary and indispensable source of the true Christian spirit, and that pastors must zealously strive to bring about this participation, *Sacrosanctum Concilium* 14 continues,

> Yet it would be futile to entertain any hopes of realizing this unless, in the first place, pastors themselves become thoroughly imbued with the spirit and power of the liturgy and make themselves its teachers. A prime need, therefore, is that attention be directed, first of all, to the liturgical formation of the clergy.

The Constitution then provides basic norms for academic instruction and formation in liturgy, which were developed in postconciliar documents.[103] Annibale Bugnini, one of the *periti* on the commission that drafted *Sacrosanctum Concilium*, noted, "everything is presented with an eye on the conscious and devout participation that should result from the properly organized instruction of the faithful and, even before that, from the development in priests and seminarians of a strong and comprehensive sense of the liturgy."[104] In 1979, the Congregation for Catholic Education published the *Instruction on Liturgical Formation in Seminaries*, rooted in extended reflection on the norms for seminary education given by the Constitution and providing "suitable directives" for how those norms should be embodied in a seminary liturgy program. Yet, like *Sacrosanctum Concilium's* call for catechesis and emphasis on the importance of the Word of God in the liturgy, the Constitution's requirements for the liturgical formation of seminarians could still be more fully implemented in the United States today.

As a foundation for mastering the contents of academic coursework, seminarians need to begin to assimilate and live *Sacrosanctum Concilium's* vision of the nature of the liturgy, participation in the liturgy, and the role of the Word in it. In 1988, Pope John Paul II named as "the most urgent task" in regard to the Church's liturgy, "the biblical and liturgical formation of the people of God, *both pastors and faithful.*"[105] Citing the Constitution's statement that it would not be possible for priests to lead people to the participation required by the very nature of the liturgy "unless pastors of souls themselves become imbued more deeply with the spirit and power of the liturgy," he added, "This is a long-term programme, which must begin in the seminaries and houses of formation and continue throughout their priestly life."[106]

In the case of the biblical formation necessary for liturgical renewal, seminarians need to learn *lectio divina* as part of their daily prayer; only if they know how to listen to the Lord speaking in His living Word will they be able to help the faithful learn how to do this in preparation for the proclamation of the Word in the liturgy, as both Pope Paul VI and Pope John Paul II have envisioned. Seminarians also need to be shown how to integrate what they learn in their academic Scripture courses with a deep understanding of the liturgical use of Scripture, as well as with the wisdom they receive by meditating on it, so that they can preach the kind of homilies called for by *Sacrosanctum Concilium* 35 and 52. While modern methods of studying Scripture yield valuable insights into the meaning of texts, and are a necessary part of the seminary curriculum, over the past 40 years they have also sometimes resulted in homilies that begin, "We all know this never happened," or "Scripture scholars tell us this isn't true, so let me tell you an old folk legend. . . ." Seminarians need to be taught to use their academic knowledge of the methodologies of contemporary Scripture scholarship in the service of opening up the living Word of God for His people.

Areas of seminary liturgical formation

Because of the liturgy's vital importance in the life of the Church, *Sacrosanctum Concilium* calls for the study of liturgy "to be ranked among the compulsory and major courses in seminaries and religious houses of studies."[107] Due to budgetary constraints, during the last 40 years many seminaries in the United States have had only a single required academic course in liturgy, which has often been taught in the very first semester of a four-year program, so that even a dedicated priest can admit he remembers little about it by the time he is ordained. The practicum courses in liturgy, in which seminarians practice performing the rites at which they will soon preside, are normally given immediately prior to ordination, making it possible for seminarians to learn *what* a priest (or deacon) is supposed to do without necessarily recalling the theological and spiritual *why* he does it this way.

The Constitution goes on to say that liturgy is to be taught "under its theological, historical, spiritual, pastoral, and canonical aspects."[108] While describing everything that should be taught under these headings and how it should be organized into courses is beyond the scope of this essay, it is possible to summarize some points made by *Liturgical Formation in Seminaries* that deserve renewed attention.[109]

In regard to the theological aspect, *Liturgical Formation in Seminaries* explicitly states that "the very nature of the entire liturgy should be theologically explained, following the mind of the Constitution *Sacrosanctum Concilium* nn. 5–11."[110] In other words, seminarians should be led into an appreciation of the Church's deep theological insight into the very nature of the liturgy, from its origin in the context of salvation history, to its eschatological dimension, which was briefly summarized in the first part of this present essay but is rarely mentioned from the pulpit. Also, seminarians are to be "introduced into understanding that symbolical, liturgical language by which, through sensible signs, words, and gestures, divine things are signified and, in the case of the sacraments, actually caused,"[111] and shown "how all liturgical actions and signs derive their meaning from Holy Scripture," especially elements coming from nature.[112] The only way priests will be able to help congregations enter into the profoundly biblical world of the liturgy and understand its symbolic language is if they themselves are at home in that world and know its language so well they think in it as well as speak it.

Another crucial component of the theological aspect of liturgical education is what *Liturgical Formation in Seminaries* refers to as "the strict connection between the liturgy and the doctrine of the faith."[113] Priests who understand that the Church's prayers are bearers of its theological tradition will understand that to preside at the liturgy and pronounce those prayers is to hand on that tradition, so they will not feel a need to substitute their own ideas for the faith of the Church community.

Similarly, when studying the historical aspect of the liturgy, seminarians need to be given a good grasp of the history of the rites and to read the classic liturgical sources,[114] so that they will understand what they will do as presiders as taking place in continuity with the Church's tradition of prayer for almost two millennia. *Liturgical Formation in Seminaries* affirms that "it is of the highest importance that liturgical renewal promoted by the Second Vatican Council be correctly and fully grasped by future priests in light of sound doctrine, both Western and Eastern,"[115] so that they will understand the Council's reasons for reforming the liturgy and for the specific changes made.

In discussing difficulties in the practical application of the reform, Pope John Paul II explicitly refers to those who received the new books "without trying to understand or help others to understand the reasons for the changes."[116] The liturgy as it is today, understood as a reform of the Tridentine liturgy, in continuity with the Church's two-thousand-year living tradition of corporate prayer, generates one set of meanings; the same liturgy, taken out of its historical context and understood in isolation, interpreted through the lens of contemporary American culture, generates an entirely different set of meanings. Understanding how, over the course of centuries, the Church's liturgy came to have the form it has today is invaluable in understanding why it has that form and how that form is intended to serve as vehicle through which worshippers can be drawn into union with God.

The spiritual aspect of liturgical formation also needs attention, since *Sacrosanctum Concilium* expects that priests will be helping the laity to enter into the spiritual dimension of the liturgy. The Constitution states that it is priests' duty "to ensure that the faithful take part fully aware of what they are doing, actively engaged in the rite, and enriched by its effects."[117] *Presbyterorum Ordinis* states that priests must instruct the congregation "to offer to God the Father the divine Victim in the sacrifice of the Mass, and to join to it the offering of their own lives."[118] *Sacrosanctum Concilium* desires that priests be "living the liturgical life" and sharing it with the faithful entrusted to their care, but unless seminarians are initiated into actually living the liturgical life—a life rooted in the Church's encounter with God in the liturgy—they will not be able to share that life with others. The Constitution therefore calls for seminarians to "be given a liturgical formation in their spiritual life," and *Liturgical Formation in Seminaries* states that one of the responsibilities of seminary liturgy professors is to "introduce students into the liturgical life and into its spiritual character."[119]

At the heart of the spiritual aspect of the liturgy is an understanding of how the liturgy functions as locus for encounter with God, and of how worshippers participate in the liturgy's external forms as vehicle through which they participate internally in the theological and spiritual realities the liturgy mediates. Since priests are to promote this kind of participation in the faithful, they must understand what it means before they are ordained, so that they can describe it in such a way that their congregations can enter into it. Once seminarians are ordained as priests, their attention during the celebration of the liturgy will be given to performing the rites reverently and correctly, and their interior participation will be shaped by the fact that they are praying and acting *in persona Christi*. If, during liturgies they attended before their ordination, much of their attention was taken up with imagining themselves as presiders, making decisions about their own future presidential style, or evaluating the performance of the ministers, they will not know how to articulate to their parishioners what it means to participate internally in the way appropriate for the congregation. Unless a seminarian learns to "pray the Mass" himself, he will not be able to explain to his future parishioners how he learned to do this, and so enable congregations to come to experience it themselves. *Liturgical Formation in Seminaries* links knowledge about given subject areas of the liturgy with experience of their spiritual dimension. In discussing how seminarians should be instructed in the "history and spiritual character of Easter and the Easter season," for example, *Liturgical Formation in Seminaries* concludes, "Most of all the seminarians should be trained to live the paschal mystery in the depths of their souls and to prepare themselves for their future paschal ministry." [120]

In regard to the pastoral aspect of the liturgy, *Liturgical Formation in Seminaries* states that "above all else" the texts and ceremonies of all "liturgical acts" must be explained to seminarians, and it calls for careful instruction in the *General Instruction of the Roman Missal,* the *Pastoral Introductions* of the rites, and the *General Instruction of the Liturgy of the Hours,* in order to accomplish this. [121] Seminarians are thus to be given a thorough knowledge of the Church's liturgy as the Church celebrates it, and to be trained to prayerfully perform it this way. [122] In the decades since the Council, celebrating the liturgy in a way that is "pastoral" has often been misunderstood to mean spontaneously re-writing the liturgy in a way that a presider thinks makes his congregation feel good. A celebration that is truly "pastoral," however, is one that is so alive with faith and reverence that the congregation can recognize its prayers and rites as sustenance given them on behalf of the Good Shepherd, and be nourished by them.

In their training on the pastoral aspect of the liturgy, then, seminarians must be enabled to see that ultimately, "doing things by the book" *is* the pastoral way of doing things, because it doesn't impose the celebrant's private tastes or personality on defenseless worshippers, thereby setting them against him, but rather invites the congregation to join with the presider in their common worship as Church. Similarly, in regard to the canonical aspect of the liturgy, seminarians who have learned the liturgy's historical and theological aspects will see that the Church's laws for valid performance of liturgical rites are not arbitrary rules, but a means for protecting the Church community's tradition of believing and praying.

In order to provide seminarians with the necessary knowledge in all these five aspects, *Sacrosanctum Concilium* calls for professors who are "thoroughly trained for their work in institutions specializing in this subject."[123] During the years since its promulgation, however, not all seminaries in the United States have been able to hire a professor with a doctorate (or even licentiate) in liturgy.[124] The Constitution adds that seminary professors in other disciplines must present their course material "in a way that will clearly bring out the connection between their subjects and the liturgy";[125] but this, too, has not always been possible.

Finally, the context within which seminary academic training in liturgy takes place is the celebrations of the liturgy in the life of the seminary community; the way in which the seminary Mass is celebrated becomes the lens through which the knowledge imparted in academic courses is understood. *Liturgical Formation in Seminaries* therefore states that those celebrations must be exemplary in regard to ritual and texts, "the spiritual and pastoral mentality adopted," and the observance of liturgical norms and laws.[126] Preaching should demonstrate the characteristics of preaching expected by *Sacrosanctum Concilium* so the seminarians will have a model of the kind of preaching the reformed liturgy requires. The Constitution calls for pastors to foster external participation in the liturgy in their parishioners, as well as internal, and to lead them by example;[127] the seminarian's participation in the seminary liturgy should prepare them to do this. *Liturgical Formation in Seminaries* expects that seminary faculty will work with the seminarians in regard to the various ministries they perform in the liturgy, "so that there is formed in them a genuine notion of the liturgy solidly rooted in the doctrine and sense of the Church."[128]

Sacrosanctum Concilium's requirements for the liturgical formation and education of the clergy flow directly from the affirmation that the "aim to be considered before all else" in the renewal of the liturgy is the active participation of the people, and they are shaped toward this end. The better the Constitution's norms for the liturgical formation of seminarians are met, the better able priests will be to help worshippers enter into that participation. After admitting that only a tireless catechesis could help the faithful "enter the world of the liturgy," Bugnini added, "No results may be expected, however, unless priests themselves are first given a liturgical formation."[129] Today there is still a need for qualified seminary professors providing the knowledge required for future priests to "become thoroughly imbued with the spirit and power of the liturgy,"[130] and to understand "what it is they are doing in their liturgical functions,"[131] how the words and rites are speaking about what is taking place in the liturgy, and how to help the faithful understand what God is doing for them through the liturgy of the Church, so they can enter into it. As *Liturgical Formation in Seminaries* explains, the main task of seminary liturgy professors is to lead seminarians

> to study the liturgical texts which the seminarians must understand. This is so that, when they become celebrants of the liturgy, they will be capable of leading the people to a knowledgeable and fruitful participation in the mystery of Christ.[132]

4. The Dispositions Necessary for Liturgical Participation

When worshippers are aware of all that God is doing for them in the liturgy and of how to participate in it, and of the important role of God's Word in the liturgy, a further element is needed in order for the Council's reforms to accomplish their intended purpose. As *Sacrosanctum Concilium* 11 makes clear, "in order that the liturgy may possess its full effectiveness, it is necessary that the faithful come to it with proper dispositions, that their minds be attuned to their voices, and that they cooperate with divine grace, lest they receive it in vain." How many of those at Mass each week could describe what "proper dispositions" are, or what they are doing in order to "co-operate with grace"? How many worshippers are comfortable when they profess that Jesus Christ is "begotten, not made, one in being with the Father," that they know what this means and why it is so important that they affirm it aloud every Sunday? How many find it natural to "attune their minds to their voices" when they say, "I have sinned through my own fault, in my thoughts and in my words, in what I have done and in what I have failed to do" and ask a room full of people (many of whom they do not know) to pray that God will forgive their sins?

The Council's liturgical reforms restored various forms of external participation to make it easier for worshippers to participate internally in the spiritual realities mediated by the liturgy. But in order to receive the reforms' intended benefits, worshippers need to *believe* that God is actually acting in the liturgy in the way described by *Sacrosanctum Concilium,* and *want* to participate in this. The liturgy mandated by the Constitution was designed for worshippers who believe in what the Church teaches and are seeking to live as faithful disciples of Jesus Christ, by the power of the Holy Spirit, to the glory of God the Father. In order to be able to participate "fully, consciously, and actively" in the liturgy reformed for this purpose, worshippers need to be disciples.

Discipleship and participation

How would this life of discipleship express itself in regard to cooperating with grace in the liturgy? The foundation of a life of discipleship is, of course, faith in Jesus Christ as Lord, as the one who, through his saving death and resurrection, brought forgiveness of sins and the promise of eternal life to those who repent and believe in him. In order to be able to enter into the re-presentation of Christ's Paschal Mystery—his dying and rising—in the liturgy, worshippers must believe in this as source of their salvation. As Pope John Paul II explains, "we must have a sufficient awareness that through the 'paschal mystery we have been buried with Christ in baptism, so that we may rise with him to a new life.' "[133] This means worshippers need to approach liturgical celebrations with a deep sense of their baptismal identity of being dead and risen with Christ and members of his Body that has gathered to be united to him by his Spirit as he offers himself to the Father. A key aspect of disciples living out their baptismal identity and preparing for its unique fulfillment in liturgical celebration is pondering the Word of God in Scripture, so that their lives are increasingly penetrated and shaped by the way God perceives things, which is the context in which the liturgy makes sense. One of the bishops on the commission who wrote *Sacrosanctum Concilium* noted that "the Constitution will demand new efforts in all fields of Christian life. Catholics will have to read the Bible and mold their lives according to it." [134]

As re-presentation of the Paschal Mystery, the liturgy is "the privileged place for the encounter of Christians with God and the one whom he has sent, Jesus Christ." [135] In order to be able to recognize Christ when they encounter him in the liturgy, those who seek to follow him as disciples need to spend time outside the liturgy coming to know him and growing in relationship with him. If parishioners are faithful to entering into the presence of God in times of prayer during the week, they will be better prepared to enter into his presence at Sunday Eucharist. This prayer needs to include repentance from sin and asking for mercy, as well as thanksgiving for redemption, and praise; when these things are experiential realities in parishioners' day-to-day lives, they are able to be "fully aware of what they are doing," with their "minds attuned to their voices," when they express them aloud during the liturgy.

Further, worshippers need to enter into the liturgy consciously seeking to encounter God in Christ in the Spirit, and believing that God is seeking that encounter with them:

> Since the liturgy is the exercise of the priesthood of Christ, it is necessary to keep ever alive the affirmation of the disciple faced with the mysterious presence of Christ: "It is the Lord!"(Jeremiah 2:7). Nothing of what we do in the liturgy can appear more important than what in an unseen but real manner Christ accomplishes by the power of his Spirit. [136]

Those who are seeking to live as disciples therefore need to nurture in themselves the living faith that can receive all that Christ does in the liturgy. [137] They should also seek to learn enough about the purpose of the liturgy and why it has the form it does so that they can genuinely pray it.

The effect of participation with "proper dispositions"

The active participation the reformed liturgy was designed to promote is not a skill which, once acquired, remains static, but a dynamic reality. As part of the life of discipleship, participation in the liturgical encounter with Christ deepens as the disciple's relationship to Christ deepens:

> Since Christ's death on the cross and his resurrection constitute the con-
> tent of the daily life of the Church and the pledge of his eternal Passover,
> the liturgy has as its first task to lead us untiringly back to the Easter
> pilgrimage initiated by Christ, in which we accept death in order to enter
> into life.[138]

Participating in the liturgy draws worshippers into ever-deepening
union with Christ in his dying and rising, which enables them to
live in a more Christ-like way outside of the liturgy, which in turn
prepares them to enter into yet deeper union with Christ in the
liturgy. Similarly, after explaining that in order to be "integrated into
the life of Christ's faithful, the Word of God demands a living faith,"
the *Introduction to the Lectionary* affirms that "hearing the Word of
God unceasingly proclaimed arouses that faith."[139] God's Word proclaimed in the liturgy Sunday by Sunday inspires the faithful to live
in the power of, and obedient to, that Word week by week. Since the
liturgy was reformed to make it easier for the faithful to derive the
graces needed to live out the universal call to holiness, the further worshippers progress on the path of discipleship, the more deeply they are
able to participate in the mystery of Christ made present in the liturgy,
and *vice versa*.

    As Virgil Michel described it, the first goal of the Liturgical
Movement was to bring about intelligent internal participation in the
Church's liturgical worship.

> But that once attained, the liturgy urges to ever greater assimilation to
> Christ the divine head, so that the member should continue to grow
> spiritually and supernaturally in his participation in the divine action of
> Christ enacted in the liturgy.[140]

That growth, Michel explained, included a deeper understanding of
the worshipper's status as a member of Christ, of his or her part in
the corporate worship of the Mystical Body, of the commandment
to love both God and neighbor and to serve God directly in worship
and indirectly in serving fellow human beings, "and especially of the
two-fold truth that in the supernatural life of the Christian it is always
Christ who is acting and producing the effects of supernatural value,
but that the abundance of such fruitful actions, even while they are
Christ's, is directly proportionate also to the good will and effort put
forth by the Christian himself."[141]

Growth in "participation in the divine action of Christ enacted in the liturgy" also includes

> A constant putting into effect of these sublime truths of membership in Christ, it means the will to live for the glory of God above all, to give oneself over wholly to the service of God and His children, in other words, to seek above all the kingdom of heaven, and to relate and co-ordinate all else properly to this supreme aim of the Christian life. [142]

This will to live fully "as 'another Christ,' as a regenerated child of God and member of Christ," must manifest itself "wholeheartedly in every action of the day." [143] Liturgical participation that is genuine thus results in worshippers desiring to live out what they are celebrating in the liturgy when the celebration is over, and in growing in laying down their lives for fellow members of Christ's Body and for those in need.

The liturgy reformed by the Council, then, was designed for worshippers seeking to live as disciples of Jesus Christ "so that they could more securely derive" the graces to enable them to grow in their faithfulness as disciples. The "full, conscious, and active participation" that *Sacrosanctum Concilium* states is called for by the liturgy's very nature is simply the liturgical mode of discipleship. The liturgy now reformed to facilitate this, requires participation that consists of worshippers "fully aware of what they are doing" participating internally in the spiritual realities mediated by the liturgy, by means of external participation in rites and prayers, as a body. Once believers have committed themselves to a life of following Jesus as disciples, they enter into an ever-deepening relationship with him, and learn to express that relationship through the external prayers and rites of the liturgy. Simultaneously—since discipleship is lived out within the matrix of committed relationships with other members of Christ's Body and their shared understanding of what it means to follow Christ—worshippers learn to coordinate their internal-by-means-of-external participation with that of their fellow worshippers. All the while, the community of disciples, transformed into Christ's likeness through union with him in the liturgy, seeks to bring his life to all they encounter. [144]

In the decades since the Council, some have been disappointed that the external reforms of the liturgy did not automatically result in the deep spiritual renewal they were expected to bring. But for true renewal to take place—not just outward reform but true spiritual renewal—worshippers need not only a new form of liturgy and cate-chesis to explain it to them, but they also need to know how to "co-operate with grace" in that liturgy, and want to. As Pope John Paul II has emphasized, the changes in the liturgy's outward form "demand a new spiritual awareness and maturity" of both celebrant and congrega-tion. [145] The liturgy will have its "full effectiveness," when worshippers approach it with "proper dispositions," and those dispositions are the result of graced conversion to Jesus Christ as Lord, lived out as his disciples and members of his Body.

♦

This essay has considered why the Second Vatican Council called for a reform of the liturgy, and which aspects of the Constitution autho-rizing that reform might deserve further attention today. Many of those who voted for *Sacrosanctum Concilium* or wrote about it when it was promulgated, expected that renewal of the liturgy would lead to renewal of the Church. As Pope John Paul II would later explain,

> A very close and organic *bond exists between the renewal of the liturgy and the renewal of the whole life of the Church.* The Church not only acts but also expresses herself in the liturgy, lives by the liturgy, and draws from the liturgy the strength for her life.[146]

This expectation was grounded in the assumption that it would be made clear to all that changes in the liturgy's outward form were being made as means to spiritual renewal. The first *Instruction on the Proper Implementation of the Constitution on the Sacred Liturgy* notes that "it is essential that everybody be persuaded that the scope of the *Constitution on the Sacred Liturgy* is not limited merely to the changing of liturgical rites and texts," and that the Constitution "will yield fruit more abun-dantly the more profoundly pastors and the faithful are truly imbued with its spirit and the more willingly they implement it." [147]

    If the changes in the liturgy's outward form have not resulted in as powerful a renewal of the Church as so many hoped for, it is because the changes happened before there was time for pastors and congregations to be "truly imbued with" the Constitution's "spirit." To be able to hear Scripture read in the vernacular is helpful, but what if Catholics knew how to hear God speak and form them as His people through that proclamation? To be able to sing the Holy, Holy is better than remaining silent, but what if the whole congregation understood what it meant, what they are doing spiritually when they sing it at that point in the liturgy, and what if their hearts were "fully attuned to their voices" when they sang it? To be able to offer the sign of peace is a fitting expression of worshippers' reconciliation with each other and unity as Body of Christ, but what if they lived out those words in their relationships with each other when Mass was over, and, as Christ's Body on earth, to the poor he came to serve? A renewed attempt by all the faithful to "be imbued with" *Sacrosanctum Concilium's* teaching on the spiritual and theological nature of the liturgy would enable it even now to bear more abundant fruit.

Many of those who worked for the liturgical reforms or contributed to them, including three popes and such eminent scholars as Romano Guardini, stated explicitly that the efforts of the Liturgical Movement toward renewing the liturgy were the work of the Holy Spirit. Pope Pius XII told the Assisi Congress that

> the Liturgical Movement is thus shown forth as a sign of the providential dispositions of God for the present time, of the movement of the Holy Ghost in the Church, to draw men more closely to the mysteries of the faith and the riches of grace which flow from the active participation of the faithful in the liturgical life.[148]

In the Apostolic Constitution promulgating the new *Roman Missal* in 1969, Pope Paul VI cited those very words.[149]

Sacrosanctum Concilium itself had affirmed: "Zeal for the promotion and restoration of the liturgy is rightly held to be a sign of the providential dispositions of God in our time, a movement of the Holy Spirit in his Church";[150] and on its twenty-fifth anniversary Pope John Paul II gave "thanks to God for the movement of the Holy Spirit in the Church which the liturgical renewal represents."[151] The work of the Holy Spirit is to glorify Jesus Christ. If the Holy Spirit inspired the Liturgical Movement, it was toward the end of bringing about whatever reforms in the liturgy would best draw the faithful into a deeper understanding and love of Jesus Christ and union with him through the liturgy, and to enable them, thereby empowered, to live more faithfully as Christ's Body in the world, to the glory of the Father.

After 40 years of reforms touching every aspect of the Church's worship, it is important to remember that those who promulgated *Sacrosanctum Concilium* believed it to be the work of the Holy Spirit to renew the Church. That the ultimate goal of the changes in the liturgy's outward form was a spiritual one, is clearly seen in the words of Cardinal Lercaro to the Consilium at its second general meeting:

> This is the purpose and raison d' être of the conciliar Constitution on the Liturgy, that truly blessed and ever to be praised gift of the Holy Spirit in response to the expectation, even to the hunger and thirst, of all the clergy and the entire Christian people. The purpose is that the clergy and people may at last attain to an authentic and deeper understanding of the sacred liturgy and *may be allowed truly to taste it.* The purpose is that the sacred rites, now made simpler and almost transparent, may more easily promote the understanding and participation of all. The purpose, finally, is that the Christian people, "a holy nation, God's own people," may exercise the right and duty it has acquired in baptism; that it may give full and solemn praise to the divine Majesty; *and that in Christ and through Christ the fountain of sanctification and salvation may be opened in souls so that their hope of eternal life with God in the heavenly fatherland may grow ever stronger.*
>
> Our entire work is aimed at making it easier for all the children of God to come to grips with matters so holy, serious, and necessary, *in order that they may taste how sweet the Lord is and how important it is for the family of God to share in these riches.*[152]

What is needed now, on *Sacrosanctum Concilium's* fortieth anniversary, is prayer for a fresh outpouring of the Spirit, that the outward reforms it set in motion may accomplish yet more fully their stated purpose "that the Christian people may more surely derive an abundance of graces from the liturgy."[153]

Notes

Part I

1. Pope Paul VI, Address at the close of the second session of the Vatican Council, 4 December 1963, in Austin Flannery, ed., *Vatican II: The Liturgy Constitution.* (Dublin: Scepter Books, 1964), p. 9.

2. *Final Report of the Extraordinary Assembly of the Synod of Bishops* (7 December 1985), II, B, b, 1, in *Origins:* Vol. 15, No. 27 (December 19, 1985), p. 448.

3. For example, on the Constitution's twenty-fifth anniversary, Pope John Paul II gave thanks for the translations of the liturgical books and lectionary, for the increased participation of the faithful, for new responsibilities of the laity, and for the vitality of many Christian communities drawn from the liturgy, in his Apostolic Letter *On the Twenty-fifth Anniversary of the Promulgation of the Conciliar Constitution Sacrosanctum Concilium on the Sacred Liturgy (Vicesimus Quintus Annus), December 4, 1988* (Washington, DC: USCC, 1988), 12. Subsequent references to this letter will use the abbreviation VQA.

4. In the Apostolic Constitution promulgating the New Order of Mass that resulted from *Sacrosanctum Concilium,* Pope Paul VI discussed the work that led up to it and wrote, "However, one should think that this renewal of the Roman Missal has taken place all of a sudden and without adequate preparation; rather has the way to its achievement been well prepared by progress in liturgical studies made during the past four centuries." *Missale Romanum,* in Austin Flannery, ed., Vatican Council II: *The Conciliar and Post-Conciliar Documents, Vol. I,* Revised edition. (Northport, NY: Costello Publishing Co., 1992), p. 138. Similarly, Pope John Paul II in his Apostolic Letter on the Constitution's twenty-fifth anniversary notes that the promulgation of *Sacrosanctum Concilium* "had been prepared for by a great liturgical and pastoral movement, and was a source of hope for the life and renewal of the Church," VQA 1. For a brief summary of the work of the principal figures of the Liturgical Movement, see Pierre Jounel, "From the Council of Trent to Vatican II," in A. G. Martimort, ed., *The Church at Prayer, Vol. I: Principles of the Liturgy* (Collegeville, MN: The Liturgical Press, 1987), pp. 72–76.

5. *"horum omnium fons et caput bonorum,"* Leo XIII, *Mirae caritatis,* in *Acta Sanctae Sedis,* Vol. XXXIV (1901–1902), p. 644.

    Sacrosanctum Concilium 10 refers to the liturgy as *fons* and *culmen* ("font" and "summit"): *"Attamen Liturgia est culmen ad quod actio Ecclesiae tendit et simul fons unde omnis eius virtus emanat." Sacrosanctum Oecumenicum Concilium Vaticanum II. Constitutiones, Decreta, Declarationes. Cura et Studio Secretariae*

Generalis Concilii Oecumenici Vatican II. (Typis Polyglottis Vaticanis, 1966), p. 11. *Lumen Gentium* 11 also refers to the liturgy as *fons* and *culmen,* pp. 111–12.

6. *"Augustum altaris Sacrificium divini cultus praecipua actio est; oportet igitur christianiae etiam pietatis sit fons ac veluti centrum,"* Pius XII, *Mediator Dei* IV, 2, in *Acta Apostolicae Sedis* (henceforth AAS) 39. Series II, Vol. 14 (1947), p. 592. This is paragraph 201 in English translations; cf. paragraph 66. Subsequent references will be to the English translation found in *The Encyclical Letter of Pope Pius XII on the Sacred Liturgy: Mediator Dei* (Boston: Daughters of St. Paul).

7. *"Essendo infatti Nostro vivissimo desiderio che il vero spirito cristiano riflorisca per ogni modo e si mantenga nei fedeli tutti, è necessario provvedere prima di ogni altra cosa alla santità e dignità del tempio, appunto i fedeli si radunano per attingere tale spirito dalla sua prima ed indispensabile fonte, che è la partecipazione attiva ai sacrosanti misteri e alla preghiera pubblica e solenne della Chiesa." Pius X, Tra le sollecitudini, Acta Sanctae Sedis* Vol. XXXVI (1903–4), p. 331.

    Sacrosanctum Concilium 14 states, "In the reform and promotion of the liturgy, this full and active participation by all the people is the aim to be considered before all else. For it is the primary and indispensable source from which all the faithful are to derive the true Christian spirit . . ." *("Quae totius populi plena et actuosa participatio, et instauranda et fovenda sacra Liturgia, summopere est attendenda: est enim primus, isque necessarius fons, e quo spiritum vere christianum fideles hauriant"; Constitutiones, Decreta, Declarationes,* p. 14).

8. *"Ac revera pernecesse est ut fideles non tamquam extranei vel muti spectatores, sed penitus liturgiae pulchritudine affecti; sic caeremoniis sacris intersint . . ."* Pius XI, *Divini cultus* IX, in *Acta Apostolicae Sedis 21 (1929),* p. 40. This is cited word for word in *Mediator Dei* 192. *Sacrosanctum Concilium* 48 states: "The Church, therefore, earnestly desires that Christ's faithful, when present at this mystery of faith, should not be there as strangers or silent spectators . . ." (*Itaque Ecclesia sollicitas curas eo intendit ne christifideles hunc fidei mysterio tamquam extranei vel muti spectatores intersint . . . ," Constitutiones, Decreta, Declarationes, p.* 28).

9. *Mediator Dei* 22; 92; 20.

10. E.g. Pierre-Marie Gy, "The Constitution in the Making," in Flannery, ed., *Vatican II: The Liturgy Constitution,* p. 16. Cf. Sacred Congregation of Rites, *Instruction on the Worship of the Eucharistic Mystery (Eucharisticum Mysterium)* 1, in Flannery, ed., *Vatican Council II: The Conciliar and Post-conciliar Documents* Vol. I, p. 101.

11. Cf. Sonya A. Quitslund, *Beauduin: A Prophet Vindicated* (New York: Newman Press, 1973); Lambert Beauduin, *Liturgy, the Life of the Church,* trans. Virgil Michel (Collegeville, MN: The Liturgical Press, 1926, 1929).

12. Pope John Paul II, in his Apostolic Letter on the Constitution's twenty-fifth anniversary, states that its guiding principles were: a) the reenactment of the paschal mystery; b) the reading of the Word of God; c) the self-manifestation of the Church, VQA 5–9. For Casel's work, see: Odo Casel, *The Mystery of Christian Worship* (Westminster, MD: The Newman Press, 1962).

13. See, e.g., Virgil Michel, OSB, "The Scope of the Liturgical Movement," *Orate Fratres* 10 (1935–36), pp. 485–490.

14. See *The Assisi Papers: Proceedings of the First International Congress of Pastoral Liturgy, Assisi-Rome, September 18–22, 1956.* (Collegeville, MN: The Liturgical Press, 1957). The addresses of Jungmann and Bea are discussed further in the second and third parts of this essay.

15. *The Assisi Papers,* pp. vi–vii.

16. *Constitution on the Sacred Liturgy* 5, in *Documents on the Liturgy 1963–1979: Conciliar, Papal and Curial Texts* (Collegeville, MN: The Liturgical Press, 1982). Paragraphs 1–4 serve as the introduction to the document; the body of the Constitution begins with the foundational theological section at the beginning of Chapter I, paragraph 5ff. Further references to the Constitution will use the standard abbreviation SC.

17. SC 6.

18. SC 6, citing John 4:23.

19. SC 6, citing the Council of Trent.

20. SC 47, citing Saint Augustine, and the Liturgy of the Hours for Corpus Christi.

21. The Paschal Mystery is explicitly mentioned in paragraphs 5, 6 (twice), 61, 104, 106, 107, 109; see also 12, 47, 81, 102.

22. SC 61.

23. SC 102; cf. *Mediator Dei* 152.

24. SC 106, 102.

25. SC 102, 105, 107–110.

26. SC 104.

27. SC 7. Cf., e.g., *Mediator Dei* 1–3 (citing Trent); *Mediator Dei* will be discussed in greater detail in the second part of this essay.

28. SC 7.

29. VQA 7.

30. SC 7.

31. SC 84.

32. SC 83.

33. SC 7; 33.

34. SC 5, citing the *Verona Sacramentary.*

35. SC 7; 10.

36. SC 8.

37. SC 6, citing 1 Corinthians 11:26; SC 8, citing Philippians 3:20, Colossians 3:4.

38. SC 10.

39. SC 2, citing the *Roman Missal;* SC 10.

40. SC 10; for "one in holiness" *(pietate concordes)* SC cites the *Roman Missal.*

41. SC 9–10.

42. SC 48.

Part II

1. SC 14.

2. SC 19; cf. 11, 33, 48.

3. SC 30.

4. SC 48 (" . . . *immaculatam hostiam, non tantum per sacerdotis manus, sed etiam una cum ipso offerentes, seipsos offere, discant"), Constitutiones, Decreta, Declarationes,* p. 28.
    Mediator Dei 92 states: "Now the faithful participate in the oblation, understood in this limited sense, after their own fashion and in a two-fold manner, namely because they not only offer the Sacrifice by the hands of the priest, but also, to a certain extent, in union with him." (*"Hanc autem restricti nominis oblationem christifideles suo modo duplicique ratione participant: quia nempe non tantum per sacerdotis manus, sed etiam una cum ipso quodammodo Sacrificium offerunt,"*AAS 39 (ser. II, vol. 14), pp. 555–56. *Mediator Dei* 80 states: "And together with him (sc. Christ) and through him let them make their oblation, and in union with him let them offer up themselves." *("atque una cum ipso (sc. Christus) et per ipsum allud offerant, unaque cum eo se devoveant"),* AAS 39 (ser. II, vol. 14), p. 552.
    NB: Both of these citations are made in the context of *Mediator Dei's* substantive explanation of the nature of eucharistic sacrifice, and the difference between the offering of the sacrifice by the priest acting *in persona Christi,*

and the sense in which the people offer it, 66–104; a complete understanding of what *Mediator Dei* means by these citations requires study of this entire section.

5. *Mediator Dei* 24.

6. *Mediator Dei* 80.

7. *Mediator Dei* 105–106.

8. *Mediator Dei* 111; cf. 124.

9. Virgil Michel, "The Scope of the Liturgical Movement," *Oratre Fratres* 10 (1935–36) p. 485; cf. SC 9–10. Note that when Michel is discussing Pope Pius X's affirmation of active participation in *Tra le sollecitudini*, he affirms that it is the "sacrifice of the altar," which as "the source and center of the life" of the Church, is the source of the "true Christian spirit which must be reflected in all the contacts of a Christian's daily life," rather than outward actions that worshippers perform, p. 486.

10. Michel, "The Scope of the Liturgical Movement," p. 485.

11. Ibid., p. 486.

12. Ibid.

13. SC 14.

14. Michel, "The Scope of the Liturgical Movement," p. 487. Further, "The Christian who drinks deep at the liturgical sources of the Christ-life will appreciate the seal of Christ with which he was indelibly marked at his baptism, and he will endeavor to put his same seal on everything with which he comes in contact throughout his daily life," p. 488.

15. *Mediator Dei* 88; cf. *Lumen Gentium* 11.

16. *Tra le sollecitudini* in *Acta Sanctae Sedis* 36, p. 331.

17. Odo Casel, *The Mystery of Christian Worship* (Westminster, MD: The Newman Press, 1962) p. 48. Two sections of *The Mystery of Christian Worship* deserve quoting here at length.

In discussing how the people share in the offering of the Church's sacrifice at Mass, Casel states: "The co-offering of the faithful rests first of all on the objective sacramental engrafting of every Christian into the body of Christ by baptism. What the body does, the members do in company with it. The more conscious this participation is, the more deeply it is experienced, the more intensive the participation. *This explains the necessity of active participation in the liturgical celebration and in its external form; the external strengthens what is within.* See section iii," p. 23n., *emph. added.*

In section iii, Casel discusses lay participation at greater length, including the paragraph containing the quotation in the body of this essay: ". . . the whole church, not merely the clergy is to take an active part in the liturgy, each according to sacred order, in his proper rank, place and measure. All members are truly, sacramentally conjoined to Christ their head; every believer, because of the sacramental character he received in baptism and confirmation, has part in the priesthood of Christ the head. This means that the layman does not merely assist with private devotion and prayer at the priest's liturgy, but is, by his objective membership in Christ's body, a necessary and real sharer in the liturgical fellowship. It belongs to the perfection of this liturgical participation, of course, that this objective priesthood should be made real and brought up to its highest pitch by a personal sharing of life. As psychology teaches us, the inner life grows stronger to the extent that the external act corresponding to an interior one is consciously made; we hear a song, but the interior participation in it will be greatly heightened and made easier if we sing it ourselves. So with the liturgy, the decisive thing is inward participation which does not require unconditionally to be made external; *but external participation does belong to the intense sharing of the experience, and to the completion of its symbolic expression,"* p. 48, *emph. added.*

18. *Mediator Dei* 23–27.

19. SC 33.

20. SC 21. Cf. the statement of Cardinal Lercaro, President of the Consilium, at the beginning of the Consilium's second general meeting, in Annibale Bugnini, *The Reform of the Liturgy 1948–1975,* trans. Matthew J. O'Connell (Collegeville, MN: The Liturgical Press, 1990), p. 933.

21. By "pastoral care" Jungmann means leading people to salvation in Christ and eternal life and leading them to "come together in holy and glorious fellowship to glorify God." Joseph Jungmann, "The Pastoral Idea in the History of the Liturgy," in *The Assisi Papers: Proceedings of the First International Congress of Pastoral Liturgy, Assisi-Rome, September 18–22, 1956* (Collegeville, MN: The Liturgical Press, 1957), p. 29.

22. Jungmann, "The Pastoral Idea in the History of the Liturgy," p. 30. For a history of how the form of the eucharistic liturgy changed through the centuries, see Robert Cabié, *The Eucharist,* in A. G. Martimort, ed., *The Church at Prayer, Vol. 2* (Collegeville, MN: The Liturgical Press, 1986).

23. Jungmann, "The Pastoral Idea in the History of the Liturgy," p. 31. In his Allocution to the Assisi Congress, Pope Pius XII himself said of the decree on Holy Week (November 16, 1955) that it "had helped the faithful to a better understanding and closer participation in the love, suffering and triumph of our Lord," *The Assisi Papers,* p. 224.

24. Augustin Bea, SJ, "The Pastoral Value of the Word of God in the Sacred Liturgy," in *The Assisi Papers,* p. 74; 90.

25. John Paul II, *On the Twenty-fifth Aniversary of the Constitution on the Sacred Liturgy* (VQA) 3. In regard to the psalter, Bea had commented in his address at Assisi: "The same 'pastoral solicitude' is manifested in the *Motu Proprio* of our Holy Father Pius XII in which he approves the new Latin translation of the psalms, which he had desired 'in order that from the recitation of the divine office one may daily derive ever more abundant light, grace and consolation . . . and thus imitate more closely . . . . the models of holiness that shine forth in the psalms,'" pp. 74–75.

26. SC 23.

27. Bugnini, *The Reform of the Liturgy 1948–1975*, p. 48.

28. *Eucharisticum Mysterium* 4, *emph. added*, citing the Council of Trent and SC 33 and 59; in Sacred Congregation of Rites, *Instruction on the Worship of the Eucharistic Mystery (Eucharisticum Mysterium)*, in Flannery, ed., *The Conciliar and Post-conciliar Documents, Vol. I*, p. 105.

29. William Barauna, OFM, "Active Participation, the Inspiring and Directive Principle of the Constitution," in William Barauna, ed., *The Liturgy of Vatican II*, English edition ed. Jovian Lang, OFM, Vol. I (Chicago: Franciscan Herald Press, 1966), p. 133.

30. SC 33; 34. In recalling the Council's desire for "noble simplicity" and signs that were easily understood, Paul John Paul II (a participant in the Council) insists that "the desired simplicity must not degenerate into an impoverishment of the signs. On the contrary, the signs, above all the sacramental signs, must be easily grasped but carry the greatest possible expressiveness," VQA 10.

31. Romano Guardini, "A Letter from Romano Guardini," *Herder Correspondence* 1: *Special Issue* (1964), p. 25. This editorial note precedes Guardini's letter: "Romano Guardini—priest, author, and professor for many years at Munich University—is generally regarded as the "father" of the German Liturgical Movement. Unable to attend the Third German Liturgical Congress, which was held in April of this year in Mainz, he sent a letter to the organizer of the Congress, Mgr. Wagner, on a matter which he believed to be 'of the first importance.' We print the full text of the letter here."

32. SC 21.

33. Cf. *Sacrosanctum Concilium* 26; *Catechism of the Catholic Church* 1396.

34. *Mediator Dei* 106.

35. SC 27. Note that many of the norms that made possible a greater sense of the liturgy as corporate action are contained in the section "Norms drawn from the Heirarchic and Communal Nature of the Liturgy." SC's affirmation of the communal nature of the liturgy was thus not a negation of its

heirarchic nature, but a desire to recover an earlier tradition of outward expression of the liturgy's communal nature.

36. Guardini, "A Letter from Romano Guardini," p. 25.

37. SC 21; 30.

38. SC 26, 28. While all liturgical ministers perform important services, only the priest acts *in persona Christi,* joining "the offering of the faithful to the sacrifice of their Head," *Lumen Gentium* 28, in Walter M. Abbott, SJ, ed., *The Documents of Vatican II* (New York: Guild Press, 1966), p. 53; cf. *Catechism of the Catholic Church* 1547–48.

39. SC 42; cf. John Paul II, *Observing and Celebrating the Day of the Lord (Dies Domini)* 35, in *Origins* 28:9 (July 30, 1998).

40. SC 21; 26–27; 30.

41. Pope John Paul II refers to "the liturgy as the self-manifestation of the Church" as one of the guiding principles of SC and affirms that "it is especially in the liturgy that the Mystery of the Church is proclaimed, experienced and lived," VQA 9.

42. SC 49. Note: SC 47 and 48 had recounted how Christ instituted the eucharistic sacrifice to perpetuate the sacrifice of the cross, and described how the faithful were to take part in this mystery. SC 49 begins, "Thus," in other words—in order to enable the faithful to enter into this re-presentation of the Paschal Mystery, and be united to God in Christ as just described in SC 47 and 48—the Council authorizes the specified changes in the rites. The term "pastorally effective" means enabling the rites to better help the faithful enter into the reality described in SC 47 and 48; cf. SC 21.

43. SC 21, 50.

44. SC 33; 7; 51.

45. SC 52.

46. SC 35.

47. SC 33; see Justin Martyr, *The First Apology* 65, in Bard Thompson, ed., *Liturgies of the Western Church.* (Cleveland, OH: World Publishing Co., 1962), p. 8.

48. SC 54.

49. SC 55; *Mediator Dei* 118, 121. Note that extending permission for reception from the chalice (SC 55) also makes possible a fuller sign of the whole Church being made one in Christ: "Holy Communion, considered as a sign, has a fuller form when it is received under both kinds. For under this form (leaving intact the principles of the Council of Trent, by which under either

species or kind there is received the true sacrament and Christ whole and entire), the sign of the eucharistic banquet appears more perfectly. Moreover, it is more clearly shown how the new and eternal Covenant is ratified in the blood of the Lord, as it also expresses the relation of the eucharistic banquet to the eschatological banquet in the kingdom of the Father (cf. Matthew 26:27–29)," *Eucharisticum Mysterium* 32, in Flannery, ed., *The Conciliar and Post-conciliar Documents, Vol. I,* p. 121.

50. SC 59. Since Trent, treatment of the sacraments had emphasized their power to sanctify more than their ecclesial dimension (or doxological or sign-character). By including "building up the Body of Christ" in its description of the purpose of the sacraments, SC calls attention to the fact that the faithful are made holy in the Church and as part of it, therefore to the sacraments' communal dimension.

51. SC 59.

52. SC 62; 63.

53. SC 64.

54. SC 66–69.

55. SC 71.

56. SC 72.

57. SC 77.

58. SC 73–76.

59. SC 81; 77.

60. E.g.: The centrality of the Paschal Mystery and its weekly celebration on the Lord's Day means that other celebrations should not take precedence over it, unless they are of greatest importance (102; 106); the baptismal and penitential character of aspects of Lent are to be given greater prominence so that the season can better fulfill its purpose of providing an occasion for conversion in preparation for the yearly celebration of the Paschal Mystery (109–110). "Because the purpose of the office is to sanctify the day, the traditional sequence of the hours is to be restored so that once again they may be genuinely related to the hour of the day when they are prayed, as far as it is possible" (88).

61. SC 19.

62. SC 14–18.

63. *Mediator Dei* 31; 32-37.

64. Michel, *"The Scope of the Liturgical Movement,"* p. 486.

65. SC 11.

66. SC 11.

67. SC 12–13; cf. *Mediator Dei* 31ff.

68. SC 48.

69. SC 61.

70. The complex and thorny question of what the Council intended in regard to inculturation is beyond the scope of this essay. See: Congregation for Divine Worship and Discipline of the Sacraments, *The Roman Liturgy and Inculturation, Fourth Instruction for the Right Application of the Conciliar Constitution on the Liturgy (Varietates Legitimae)* (Rome: 1984).

71. Paul VI, *Motu Proprio on the Sacred Liturgy* (January 25, 1964) *(Sacram Liturgiam)*, in Flannery, ed. , *The Conciliar and Post-conciliar Documents, Vol. I,* p. 42.

72. Ibid.

73. Ibid, *emph. added.*

74. Paul VI, in Flannery, ed., *Vatican II: The Liturgy Constitution,* pp. 9–10.

Part III

1. "The Constitution is strikingly clear and at the same time profound. Rich in Biblical and Patristic references, it has a studied felicity of expression and a diction that is crisp and concise. In other words, it is full of meaning, and so requires study and reflection," Giacomo Cardinal Lercaro, in Barauna, ed., *The Liturgy of Vatican II, Vol. 1,* p. xiii.

2. SC 19; cf. SC 14.

3. SC 11; cf. SC 35.

4. SC 18.

5. Annibale Bugnini, *The Reform of the Liturgy 1948–1975,* trans. Matthew J. O'Connell (Collegeville, MN: The Liturgical Press, 1990) pp. 46–47.

6. VQA 10, *emph. added.*

7. Henri Jenny (Auxiliary Bishop of Cambrai), "The Paschal Mystery is Central," *Worship* 37:8, August–September, 1963), p. 485. In describing the Paschal Mystery as heart of the liturgy, Bugnini wrote, "Only by entering ever anew into this mystery (or, as Tertullian would say, 'immersing itself in it') and drawing all the practical conclusions from this relationship will the world find salvation; only thus will Christian life be radically renewed," *The Reform of the Liturgy 1948–1975,* p. 40.

8. VQA 6, citing the *Roman Missal,* Evening Mass *In Cena Domini,* Prayer over the Gifts; and alluding to the Preface of the Sundays in Ordinary Time I.

9. The beautiful treatment of how the Church's liturgy and sacraments are rooted in the Paschal Mystery found in the *Catechism of the Catholic Church* is very helpful in developing catechesis on what is going on in the liturgy.

10. Cf. Pamela Jackson, "Eucharist," in Allan D. Fitzgerald, OSA, ed., *Augustine Through the Ages: An Encyclopedia* (Grand Rapids, MI: Eerdmans Publishing Co., 1999), pp. 230–34; *Catechism of the Catholic Church* 1362–1372.

11. John Paul II, *Dies Domini* 51, in *Origins* 28:9 (July 30, 1998), p. 144, citing *Lumen Gentium* 10 and 11. The complete text of *Lumen Gentium* 10 and 11 provides a fuller explanation of how the priest, acting *in persona Christi,* brings about the sacrifice and how the faithful join in the offering "by virtue of their royal priesthood."

12. Note that paragraph 48 is a single sentence in the Latin, *Constitutiones, Decreta, Declarationes,* p. 28.

13. *Conscie, pie,* and *actuose* appear in translation as "conscious of what they are doing, with devotion and full involvement," SC 48.

14. Ten years after *Sacrosanctum Concilium* was promulgated, one liturgical scholar commented, "The quantity of participation, however, seems to have grown as thoughtful reflection upon the reality of participation has declined," Aidan Kavanagh, "What is Participation? Or, Participation Revisited," *Doctrine and Life 23:7* (July 1973), p. 344.

15. Cf. SC 33, 30. Note that the text of the liturgy being in the vernacular also facilitates this interior conversation; it is easier to carry on a conversation in one's native tongue, since one's whole attention can be given to the meaning of what is being said, rather than distracted by the need to translate.

16. VQA 14, *emph. added.*

17. Cf. Virgil Michel's affirmation that what is needed is "a real understanding of the inner action of the Mass and of the supernatural relation of the individual member to the corporate sacrifice of the mystical body." Further, "a Christian participation in the Mass is the more meritorious the more it is done with an understanding of the true nature of the prayer-action of the Mass and with the willing joining of heart and soul in that action as it unfolds itself before the senses," "The Scope of the Liturgical Movement," *Oratre Fratres* 10 (1935–36) p. 486.

18. Michel believed that a renewed liturgy would help rescue society from "disintegrating individualism," Ibid., p. 489.

19. *Presbyterorum Ordinis* 5 in Walter M. Abbot, SJ, ed., *The Documents of Vatican II* (New York: Guild Press, 1966), p. 542. Pope Paul VI described the task of priests as including "winning over to a personal involvement in communal prayer the many people used to praying—or not praying—in church as they please," and "in a word, the issue is engaging the people of God in the priestly liturgical life." Further, priests "must be convinced that the objective is to reach the heart of today's people through the liturgy as the truest, most authoritative, sacred and effective way and so to re-kindle in them the love for God and neighbor, the awesome, intoxicating power to commune with God—authentically, consolingly, redemptively." Paul VI, "Address to pastors and Lenten preachers of Rome, excerpt on the liturgy, March 1, 1965," in *Documents on the Liturgy* 1963–1979: *Conciliar, Papal, and Curial Texts* (Collegeville, MN: The Liturgical Press, 1987), p. 112.

20. Romano Guardini, "A Letter from Romano Guardini," *Herder Correspondence 1: Special Issue* (1964), p. 24.

21. Ibid.

22. Ibid.

23. Ibid., *emph. added.*

24. Ibid., p. 25. He elucidates: "It is this body which is the 'we' of the prayers. Its structure is different from that of any other collection of people meeting for a common purpose. It is that of a *corpus,* an objective whole. In the liturgical act the celebrating individual becomes part of this body and he incorporates the *circumstantes* in his self-expression."

25. Ibid., p. 25. He also notes that "those whose task it is to teach and educate will have to ask themselves—and this is all-decisive—whether they themselves desire the liturgical act, or, to put it plainly, whether they know of its existence and what exactly it consists of and that it is neither a luxury nor an oddity, but a matter of fundamental importance," pp. 24–25.

26. Not long after the Council, William Barauna, drawing on the work of W. Duerig, commented on how, in some European countries that had first been touched by the Liturgical Movement, there was 50 years later a "state of stagnation." "When the novelty of the new forms of participation had passed, its attraction disappeared little by little," because the laity had not been formed in the "spirit" of the liturgy, which was alien to them because their culture did not give them an appreciation for symbolism, community life, or "living in the spirit of the mystery of the liturgy," William Barauna, OFM, "Active Participation, the Inspiring and Directive Principle of the Constitution," in William Barauna, ed., *The Liturgy of Vatican II*, English edition ed. Jovian Lang, OFM, Vol. 1, pp. 148–49.

27. The *Instruction on the Proper Implementation of the Constitution on the Sacred Liturgy* states that the faithful "by perfect participation in the liturgy will receive the divine life abundantly and, having become Christ's leaven

and the salt of the earth, they will announce and transmit it to others," *Inter Oecumenici* 8, in Flannery, ed., *The Conciliar and Post-conciliar Documents, Vol. I*, p. 47.

The Council's *Decree on the Apostolate of the Laity (Apostolicam Actuositatem)* had already taught that "the success of the lay apostolate depends on the laity's living union with Christ," and that "this life of intimate union with Christ in the Church is nourished by spiritual aids which are common to all the faithful, especially active participation in the sacred liturgy," *Apostolicam Actuositatem* 4; cf. 10, in Abbot, ed., *The Documents of Vatican II*, p. 493.

28. *Dominicae Cenae* 9, as cited in VQA 14.

29. Compare SC 10 with *Mediator Dei* 201: "The Mass is the chief act of divine worship; it should also be the source and center of Christian piety." *Mediator Dei* 202 urges bishops to "teach the Christian people carefully about the treasures of piety contained in the sacred liturgy so that they may be able to profit more abundantly by these supernatural gifts."

30. This should be read in light of *Mediator Dei* 197: "But there is something else of even greater importance, Venerable Brethren, which We commend to your apostolic zeal, in a very special manner. Whatever pertains to the external worship has assuredly its importance; however, *the most pressing duty of Christians is to live the liturgical life and increase and cherish its supernatural spirit*" *(emph. added).*

31. Jungmann, "The Pastoral Idea in the History of the Liturgy," p. 23.

32. Ibid., p. 27.

33. Ibid., pp. 27–29. Note especially his description of how the early Roman liturgy taught the faithful to enter into Christ's sacrifice to the Father.

34. *Questions Liturgiques* 4 (1953), pp. 32–33, cited in Sonya A. Quitslund, *Beauduin: A Prophet Vindicated* (New York: Newman Press, 1973), pp. 10–11; cf. p. 12.

35. Paul VI, in Flannery, ed., *Vatican II: The Liturgy Constitution*, p. 9.

36. Pope John Paul II, VQA 10. He adds that the number of Eucharistic Prayers and Prefaces in the liturgy was increased after Vatican II "so as to enrich the Church's treasury of prayer and an understanding of the mystery of Christ."

37. SC 13.

38. *Holy Communion and Worship of the Eucharist Outside of Mass* 2; 4; 80, in *The Rites of the Catholic Church, Vol. I* (Collegeville, MN: The Liturgical Press, 1990). Drawing on SC 13 (via *Eucharisticum Mysterium* 58), the rite states that in structuring services of eucharistic adoration "account should be taken of the liturgical seasons so that they accord with the liturgy, are in some way derived from it, and lead people back to it," 79.

This idea of "extending" what happens in the Eucharist is also developed in the *General Instruction of The Liturgy of the Hours* 12: "The Liturgy of the Hours extends to the different hours of the day the praise and thanksgiving, the commemoration of the mysteries of salvation, the petitions and the foretaste of heavenly glory, that are present in the eucharistic mystery, 'the center and apex of the whole Christian community.'

The Liturgy of the Hours is an excellent preparation for the celebration of the Eucharist itself, for it inspires and deepens in a fitting way the dispositions necessary for the fruitful celebration of the Eucharist: faith, hope, love, devotion and the spirit of self-denial," in *The Liturgy of the Hours, Vol. 1* (New York: Catholic Book Publishing Co., 1975), p. 29.

39. SC 14; SC 19.

40. SC 29.

41. VQA 21.

42. *Mediator Dei* 20.

43. The other two guiding principles are the reenactment of the Paschal Mystery and the liturgy as self-manifestation of the Church, VQA 5–9.

44. Cf. Pamela Jackson, "Cyril of Jerusalem's Use of Scripture in Catechesis," *Theological Studies* 52 (1991), pp. 431–50.

45. Introduction 9, in *The Roman Missal. Lectionary for Mass* (New Jersey: Catholic Book Publishing Co., 1998). Subsequent references to the Introduction will use the abbreviation ILM. For a further account of the many ways the Holy Spirit works in the liturgy, see ILM 9 in its entirety.

46. ILM 6.

47. *Dies Domini* 41.

48. *Dies Domini* 41, drawing on ILM 6.

49. ILM 45.

50. "A speaking style on the part of the readers that is audible, clear, and intelligent is the first means of transmitting the word of God properly to the congregation," ILM 14.

51. ILM 28. Also, "the Liturgy of the Word must be celebrated in a way that fosters meditation; clearly, any sort of haste that hinders recollection must be avoided."

52. SC 33.

53. *Dei Verbum* 21, in Abbot, ed. *The Documents of Vatican II*, p. 125; cf. *Dei Verbum* 23, 24.

54. Augustin Bea, "The Pastoral Value of the Word of God in the Sacred Liturgy," in *The Assisi Papers*, p. 79. As examples of lay apologists, Bea names Aristedes, Justin, Athenagoras, Minucius Felix, and Lactantius.

55. Ibid., pp. 85–86.

56. Ibid., pp. 89–90, referring to Thomas à Kempis' *The Imitation of Christ* 4, 11.

57. SC 35. SC 92 states that in The Liturgy of the Hours "Readings from Sacred Scripture should be arranged so that the riches of God's Word may be easily accessible in more abundant measure."

58. *"Quo ditior mensa verbi dei paretur fidelibus, thesauri biblici largius aperiantur, ita ut . . ."* SC 51.

59. *Missale Romanum,* in Flannery, ed., *The Conciliar and Post-conciliar Documents, Vol. I,* p. 140. In Eastertide, the first reading is from Acts.

60. *Missale Romanum,* in Flannery, ed. *The Conciliar and Post-conciliar Documents,* Vol. I, p. 140. "Thus, in accordance with the exhortation of the Second Vatican Council, the sacred writings will be recognized by all as the unfailing source of the spiritual life, the basis of Christian instruction, and the very kernel of theological study."

61. VQA 12.

62. ILM 47; cf. ILM 5: "the Scriptures are the living waters from which all who seek life and salvation must drink."

63. SC 7.

64. ILM 41, which goes on to cite *Presbyterorum Ordinis* 4.

65. ILM 46.

66. Pontifical Biblical Commission, *The Interpretation of the Bible in the Church* IV, C, in *Origins* 23:29 (January 6, 1994), p. 522.

67. SC 33.

68. Colman O'Neill, "General Principles," in Flannery, ed., *Vatican II: The Liturgy Constitution,* p. 31.

69. VQA 7.

70. SC 52.

71. SC 35.

72. SC 52.

73. SC 35.

74. ILM 7.

75. ILM 47.

76. ILM 7.

77. ILM 10. Cf. 24: "Through the readings and homily, Christ's paschal mystery is proclaimed; through the sacrifice of the Mass it becomes present."

78. ILM 61.

79. For further reflection on how the Scriptures proclaimed extend outward to draw the listeners into the scriptural story, etc., see Pamela E. J. Jackson, *Journeybread for the Shadowlands: The Readings for the Rites of the Catechumenate, RCIA* (Collegeville, MN: The Liturgical Press, 1993).

80. P*resbyterorum Ordinis* 13. Further, "Clearly, much depends on those who exercise the ministry of the Word. It is their duty to prepare the reflection on the Word of the Lord by prayer and study of the sacred text, so that they may then express its contents faithfully and apply them to people's concerns and to their daily lives," *Dies Domini* 40. Cf. *Ecclesia in America* 31.

81. ILM 41.

82. SC 49.

83. SC 24.

84. "Because of the Holy Spirit's inspiration and support, the Word of God becomes the foundation of the liturgical celebration and the rule and support of all our life," ILM 9.

85. "Since the liturgy is totally permeated by the Word of God, any other word must be in harmony with it, above all in the homily but also in the various interventions of the minister and in the hymns which are sung. No other reading may supplant the Biblical word, and the words of men must be at the service of the Word of God without obscuring it," VQA 10.

86. ILM 6.

87. Louis Bouyer, *The Liturgy Revised. A Doctrinal Commentary on the Conciliar Constitution on the Liturgy* (Notre Dame, IN: University of Notre Dame Press, 1964), p. 97.

88. Bouyer, p. 98.

89. VQA 8. The Latin word in SC 24 translated as "knowledge" is *affectus*.

90. VQA 8. In *Dominicae Cenae* 10 (1980), he had already stated that beyond the faithful's involvement in a vernacular Liturgy of the Word, "complete renewal" makes further demands, consisting in *"a new sense of responsibility*

towards the Word of God" and even *"concerns the inner attitude* with which the ministers of the word perform their function in the liturgical assembly" in Austin Flannery, ed. *More Post-conciliar Documents* (Collegeville, MN: The Liturgical Press, 1982), p. 79 *(emph. in original)*.

91. *Dies Domini* 40.

92. *Dies Domini* 40, citing *Dominicae Cenae* 10.

93. *Dies Domini* 40.

94. *Dies Domini* 40; cf. *Ecclesia in America* 31.

95. *Dies Domini* 40.

96. ILM 48.

97. ILM 47.

98. ILM 45.

99. ILM 48; cf. 9.

100. ILM 6. Part of the task of the homilist in opening up the Scripture proclaimed is to invite the faithful "to take upon themselves the demands of the Christian life," ILM 41.

101. ILM 5.

102. ILM 4.

103. For a list of these documents, as well as of twentieth-century papal documents urging good liturgical formation of seminarians, see: *Liturgical Formation in Seminaries: A Commentary* (Washington, DC: USCC, 1984), pp. 53–54. Future references to the *Instruction on Liturgical Formation in Seminaries* (1979), which is also contained in this book, will use the abbreviation LFS.

104. Bugnini, p. 4l. After summarizing the Constitution's norms for the training of seminarians and their professors, and for liturgical commissions of experts at all levels, Bugnini concluded, "The Constitution thus calls for the efforts of the entire Church structure; without these efforts the prospects opened up by the Constitution will remain simply words on a page."

105. VQA 15, *emph. added.* Cf., "That understanding of the liturgy which is considered necessary for priests and which seminarians must acquire demands a diligent familiarity with the Bible, as the conciliar Constitution *Sacrosanctum Concilium* recommends, and also some familiarity with the writings of the Fathers of the Church," LFS 11.

106. VQA 15. He goes on to call for appropriate liturgical formation for lay people, especially those with responsibilities in the Church community.

107. SC 16.

108. SC 16.

109. In a forthcoming essay I will propose one way this could be done.

110. LFS 49.

111. LFS 11.

112. LFS 52, citing SC 24 and also urging that seminarians receive that "warm and living love" it calls for; LFS, Appendix, 20.

113. LFS 44.

114. LFS 47.

115. LFS 44.

116. VQA 11.

117. *"ut fideles scienter, actuose, et fructuose participent,"* SC 11.

118. *Presbyterorum Ordinis* 5.

119. SC 17; LFS 51.

120. LFS 63. Cf. LFS 18: "The students are to be helped to penetrate more profoundly [the most important] parts of the liturgy and to meditate on them and think about them. They are to learn to draw out and to take from them ever fresh spiritual nourishment."

121. LFS 46; LFS, Appendix, 42.

122. SC 22; cf. *Mediator Dei* 58.

123. SC 15.

124. Further, not all of the programs in the United States which offer advanced training in liturgy are geared toward providing the kind of preparation necessary for teaching liturgy in a seminary, which requires a kind of formation and body of knowledge not needed to teach undergraduates.

125. SC 16.

126. LFS 16; cf. SC 17, 29, and *Eucharisticum Mysterium* 20.

127. SC 19.

128. LFS 17.

129. Bugnini, *The Reform of the Liturgy 1948–1975*, p. 47.

130. SC 14.

131. SC 18.

132. LFS, Appendix, 5.

133. VQA 6, citing the *Roman Missal,* Easter Vigil, Renewal of Baptismal Promises.

134. D. H. Jenny, auxiliary bishop of Cambrai, cited in Barauna, Vol. 1, p. 149.

135. VQA 7.

136. Ibid., 10.

137. "A faith alive in charity, adoration, praise of the Father and silent contemplation will always be the prime objective of liturgical and sacramental pastoral care," VQA 10.

138. VQA 6.

139. ILM 47.

140. Michel, p. 487.

141. Ibid.

142. Ibid.

143. Ibid.

144. Pope John Paul II thus speaks of the "genuine liturgical life" fostered by *Sacrosanctum Concilium* as sustaining the Church "along the paths of renewal and holiness," VQA 14.

145. *Dominicae Cenae* 9, in Flannery, ed. *More Post-conciliar Documents,* p. 77.

146. *Dominicae Cenae* 13, in Flannery, ed., *More Post-conciliar Documents,* p. 86, *emph. in original.* Cf. Pope John Paul II's statement at the beginning of *Vicesimus Quintus Annus* that the promulgation of *Sacrosanctum Concilium* "had been prepared for by a great liturgical and pastoral movement, and was a source of hope for the life and the renewal of the Church," VQA 1.

147. *Instruction on the Proper Implementation of the Constitution on the Sacred Liturgy (Inter Oecumenici)* (26 September, 1964) 5; 1, in Flannery, ed., *The Conciliar and Post-conciliar Documents, Vol. I,* p. 46; 45. The *Instruction* goes on to explain the importance of the Paschal Mystery in the liturgy.

148. *The Assisi Papers,* p. 224.

149. "In recent times, however, there has been at work with ever increasing intensity among the faithful a liturgical renewal which our predecessor Pius XII described as a manifest sign of God's benign providence towards the present generation of mankind, and as a movement of the Holy Spirit bringing grace to his Church," *Missale Romanum,* in Flannery, ed. *Conciliar and Post-conciliar Documents,* Vol. I, p. 137.

150. SC 43.

151. VQA 12.

152. Cited in Bugnini, p. 933, *emph. added.*

153. SC 21.

Appendix

Constitution on the Sacred Liturgy
Sacrosanctum Concilium

Second Vatican Council

4 December 1963

Outline

Introduction 1–4

Chapter I: General Principles for the Reform and Promotion of the
      Sacred Liturgy 5–46
      I. Nature of the Liturgy and its Importance in the Church's
          Life 5–13
      II. Promotion of Liturgical Instruction and Active
      Participation 14–20
      III. The Reform of the Sacred Liturgy 21–40
          A. General Norms 22–25
          B. Norms Drawn from the Hierarchic and Communal
              Nature of the Liturgy 26–32
          C. Norms Based on the Teaching and Pastoral
              Character of the Liturgy 33–36
          D. Norms for Adapting the Liturgy to the Culture
              and Traditions of Peoples 37–40
      IV. Promotion of Liturgical Life in Diocese and
          Parish 41–42
      V. Promotion of Pastoral-Liturgical Action 43–46
Chapter II: The Most Sacred Mystery of the Eucharist 47–58
Chapter III: The Other Sacraments and the Sacramentals 59–82
Chapter IV: Divine Office 83–101
Chapter V: The Liturgical Year 102–111
Chapter VI: Sacred Music 112–121
Chapter VII: Sacred Art and Sacred Furnishings 122–130
Appendix: Declaration of the Second Vatican Ecumenical Council on
      Revision of the Calendar 131

Constitution on the Sacred Liturgy

1. This Sacred Council has several aims in view: it desires to impart an ever increasing vigor to the Christian life of the faithful; to adapt more suitably to the needs of our own times those institutions that are subject to change; to foster whatever can promote union among all who believe in Christ; to strengthen whatever can help to call the whole of humanity into the household of the Church. The Council therefore sees particularly cogent reasons for undertaking the reform and promotion of the liturgy.

2. For the liturgy, "making the work of our redemption a present actuality,"[1] most of all in the divine sacrifice of the eucharist, is the outstanding means whereby the faithful may express in their lives and manifest to others the mystery of Christ and the real nature of the true Church. It is of the essence of the Church to be both human and divine, visible yet endowed with invisible resources, eager to act yet intent on contemplation, present in this world yet not at home in it; and the Church is all these things in such wise that in it the human is directed and subordinated to the divine, the visible likewise to the invisible, action to contemplation, and this present world to that city yet to come which we seek.[2] While the liturgy daily builds up those who are within into a holy temple of the Lord, into a dwelling place for God in the Spirit,[3] to the mature measure of the fullness of Christ,[4] at the same time it marvelously strengthens their power to preach Christ and thus shows forth the Church to those who are outside as a sign lifted up among the nations,[5] under which the scattered children of God may be gathered together,[6] until there is one sheepfold and one shepherd.[7]

3. Wherefore the Council judges that the following principles concerning the promotion and reform of the liturgy should be called to mind and practical norms established.

Among these principles and norms there are some that can and should be applied both to the Roman Rite and also to all the other rites. The practical norms that follow, however, should be taken as applying only to the Roman Rite, except for those that, in the very nature of things, affect other rites as well.

4. Lastly, in faithful obedience to tradition, the Council declares that the Church holds all lawfully acknowledged rites to be of equal right and dignity and wishes to preserve them in the future and to foster them in every way. The Council also desires that, where necessary, the rites be revised carefully in the light of sound tradition and that they be given new vigor to meet the circumstances and needs of modern times.

Chapter I
General Principles for the Reform and Promotion of the Sacred Liturgy

I. Nature of the Liturgy and Its Importance in the Church's Life

5. God who "wills that all be saved and come to the knowledge of the truth" (1 Tm. 2:4), "who in many and various ways spoke in times past to the fathers by the prophets" (Heb. 1:1), when the fullness of time had come sent his Son, the Word made flesh, anointed by the Holy Spirit, to preach the Gospel to the poor, to heal the contrite of heart;[1] he is "the physician, being both flesh and of the Spirit,"[2] the mediator between God and us.[3] For his humanity, united with the person of the Word, was the instrument of our salvation. Therefore in Christ "the perfect achievement of our reconciliation came forth and the fullness of divine worship was given to us.[4]

The wonderful works of God among the people of the Old Testament were a prelude to the work of Christ the Lord. He achieved his task of redeeming humanity and giving perfect glory to God, principally by the paschal mystery of his blessed passion, resurrection from the dead, and glorious ascension, whereby "dying, he destroyed our death and, rising, he restored our life."[5] For it was from the side of Christ as he slept the sleep of death upon the cross that there came forth the sublime sacrament of the whole Church.[6]

6. As Christ was sent by the Father, he himself also sent the apostles, filled with the Holy Spirit. Their mission was, first, by preaching the Gospel to every creature,[7] to proclaim that by his death and resurrection Christ has freed us from Satan's grip[8] and brought us into the Father's kingdom. But the work they preached they were also to bring into effect through the sacrifice and the sacraments, the center of the whole liturgical life. Thus by baptism all are plunged into the paschal mystery of Christ: they die with him, are buried with him, and rise with him;[9] they receive the spirit of adoption as children "in which we cry: Abba, Father" (Rom. 8:15), and thus become true adorers whom the Father seeks.[10] In like manner, as often as they eat the supper of the Lord they proclaim the death of the Lord until he comes.[11] For that reason, on the very day of Pentecost when the Church appeared before the world, "those who received the word" of Peter "were baptized." And "they continued steadfastly in the teaching of the apostles and in the communion of the breaking of bread and in prayers . . . praising God and being in favor with all the people" (Acts 2:41–47). From that time onward the Church has never failed to come together to celebrate the paschal mystery: reading those things "which were in all the Scriptures concerning him" (Lk. 24:27); celebrating the eucharist, in which "the victory and triumph of his death are again made present";[12] and at the same time giving thanks "to God for his inexpressible gift" (2 Cor. 9:15) in Christ Jesus, "in praise of his glory" (Eph. 1:12), through the power of the Holy Spirit.

7. To accomplish so great a work, Christ is always present in his Church, especially in its liturgical celebrations. He is present in the sacrifice of the Mass, not only in the person of his minister, "the same now offering, through the ministry of priests, who formerly offered himself on the cross,"[13] but especially under the eucharistic elements. By his power he is present in the sacraments, so that when a man baptizes it is really Christ himself who baptizes.[14] He is present in his word, since it is he himself who speaks when the holy Scriptures are read in the Church. He is present, lastly, when the Church prays and sings, for he promised: "Where two or three are gathered together in my name, there am I in the midst of them" (Mt. 18:20).

Christ always truly associates the Church with himself in this great work wherein God is perfectly glorified and the recipients made holy. The Church is the Lord's beloved Bride who calls to him and through him offers worship to the eternal Father.

Rightly, then, the liturgy is considered as an exercise of the priestly office of Jesus Christ. In the liturgy, by means of signs perceptible to the senses, human sanctification is signified and brought about in ways proper to each of these signs; in the liturgy the whole public worship is performed by the Mystical Body of Jesus Christ, that is, by the Head and his members.

From this it follows that every liturgical celebration, because it is an action of Christ the Priest and of his Body which is the Church, is a sacred action surpassing all others; no other action of the Church can equal its effectiveness by the same title and to the same degree.

8. In the earthly liturgy we take part in a foretaste of that heavenly liturgy celebrated in the holy city of Jerusalem toward which we journey as pilgrims, where Christ is sitting at the right hand of God, a minister of the holies and of the true tabernacle;[15] we sing a hymn to the Lord's glory with the whole company of heaven; venerating the memory of the saints, we hope for some part and fellowship with them; we eagerly await the Savior, our Lord Jesus Christ, until he, our life, shall appear and we too will appear with him in glory.[16]

9. The liturgy does not exhaust the entire activity of the Church. Before people can come to the liturgy they must be called to faith and to conversion: "How then are they to call upon him in whom they have not yet believed? But how are they to believe him whom they have not heard? And how are they to hear if no one preaches? And how are men to preach unless they be sent?" (Rom. 10:14–15).

Therefore the Church announces the good tidings of salvation to those who do not believe, so that all may know the true God and Jesus Christ whom he has sent and may be converted from their ways, doing penance.[17] To believers, also, the Church must ever preach faith and penance, prepare them for the sacraments, teach them to observe all that Christ has commanded,[18] and invite them to all the works of charity, worship, and the apostolate. For all these works make it clear that Christ's faithful, though not of this world, are to be the light of the world and to glorify the Father in the eyes of all.

10. Still, the liturgy is the summit toward which the activity of the Church is directed; at the same time it is the fount from which all the Church's power flows. For the aim and object of apostolic works is that all who are made children of God by faith and baptism should come together to praise God in the midst of his Church, to take part in the sacrifice, and to eat the Lord's Supper.

The liturgy in its turn moves the faithful, filled with "the paschal sacraments," to be "one in holiness";[19] it prays that "they may hold fast in their lives to what they have grasped by their faith";[20] the renewal in the eucharist of the covenant between the Lord and his people draws the faithful into the compelling love of Christ and sets them on fire. From the liturgy, therefore, particularly the eucharist, grace is poured forth upon us as from a fountain; the liturgy is the source for achieving in the most effective way possible human sanctification and God's glorification, the end to which all the Church's other activities are directed.

11. But in order that the liturgy may possess its full effectiveness, it is necessary that the faithful come to it with proper dispositions, that their minds be attuned to their voices, and that they cooperate with divine grace, lest they receive it in vain.[21] Pastors must therefore realize that when the liturgy is celebrated something more is required than the mere observance of the laws governing valid and lawful celebration; it is also their duty to ensure that the faithful take part fully aware of what they are doing, actively engaged in the rite, and enriched by its effects.

12. The spiritual life, however, is not limited solely to participation in the liturgy. Christians are indeed called to pray in union with each other, but they must also enter into their chamber to pray to the Father in secret;[22] further, according to the teaching of the Apostle, they should pray without ceasing.[23] We learn from the same Apostle that we must always bear about in our body the dying of Jesus, so that the life also of Jesus may be made manifest in our bodily frame.[24] This is why we ask the Lord in the sacrifice of the Mass that "receiving the offering of the spiritual victim," he may fashion us for himself "as an eternal gift."[25]

13. Popular devotions of the Christian people are to be highly endorsed, provided they accord with the laws and norms of the Church, above all when they are ordered by the Apostolic See.

Devotions proper to particular Churches also have a special dignity if they are undertaken by mandate of the bishops according to customs or books lawfully approved.

But these devotions should be so fashioned that they harmonize with the liturgical seasons, accord with the sacred liturgy, are in some way derived from it, and lead the people to it, since, in fact, the liturgy, by its very nature far surpasses any of them.

II. Promotion of Liturgical Instruction and Active Participation

14. The Church earnestly desires that all the faithful be led to that full, conscious, and active participation in liturgical celebrations called for by the very nature of the liturgy. Such participation by the Christian people as "a chosen race, a royal priesthood, a holy nation, God's own people" (1 Pt. 2:9; see 2:4–5) is their right and duty by reason of their baptism.

In the reform and promotion of the liturgy, this full and active participation by all the people is the aim to be considered before all else. For it is the primary and indispensable source from which the faithful are to derive the true Christian spirit and therefore pastors must zealously strive in all their pastoral work to achieve such participation by means of the necessary instruction.

Yet it would be futile to entertain any hopes of realizing this unless, in the first place, the pastors themselves become thoroughly imbued with the spirit and power of the liturgy and make themselves its teachers. A prime need, therefore, is that attention be directed, first of all, to the liturgical formation of the clergy. Wherefore the Council has decided to enact what follows.

15. Professors appointed to teach liturgy in seminaries, religious houses of study, and theological faculties must be thoroughly trained for their work in institutes specializing in this subject.

16. The study of liturgy is to be ranked among the compulsory and major courses in seminaries and religious houses of studies; in theological faculties it is to rank among the principal courses. It is to be taught under its theological, historical, spiritual, pastoral, and canonical aspects. Moreover, other professors, while striving to expound the mystery of Christ and the history of salvation from the angle proper to each of their own subjects, must nevertheless do so in a way that will clearly bring out the connection between their subjects and the liturgy, as also the underlying unity of all priestly training. This consideration is especially important for professors of dogmatic, spiritual, and pastoral theology and for professors of holy Scripture.

17. In seminaries and houses of religious, clerics shall be given a liturgical formation in their spiritual life. The means for this are: proper guidance so that they may be able to understand the sacred rites and take part in them wholeheartedly; the actual celebration of the sacred mysteries and of other, popular devotions imbued with the spirit of the liturgy. In addition they must learn how to observe the liturgical laws, so that life in seminaries and houses of religious may be thoroughly permeated by the spirit of the liturgy.

18. Priests, both secular and religious, who are already working in the Lord's vineyard are to be helped by every suitable means to understand ever more fully what it is they are doing in their liturgical functions; they are to be aided to live the liturgical life and to share it with the faithful entrusted to their care.

19. With zeal and patience pastors must promote the liturgical instruction of the faithful and also their active participation in the liturgy both internally and externally, taking into account their age and condition, their way of life, and their stage of religious development. By doing so, pastors will be fulfilling one of their chief duties as faithful stewards of the mysteries of God; and in this matter they must lead their flock not only by word but also by example.

20. Radio and television broadcasts of sacred rites must be marked by discretion and dignity, under the leadership and direction of a competent person appointed for this office by the bishops. This is especially important when the service to be broadcast is the Mass.

III. The Reform of the Sacred Liturgy

21. In order that the Christian people may more surely derive an abundance of graces from the liturgy, the Church desires to undertake with great care a general reform of the liturgy itself. For the liturgy is made up of immutable elements, divinely instituted, and of elements subject to change. These not only may but ought to be changed with the passage of time if they have suffered from the intrusion of anything out of harmony with the inner nature of the liturgy or have become pointless.

In this reform both texts and rites should be so drawn up that they express more clearly the holy things they signify and that the Christian people, as far as possible, are able to understand them with ease and to take part in the rites fully, actively, and as befits a community.

Wherefore the Council establishes the general norms that follow.

A. General Norms

22. §1. Regulation of the liturgy depends solely on the authority of the Church, that is, on the Apostolic See and, accordingly as the law determines, on the bishop.

§2. In virtue of power conceded by the law, the regulation of the liturgy within certain defined limits belongs also to various kinds of competent territorial bodies of bishops lawfully established.

§3. Therefore, no other person, not even if he is a priest, may on his own add, remove, or change anything in the liturgy.

23. That sound tradition may be retained and yet the way remain open to legitimate progress, a careful investigation is always to be made into each part of the liturgy to be revised. This investigation should be theological, historical, and pastoral. Also the general laws governing the structure and meaning of the liturgy must be studied in conjunction with the experience derived from recent liturgical reforms and from the indults conceded to various places. Finally, there must be no innovations unless the good of the Church genuinely and certainly requires them; care must be taken that any new forms adopted should in some way grow organically from forms already existing.

As far as possible, marked differences between the rites used in neighboring regions must be carefully avoided.

24. Sacred Scripture is of the greatest importance in the celebration of the liturgy. For it is from Scripture that the readings are given and explained in the homily and that psalms are sung; the prayers, collects, and liturgical songs are scriptural in their inspiration; it is from the Scriptures that actions and signs derive their meaning. Thus to achieve the reform, progress, and adaptation of the liturgy, it is essential to promote that warm and living love for Scripture to which the venerable tradition of both Eastern and Western rites gives testimony.

25. The liturgical books are to be revised as soon as possible; experts are to be employed in this task and bishops from various parts of the world are to be consulted.

B. Norms Drawn from the Hierarchic and Communal Nature of the Liturgy

26. Liturgical services are not private functions, but are celebrations belonging to the Church, which is the "sacrament of unity," namely, the holy people united and ordered under their bishops.[26]

Therefore liturgical services involve the whole Body of the Church; they manifest it and have effects upon it; but they also concern the individual members of the Church in different ways, according to their different orders, offices, and actual participation.

27. Whenever rites, according to their specific nature, make provision for communal celebration involving the presence and active participation of the faithful, it is to be stressed that this way of celebrating them is to be preferred, as far as possible, to a celebration that is individual and, so to speak, private.

This applies with special force to the celebration of Mass and the administration of the sacraments, even though every Mass has of itself a public and social character.

28. In liturgical celebrations each one, minister or layperson, who has an office to perform, should do all of, but only, those parts which pertain to that office by the nature of the rite and the principles of liturgy.

29. Servers, readers, commentators, and members of the choir also exercise a genuine liturgical function. They ought to discharge their office, therefore, with the sincere devotion and decorum demanded by so exalted a ministry and rightly expected of them by God's people.

Consequently, they must all be deeply imbued with the spirit of the liturgy, in the measure proper to each one, and they must be trained to perform their functions in a correct and orderly manner.

30. To promote active participation, the people should be encouraged to take part by means of acclamations, responses, psalmody, antiphons, and songs, as well as by actions, gestures, and bearing. And at the proper times all should observe a reverent silence.

31. The revision of the liturgical books must ensure that the rubrics make provision for the parts belonging to the people.

32. The liturgy makes distinctions between persons according to their liturgical function and sacred orders and there are liturgical laws providing for due honors to be given to civil authorities. Apart from these instances, no special honors are to be paid in the liturgy to any private persons or classes of persons, whether in the ceremonies or by external display.

C. Norms Based on the Teaching and Pastoral Character of the Liturgy

33. Although the liturgy is above all things the worship of the divine majesty, it likewise contains rich instruction for the faithful.[27] For in the liturgy God is speaking to his people and Christ is still proclaiming his gospel. And the people are responding to God by both song and prayer.

Moreover, the prayers addressed to God by the priest, who presides over the assembly in the person of Christ, are said in the name of the entire holy people and of all present. And the visible signs used by the liturgy to signify invisible divine realities have been chosen by Christ or the Church. Thus not only when things are read "that were written for our instruction" (Rom 15:4), but also when the Church prays or sings or acts, the faith of those taking part is nourished and their minds are raised to God, so that they may offer him their worship as intelligent beings and receive his grace more abundantly.

In the reform of the liturgy, therefore, the following general norms are to be observed.

34. The rites should be marked by a noble simplicity; they should be short, clear, and unencumbered by useless repetitions; they should be within the people's powers of comprehension and as a rule not require much explanation.

35. That the intimate connection between words and rites may stand out clearly in the liturgy:

1. In sacred celebrations there is to be more reading from holy Scripture and it is to be more varied and apposite.

2. Because the spoken word is part of the liturgical service, the best place for it, consistent with the nature of the rite, is to be indicated even in the rubrics; the ministry of preaching is to be fulfilled with exactitude and fidelity. Preaching should draw its content mainly from scriptural and liturgical

sources, being a proclamation of God's wonderful works in the history of salvation, the mystery of Christ, ever present and active within us, especially in the celebration of the liturgy.

3. A more explicitly liturgical catechesis should also be given in a variety of ways. Within the rites themselves provision is to be made for brief comments, when needed, by the priest or a qualified minister; they should occur only at the more suitable moments and use a set formula or something similar.

4. Bible services should be encouraged, especially on the vigils of the more solemn feasts, on some weekdays in Advent and Lent, and on Sundays and holy days. They are particularly to be recommended in places where no priest is available; when this is the case, a deacon or some other person authorized by the bishop is to preside over the celebration.

36.   §1. Particular law remaining in force, the use of the Latin language is to be preserved in the Latin rites.

§2. But since the use of the mother tongue, whether in the Mass, the administration of the sacraments, or other parts of the liturgy, frequently may be of great advantage to the people, the limits of its use may be extended. This will apply in the first place to the readings and instructions and to some prayers and chants, according to the regulations on this matter to be laid down for each case in subsequent chapters.

§3. Respecting such norms and also, where applicable, consulting the bishops of nearby territories of the same language, the competent, territorial ecclesiastical authority mentioned in art. 22, §2 is empowered to decide whether and to what extent the vernacular is to be used. The enactments of the competent authority are to be approved, that is, confirmed by the Holy See.

§4. Translations from the Latin text into the mother tongue intended for use in the liturgy must be approved by the competent, territorial ecclesiastical authority already mentioned.

D. Norms for Adapting the Liturgy to the Culture and Traditions of Peoples

37. Even in the liturgy the Church has no wish to impose a rigid uniformity in matters that do not affect the faith or the good of the whole community; rather, the Church respects and fosters the genius and talents of the various races and peoples. The Church considers with sympathy and, if possible, preserves intact the elements in these peoples' way of life that are not indissolubly bound up with superstition and error. Sometimes in fact the Church admits such elements into the liturgy itself, provided they are in keeping with the true and authentic spirit of the liturgy.

38. Provisions shall also be made, even in the revision of liturgical books, for legitimate variations and adaptations to different groups, regions, and peoples, especially in mission lands, provided the substantial unity of the Roman Rite is preserved; this should be borne in mind when rites are drawn up and rubrics devised.

39. Within the limits set by the editio typica of the liturgical books, it shall be for the competent, territorial ecclesiastical authority mentioned in art. 22, §2 to specify adaptations, especially in the case of the administration of the sacraments, the sacramentals, processions, liturgical language, sacred music, and the arts. This, however, is to be done in accord with the fundamental norms laid down in this Constitution.

40. In some places and circumstances, however, an even more radical adaptation of the liturgy is needed and this entails greater difficulties. Wherefore:

1. The competent, territorial ecclesiastical authority mentioned in art. 22, §2, must, in this matter, carefully and prudently weigh what elements from the traditions and culture of individual peoples may be appropriately admitted into divine worship. They are to propose to the Apostolic See adaptations considered useful or necessary that will be introduced with its consent.

2. To ensure that adaptations are made with all the circumspection they demand, the Apostolic See will grant power to this same territorial ecclesiastical authority to permit and to direct, as the case requires, the necessary preliminary experiments within certain groups suited for the purpose and for a fixed time.

3. Because liturgical laws often involve special difficulties with respect to adaptation, particularly in mission lands, experts in these matters must be employed to formulate them.

IV. Promotion of Liturgical Life in Diocese and Parish

41. The bishop is to be looked on as the high priest of his flock, the faithful's life in Christ in some way deriving from and depending on him.

Therefore all should hold in great esteem the liturgical life of the diocese centered around the bishop, especially in his cathedral church; they must be convinced that the preeminent manifestation of the Church is present in the full, active participation of all God's holy people in these liturgical celebrations, especially in the same eucharist, in a single prayer, at one altar at which the bishop presides, surrounded by his college of priests and by his ministers.[28]

42. But because it is impossible for the bishop always and everywhere to preside over the whole flock in his Church, he cannot do otherwise than establish lesser groupings of the faithful. Among these the parishes, set up locally under a pastor taking the place of the bishop, are the most important: in some manner they represent the visible Church established throughout the world.

And therefore both in attitude and in practice the liturgical life of the parish and its relationship to the bishop must be fostered among the faithful and clergy; efforts must also be made toward a lively sense of community within the parish, above all in the shared celebration of the Sunday Mass.

V. Promotion of Pastoral-Liturgical Action

43. Zeal for the promotion and restoration of the liturgy is rightly held to be a sign of the providential dispositions of God in our time, a movement of the Holy Spirit in his Church. Today it is a distinguishing mark of the Church's life, indeed of the whole tenor of contemporary religious thought and action.

So that this pastoral-liturgical action may become even more vigorous in the Church, the Council decrees what follows.

44. It is advisable that the competent, territorial ecclesiastical authority mentioned in art. 22, §2 set up a liturgical commission, to be assisted by experts in liturgical science, music, art, and pastoral practice. As far as possible the commission should be aided by some kind of institute for pastoral liturgy, consisting of persons eminent in these matters and including the laity as circumstances suggest. Under the direction of the aforementioned territorial ecclesiastical authority, the commission is to regulate pastoral-liturgical action throughout the territory and to promote studies and necessary experiments whenever there is question of adaptations to be proposed to the Apostolic See.

45. For the same reason every diocese is to have a commission on the liturgy, under the direction of the bishop, for promoting the liturgical apostolate.

Sometimes it may be advisable for several dioceses to form among themselves one single commission, in order to promote the liturgy by means of shared consultation.

46. Besides the commission on the liturgy, every diocese, as far as possible, should have commissions for music and art.

These three commissions must work in closest collaboration; indeed it will often be best to fuse the three of them into one single commission.

Chapter II
The Most Sacred Mystery of the Eucharist

47. At the Last Supper, on the night when he was betrayed, our Savior instituted the eucharistic sacrifice of his body and blood. He did this in order to perpetuate the sacrifice of the cross throughout the centuries until he should come again and in this way to entrust to his beloved Bride, the Church, a memorial of his death and resurrection: a sacrament of love, a sign of unity, a bond of charity,[1] a paschal banquet "in which Christ is eaten, the heart is filled with grace, and a pledge of future glory given to us."[2]

48. The Church, therefore, earnestly desires that Christ's faithful, when present at this mystery of faith, should not be there as strangers or silent spectators; on the contrary, through a good understanding of the rites and prayers they should take part in the sacred service conscious of what they are doing, with devotion and full involvement. They should be instructed by God's word and be nourished at the table of the Lord's body; they should give thanks to God; by offering the immaculate Victim, not only through the hands of the priest, but also with him, they should learn to offer themselves as well; through Christ the Mediator,[3] they should be formed day by day into an ever more perfect unity with God and with each other, so that finally God may be all in all.

49. Thus, mindful of those Masses celebrated with the assistance of the faithful, especially on Sundays and holy days of obligation, the Council makes the following decrees in order that the sacrifice of the Mass, even in its ritual forms, may become pastorally effective to the utmost degree.

50. The Order of Mass is to be revised in a way that will bring out more clearly the intrinsic nature and purpose of its several parts, as also the connection between them, and will more readily achieve the devout, active participation of the faithful.

For this purpose the rites are to be simplified, due care being taken to preserve their substance; elements that, with the passage of time, came to be duplicated or were added with but little advantage are now to be discarded; other elements that have suffered injury through accident of history are now, as may seem useful or necessary, to be restored to the vigor they had in the traditions of the Fathers.

51. The treasures of the Bible are to be opened up more lavishly, so that a richer share in God's word may be provided for the faithful. In this way a more representative portion of holy Scripture will be read to the people in the course of a prescribed number of years.

52. By means of the homily the mysteries of the faith and the guiding principles of the Christian life are expounded from the sacred text during the course of the liturgical year; as part of the liturgy itself therefore, the homily is strongly recommended; in fact, at Masses celebrated with the assistance of the people on Sundays and holy days of obligation it is not to be omitted except for a serious reason.

53. Especially on Sundays and holy days of obligation there is to be restored, after the gospel and the homily, "the universal prayer" or "the prayer of the faithful." By this prayer, in which the people are to take part, intercession shall be made for holy Church, for the civil authorities, for those oppressed by various needs, for all people, and for the salvation of the entire world.[4]

54. With art. 36 of this Constitution as the norm, in Masses celebrated with the people a suitable place may be allotted to their mother tongue. This is to apply in the first place to the readings and "the universal prayer," but also, as local conditions may warrant, to those parts belonging to the people.

Nevertheless steps should be taken enabling the faithful to say or to sing together in Latin those parts of the Ordinary of the Mass belonging to them.

Wherever a more extended use of the mother tongue within the Mass appears desirable, the regulation laid down in art. 40 of this Constitution is to be observed.

55. That more complete form of participation in the Mass by which the faithful, after the priest's communion, receive the Lord's body from the sacrifice, is strongly endorsed.

The dogmatic principles laid down by the Council of Trent remain intact.[5] In instances to be specified by the Apostolic See, however, communion under both kinds may be granted both to clerics and religious and to the laity at the discretion of the bishops, for example, to the ordained at the Mass of their ordination, to the professed at the Mass of their religious profession, to the newly baptized at the Mass following their baptism.

56. The two parts that, in a certain sense, go to make up the Mass, namely, the liturgy of the word and the liturgy of the eucharist, are so closely connected with each other that they form but one single act of worship. Accordingly this Council strongly urges pastors that in their catechesis they insistently teach the faithful to take part in the entire Mass, especially on Sundays and holy days of obligation.

57. §1. Concelebration, which aptly expresses the unity of the priesthood, has continued to this day as a practice in the Church of both East and West. For this reason it has seemed good to the Council to extend permission for concelebration to the following cases:

> 1. a. on Holy Thursday, both the chrism Mass and the evening Mass;
> b. Masses during councils, bishops' conferences, and synods;
> c. the Mass at the blessing of an abbot.

2. Also, with permission of the Ordinary, who is the one to decide whether concelebration is opportune, to:
> a. the conventual Mass and the principal Mass in churches, when the needs of the faithful do not require that all the priests on hand celebrate individually;
> b. Masses celebrated at any kind of meeting of priests, whether secular or religious.

§2. 1. The regulation, however, of the discipline of concelebration in the diocese pertains to the bishop.

2. This, however, does not take away the option of every priest to celebrate Mass individually, not, however, at the same time and in the same church as a concelebrated Mass or on Holy Thursday.

58. A new rite for concelebration is to be drawn up and inserted into the Roman Pontifical and Roman Missal.

Chapter III
The Other Sacraments and the Sacramentals

59. The purpose of the sacraments is to make people holy, to build up the Body of Christ, and, finally, to give worship to God; but being signs they also have a teaching function. They not only presuppose faith, but by words and objects they also nourish, strengthen, and express it; that is why they are called "sacraments of faith." They do indeed impart grace, but, in addition, the very act of celebrating them disposes the faithful most effectively to receive this grace in a fruitful manner, to worship God rightly, and to practice charity.

It is therefore of the highest importance that the faithful should readily understand the sacramental signs and should with great eagerness frequent those sacraments that were instituted to nourish the Christian life.

60. The Church has, in addition, instituted sacramentals. These are sacred signs bearing a kind of resemblance to the sacraments: they signify effects, particularly of a spiritual kind, that are obtained through the Church's intercession. They dispose people to receive the chief effect of the sacraments and they make holy various occasions in human life.

61. Thus, for well-disposed members of the faithful, the effect of the liturgy of the sacraments and sacramentals is that almost every event in their lives is made holy by divine grace that flows from the paschal mystery of Christ's passion, death, and resurrection, the fount from which all sacraments and sacramentals draw their power. The liturgy means also that there is hardly any proper use of material things that cannot thus be directed toward human sanctification and the praise of God.

62. With the passage of time, however, certain features have crept into the rites of the sacraments and sacramentals that have made their nature and purpose less clear to the people of today; hence some changes have become necessary as adaptations to the needs of our own times. For this reason the Council decrees what follows concerning the revision of these rites.

63. Because the use of the mother tongue in the administration of the sacraments and sacramentals can often be of considerable help for the people, this use is to be extended according to the following norms:

a. With art. 36 as the norm, the vernacular may be used in administering the sacraments and sacramentals.

b. Particular rituals in harmony with the new edition of the Roman Ritual shall be prepared without delay by the competent, territorial ecclesiastical authority mentioned in art. 22, §2 of this Constitution. These rituals are to be adapted, even in regard to the language employed, to the needs of the different regions. Once they have been reviewed by the Apostolic See, they are to be used in the regions for which they have been prepared. But those who draw up these rituals or particular collections of rites must not leave out the prefatory instructions for the individual rites in the Roman Ritual, whether the instructions are pastoral and rubrical or have some special social bearing.

64. The catechumenate for adults, divided into several stages, is to be restored and put into use at the discretion of the local Ordinary. By this means the time of the catechumenate, which is intended as a period of well-suited instruction, may be sanctified by sacred rites to be celebrated at successive intervals of time.

65. With art. 37–40 of this Constitution as the norm, it is lawful in mission lands to allow, besides what is part of Christian tradition, those initiation elements in use among individual peoples, to the extent that such elements are compatible with the Christian rite of initiation.

66. Both of the rites for the baptism of adults are to be revised: not only the simpler rite, but also the more solemn one, with proper attention to the restored catechumenate. A special Mass "On the Occasion of a Baptism" is to be incorporated into the Roman Missal.

67. The rite for the baptism of infants is to be revised and it should be suited to the fact that those to be baptized are infants. The roles as well as the obligations of parents and godparents should be brought out more clearly in the rite itself.

68. The baptismal rite should contain alternatives, to be used at the discretion of the local Ordinary, for occasions when a very large number are to be baptized together. Moreover, a shorter rite is to be drawn up, especially in mission lands, for use by catechists, but also by the faithful in general, when there is danger of death and neither a priest nor a deacon is available.

69. In place of the rite called the "Order of Supplying What Was Omitted in the Baptism of an Infant," a new rite is to be drawn up. This should manifest more clearly and fittingly that an infant who was baptized by the short rite has already been received into the Church.

Similarly, a new rite is to be drawn up for converts who have already been validly baptized; it should express that they are being received into the communion of the Church.

70. Except during the Easter season, baptismal water may be blessed within the rite of baptism itself by use of an approved, shorter formulary.

71. The rite of confirmation is also to be revised in order that the intimate connection of this sacrament with the whole of Christian initiation may stand out more clearly; for this reason it is fitting for candidates to renew their baptismal promises just before they are confirmed.

Confirmation may be conferred within Mass when convenient; as for the rite outside Mass, a formulary is to be composed for use as an introduction.

72. The rite and formularies for the sacrament of penance are to be revised so that they more clearly express both the nature and effect of the sacrament.

73. "Extreme unction," which may also and more properly be called "anointing of the sick," is not a sacrament for those only who are at the point of death. Hence, as soon as any one of the faithful begins to be in danger of death from sickness or old age, the fitting time for that person to receive this sacrament has certainly already arrived.

74. In addition to the separate rites for anointing of the sick and for viaticum, a continuous rite shall be drawn up, structured so that the sick person is anointed after confessing and before receiving viaticum.

75. The number of the anointings is to be adapted to the circumstances; the prayers that belong to the rite of anointing are to be so revised that they correspond to the varying conditions of the sick who receive the sacrament.

76. Both the ceremonies and texts of the ordination rites are to be revised. The address given by the bishop at the beginning of each ordination or consecration may be in the vernacular.

When a bishop is consecrated, all the bishops present may take part in the laying on of hands.

77. The marriage rite now found in the Roman Ritual is to be revised and enriched in such a way that it more clearly signifies the grace of the sacrament and imparts a knowledge of the obligations of spouses.

"If any regions follow other praiseworthy customs and ceremonies when celebrating the sacrament of marriage, the Council earnestly desires that by all means these be retained."[1]

Moreover, the competent, territorial ecclesiastical authority mentioned in art. 22, §2 of this Constitution is free to draw up, in accord with art. 63, its own rite, suited to the usages of place and people. But the rite must always conform to the law that the priest assisting at the marriage must ask for and obtain the consent of the contracting parties.

78. Marriage is normally to be celebrated within Mass, after the reading of the gospel and the homily and before "the prayer of the faithful." The prayer for the bride, duly emended to remind both spouses of their equal obligation to remain faithful to each other, may be said in the vernacular.

But if the sacrament of marriage is celebrated apart from Mass, the epistle and gospel from the nuptial Mass are to be read at the beginning of the rite and the blessing is always to be given to the spouses.

79. The sacramentals are to be reviewed in the light of the primary criterion that the faithful participate intelligently, actively, and easily; the conditions of

our own days must also be considered. When rituals are revised, in accord with art. 63, new sacramentals may also be added as the need for them becomes apparent.

Reserved blessings shall be very few; reservations shall be in favor only of bishops and Ordinaries.

Let provision be made that some sacramentals, at least in special circumstances and at the discretion of the Ordinary, may be administered by qualified laypersons.

80. The rite for the consecration to a life of virginity as it exists in the Roman Pontifical is to be revised.

A rite of religious profession and renewal of vows shall be drawn up with a view to achieving greater unity, simplicity, and dignity. Apart from exceptions in particular law, this rite should be adopted by those who make their profession or renewal of vows within Mass.

Religious profession should preferably be made within Mass.

81. The rite of funerals should express more clearly the paschal character of Christian death and should correspond more closely to the circumstances and traditions of various regions. This applies also to the liturgical color to be used.

82. The rite for the burial of infants is to be revised and a special Mass for the occasion provided.

Chapter IV
Divine Office

83. Christ Jesus, High Priest of the new and eternal covenant, taking human nature, introduced into this earthly exile the hymn that is sung throughout all ages in the halls of heaven. He joins the entire human community to himself, associating it with his own singing of this canticle of divine praise.

For he continues his priestly work through the agency of his Church, which is unceasingly engaged in praising the Lord and interceding for the salvation of the whole world. The Church does this not only by celebrating the eucharist, but also in other ways, especially by praying the divine office.

84. By tradition going back to early Christian times, the divine office is so arranged that the whole course of the day and night is made holy by the praises of God. Therefore, when this wonderful song of praise is rightly performed by priests and others who are deputed for this purpose by the Church's ordinance or by the faithful praying together with the priest in the approved form, then it is truly the voice of a bride addressing her bridegroom; it is the very prayer that Christ himself, together with his Body, addresses to the Father.

85. Hence all who render this service are not only fulfilling a duty of the Church, but also are sharing in the greatest honor of Christ's Bride, for by offering these praises to God they are standing before God's throne in the name of the Church, their Mother.

86. Priests engaged in the sacred pastoral ministry will offer the praises of the hours with greater fervor the more vividly they realize that they must heed St. Paul's exhortation: "Pray without ceasing" (1 Thes 5:17). For the work in which they labor will effect nothing and bring forth no fruit except by the power of the Lord who said: "Without me you can do nothing" (Jn 15:5). That is why the apostles, instituting deacons, said: "We will devote ourselves to prayer and to the ministry of the word" (Acts 6:4).

87. In order that the divine office may be better and more completely carried out in existing circumstances, whether by priests or by other members of the Church, the Council, carrying further the restoration already so happily begun by the Apostolic See, has seen fit to decree what follows concerning the office of the Roman Rite.

88. Because the purpose of the office is to sanctify the day, the traditional sequence of the hours is to be restored so that once again they may be genuinely related to the hour of the day when they are prayed, as far as it is possible. Moreover, it will be necessary to take into account the modern conditions in which daily life has to be lived, especially by those who are called to labor in apostolic works.

89. Therefore, when the office is revised, these norms are to be observed:

a. By the venerable tradition of the universal Church, lauds as morning prayer and vespers as evening prayer are the two hinges on which the daily office turns; hence they are to be considered as the chief hours and celebrated as such.

b. Compline is to be so composed that it will be a suitable prayer for the end of the day.

c. The hour known as matins, although it should retain the character of nocturnal praise when celebrated in choir, shall be adapted so that it may be recited at any hour of the day; it shall be made up of fewer psalms and longer readings.

d. The hour of prime is to be suppressed.

e. In choir the minor hours of terce, sext, and none are to be observed. But outside choir it will be lawful to choose whichever of the three best suits the hour of the day.

90. The divine office, because it is the public prayer of the Church, is a source of devotion and nourishment also for personal prayer. Therefore priests and all others who take part in the divine office are earnestly exhorted in the Lord to attune their minds to their voices when praying it. The better to achieve this, let them take steps to improve their understanding of the liturgy and of the Bible, especially the psalms.

In revising the Roman office, its ancient and venerable treasures are to be so adapted that all those to whom they are handed on may more fully and readily draw profit from them.

91. So that it may really be possible in practice to observe the course of the hours proposed in art. 89, the psalms are no longer to be distributed over just one week, but over some longer period of time.

The work of revising the psalter, already happily begun, is to be finished as soon as possible and is to take into account the style of Christian Latin, the liturgical use of psalms, including their being sung, and the entire tradition of the Latin Church.

92. As regards the readings, the following shall be observed:

a. Readings from sacred Scripture shall be arranged so that the riches of God's word may be easily accessible in more abundant measure.

b. Readings excerpted from the works of the Fathers, doctors, and ecclesiastical writers shall be better selected.

c. The accounts of the martyrdom or lives of the saints are to be made to accord with the historical facts.

93. To whatever extent may seem advisable, the hymns are to be restored to their original form and any allusion to mythology or anything that conflicts with Christian piety is to be dropped or changed. Also, as occasion arises, let other selections from the treasury of hymns be incorporated.

94. That the day may be truly sanctified and the hours themselves recited with spiritual advantage, it is best that each of them be prayed at a time most closely corresponding to the true time of each canonical hour.

95. In addition to the conventual Mass, communities obliged to choral office are bound to celebrate the office in choir every day. In particular:

a. Orders of canons, of monks and of nuns, and of other regulars bound by law or constitutions to choral office must celebrate the entire office.

b. Cathedral or collegiate chapters are bound to recite those parts of the office imposed on them by general or particular law.

c. All members of the above communities who are in major orders or are solemnly professed, except for lay brothers, are bound individually to recite those canonical hours which they do not pray in choir.

96. Clerics not bound to office in choir, if they are in major orders, are bound to pray the entire office every day, either in common or individually, following the norms in art. 89.

97. Appropriate instances are to be defined by the rubrics in which a liturgical service may be substituted for the divine office.

In particular cases and for a just reason Ordinaries may dispense their subjects wholly or in part from the obligation of reciting the divine office or may commute it.

98. Members of any institute dedicated to acquiring perfection who, according to their constitutions, are to recite any parts of the divine office are thereby performing the public prayer of the Church.

They too perform the public prayer of the Church who, in virtue of their constitutions, recite any little office, provided this has been drawn up after the pattern of the divine office and duly approved.

99. Since the divine office is the voice of the Church, that is, of the whole Mystical Body publicly praising God, those clerics who are not obliged to office in choir, especially priests who live together or who meet together for any purpose, are urged to pray at least some part of the divine office in common.

All who pray the divine office, whether in choir or in common, should fulfill the task entrusted to them as perfectly as possible: this refers not only to the internal devotion of their minds but also to their external manner of celebration.

It is advantageous, moreover, that the office in choir and in common be sung when there is an opportunity to do so.

100. Pastors should see to it that the chief hours, especially vespers, are celebrated in common in church on Sundays and the more solemn feasts. The laity, too, are encouraged to recite the divine office either with the priests, or among themselves, or even individually.

101. §1. In accordance with the centuries-old tradition of the Latin rite, clerics are to retain the Latin language in the divine office. But in individual cases the Ordinary has the power of granting the use of a vernacular translation, prepared in accord with art. 36, to those clerics for whom the use of Latin constitutes a grave obstacle to their praying the office properly.

§2. The competent superior has the power to grant the use of the vernacular in the celebration of the divine office, even in choir, to nuns and to members of institutes dedicated to acquiring perfection, both men who are not clerics and women. The version, however, must be one that has been approved.

§3. Any cleric bound to the divine office fulfills his obligation if he prays the office in the vernacular together with a group of the faithful or with those mentioned in §2, provided the text of the translation has been approved.

Chapter V
The Liturgical Year

102. The Church is conscious that it must celebrate the saving work of the divine Bridegroom by devoutly recalling it on certain days throughout the course of the year. Every week, on the day which the Church has called the Lord's Day, it keeps the memory of the Lord's resurrection, which it also celebrates once in the year, together with his blessed passion, in the most solemn festival of Easter.

Within the cycle of a year, moreover, the Church unfolds the whole mystery of Christ, from his incarnation and birth until his ascension, the day of Pentecost, and the expectation of blessed hope and of the Lord's return.

Recalling thus the mysteries of redemption, the Church opens to the faithful the riches of the Lord's powers and merits, so that these are in some way made present in every age in order that the faithful may lay hold on them and be filled with saving grace.

103. In celebrating this annual cycle of Christ's mysteries, the Church honors with special love Mary, the Mother of God, who is joined by an inseparable bond to the saving work of her Son. In her the Church holds up and admires the most excellent effect of the redemption and joyfully contemplates, as in a flawless image, that which the Church itself desires and hopes wholly to be.

104. The Church has also included in the annual cycle days devoted to the memory of the martyrs and the other saints. Raised up to perfection by the manifold grace of God and already in possession of eternal salvation, they sing God's perfect praise in heaven and offer prayers for us. By celebrating their passage from earth to heaven the Church proclaims the paschal mystery achieved in the saints, who have suffered and been glorified with Christ; it proposes them to the faithful as examples drawing all to the Father through Christ and pleads through their merits for God's favors.

105. Finally, in the various seasons of the year and according to its traditional discipline, the Church completes the formation of the faithful by means of devout practices for soul and body, by instruction, prayer, and works of penance and of mercy.

Accordingly the sacred Council has seen fit to decree what follows.

106. By a tradition handed down from the apostles and having its origin from the very day of Christ's resurrection, the Church celebrates the paschal mystery every eighth day, which, with good reason, bears the name of the Lord's Day or Sunday. For on this day Christ's faithful must gather together so that, by hearing the word of God and taking part in the eucharist, they may call to mind the passion, the resurrection, and the glorification of the Lord Jesus and may thank God, who "has begotten them again unto a living hope through the resurrection of Jesus Christ from the dead" (1 Pt. 1:3). Hence the Lord's Day is the first holy day of all and should be proposed to the devotion of the faithful and taught to them in such a way that it may become in fact a day of joy and of freedom from work. Other celebrations, unless they be truly of greatest importance, shall not have precedence over the Sunday, the foundation and core of the whole liturgical year.

107. The liturgical year is to be so revised that the traditional customs and usages of the sacred seasons are preserved or restored to suit the conditions

of modern times; their specific character is to be retained, so that they duly nourish the devotion of the faithful who celebrate the mysteries of Christian redemption and above all the paschal mystery. If certain adaptations are considered necessary on account of local conditions, they are to be made in accordance with the provisions of art. 39 and 40.

108. The minds of the faithful must be directed primarily toward those feasts of the Lord on which the mysteries of salvation are celebrated in the course of the year. Therefore, the Proper of Seasons shall be given the precedence due to it over the feasts of the saints, in order that the entire cycle of the mysteries of salvation may be celebrated in the measure due to them.

109. Lent is marked by two themes, the baptismal and the penitential. By recalling or preparing for baptism and by repentance, this season disposes the faithful, as they more diligently listen to the word of God and devote themselves to prayer, to celebrate the paschal mystery. The baptismal and penitential aspects of Lent are to be given greater prominence in both the liturgy and liturgical catechesis. Hence:

a. More use is to be made of the baptismal features proper to the Lenten liturgy; some of those from an earlier era are to be restored as may seem advisable.

b. The same is to apply to the penitential elements. As regards catechesis, it is important to impress on the minds of the faithful not only the social consequences of sin but also the essence of the virtue of penance, namely, detestation of sin as an offense against God; the role of the Church in penitential practices is not to be neglected and the people are to be exhorted to pray for sinners.

110. During Lent penance should be not only inward and individual, but also outward and social. The practice of penance should be fostered, however, in ways that are possible in our own times and in different regions and according to the circumstances of the faithful; it should be encouraged by the authorities mentioned in art. 22.

Nevertheless, let the paschal fast be kept sacred. Let it be observed everywhere on Good Friday and, where possible, prolonged throughout Holy Saturday, as a way of coming to the joys of the Sunday of the resurrection with uplifted and welcoming heart.

111. The saints have been traditionally honored in the Church and their authentic relics and images held in veneration. For the feasts of the saints proclaim the wonderful works of Christ in his servants and display to the faithful fitting examples for their imitation.

Lest the feasts of the saints take precedence over the feasts commemorating the very mysteries of salvation, many of them should be left to be celebrated by a particular Church or nation or religious family; those only should be extended to the universal Church that commemorate saints of truly universal significance.

Chapter VI
Sacred Music

112. The musical tradition of the universal Church is a treasure of inestimable value, greater even than that of any other art. The main reason for this preeminence is that, as sacred song closely bound to the text, it forms a necessary or integral part of the solemn liturgy.

Holy Scripture itself has bestowed praise upon sacred song[1] and the same may be said of the Fathers of the Church and of the Roman pontiffs, who in recent times, led by St. Pius X, have explained more precisely the ministerial function supplied by sacred music in the service of the Lord.

Therefore sacred music will be the more holy the more closely it is joined to the liturgical rite, whether by adding delight to prayer, fostering oneness of spirit, or investing the rites with greater solemnity. But the Church approves of all forms of genuine art possessing the qualities required and admits them into divine worship.

Accordingly, the Council, keeping the norms and precepts of ecclesiastical tradition and discipline and having regard to the purpose of sacred music, which is the glory of God and the sanctification of the faithful, decrees what follows.

113. A liturgical service takes on a nobler aspect when the rites are celebrated with singing, the sacred ministers take their parts in them, and the faithful actively participate.

As regards the language to be used, the provisions of art. 36 are to be observed; for the Mass, those of art. 54; for the sacraments, those of art. 63; for the divine office, those of art. 101.

114. The treasure of sacred music is to be preserved and fostered with great care. Choirs must be diligently developed, especially in cathedral churches; but bishops and other pastors of souls must be at pains to ensure that whenever a liturgical service is to be celebrated with song, the whole assembly of the faithful is enabled, in keeping with art. 28 and 30, to contribute the active participation that rightly belongs to it.

115. Great importance is to be attached to the teaching and practice of music in seminaries, in the novitiates and houses of study of religious of both sexes, and also in other Catholic institutions and schools. To impart this instruction, those in charge of teaching sacred music are to receive thorough training.

It is recommended also that higher institutes of sacred music be established whenever possible.

Musicians and singers, especially young boys, must also be given a genuine liturgical training.

116. The Church acknowledges Gregorian chant as distinctive of the Roman liturgy; therefore, other things being equal, it should be given pride of place in liturgical services.

But other kinds of sacred music, especially polyphony, are by no means excluded from liturgical celebrations, provided they accord with the spirit of the liturgical service, in the way laid down in art. 30.

117. The editio typica of the books of Gregorian chant is to be completed and a more critical edition is to be prepared of those books already published since the reform of St. Pius X.

It is desirable also that an edition be prepared containing the simpler melodies for use in small churches.

118. The people's own religious songs are to be encouraged with care so that in sacred devotions as well as during services of the liturgy itself, in keeping with rubrical norms and requirements, the faithful may raise their voices in song.

119. In certain parts of the world, especially mission lands, people have their own musical traditions and these play a great part in their religious and social life. Thus, in keeping with art. 39 and 40, due importance is to be attached to their music and a suitable place given to it, not only in forming their attitude toward religion, but also in adapting worship to their native genius.

Therefore, when missionaries are being given training in music, every effort should be made to see that they become competent in promoting the traditional music of the people, both in schools and in sacred services, as far as may be practicable.

120. In the Latin Church the pipe organ is to be held in high esteem, for it is the traditional musical instrument that adds a wonderful splendor to the Church's ceremonies and powerfully lifts up the spirit to God and to higher things.

But other instruments also may be admitted for use in divine worship, with the knowledge and consent of the competent territorial authority and in conformity with art. 22, §2, art. 37 and art. 40. This applies, however, only on condition that the instruments are suitable, or can be made suitable, for sacred use, are in accord with the dignity of the place of worship, and truly contribute to the uplifting of the faithful.

121. Composers, filled with the Christian spirit, should feel that their vocation is to develop sacred music and to increase its store of treasures.

Let them produce compositions having the qualities proper to genuine sacred music, not confining themselves to works that can be sung only by large choirs, but providing also for the needs of small choirs and for the active participation of the entire assembly of the faithful.

The texts intended to be sung must always be consistent with Catholic teaching; indeed they should be drawn chiefly from holy Scripture and from liturgical sources.

Chapter VII
Sacred Art and Sacred Furnishings

122. The fine arts are deservedly ranked among the noblest activities of human genius and this applies especially to religious art and to its highest achievement, sacred art. These arts, by their very nature, are oriented toward the infinite beauty of God, which they attempt in some way to portray by the work of human hands. They are dedicated to advancing God's praise and glory to the degree that they center on the single aim of turning the human spirit devoutly toward God.

The Church has therefore always been the friend of the fine arts, has ever sought their noble help, and has trained artists with the special aim that all things set apart for use in divine worship are truly worthy, becoming, and beautiful, signs and symbols of the supernatural world. The Church has always regarded itself as the rightful arbiter of the arts, deciding which of the works of artists are in accordance with faith, with reverence, and with honored traditional laws and are thereby suited for sacred use.

The Church has been particularly careful to see that sacred furnishings worthily and beautifully serve the dignity of worship and has admitted changes in materials, design, or ornamentation prompted by the progress of the technical arts with the passage of time.

Wherefore it has pleased the Fathers to issue the following decrees on these matters.

123. The Church has not adopted any particular style of art as its very own but has admitted styles from every period, according to the proper genius and circumstances of peoples and the requirements of the many different rites in the Church. Thus, in the course of the centuries, the Church has brought into being a treasury of art that must be very carefully preserved. The art of our own days, coming from every race and region, shall also be given free scope in the Church, on condition that it serves the places of worship and sacred rites with the reverence and honor due to them. In this way contemporary art can add its own voice to that wonderful chorus of praise sung by the great masters of past ages of Catholic faith.

124. In encouraging and favoring art that is truly sacred, Ordinaries should strive after noble beauty rather than mere sumptuous display. This principle is to apply also in the matter of sacred vestments and appointments.

Let bishops carefully remove from the house of God and from other places of worship those works of artists that are repugnant to faith and morals and to Christian devotion and that offend true religious sense either by their grotesqueness or by the deficiency, mediocrity, or sham in their artistic quality.

When churches are to be built, let great care be taken that they are well suited to celebrating liturgical services and to bringing about the active participation of the faithful.

125. The practice of placing sacred images in churches so that they may be venerated by the faithful is to be maintained. Nevertheless there is to be restraint regarding their number and prominence so that they do not create confusion among the Christian people or foster religious practices of doubtful orthodoxy.

126. When deciding on works of art, local Ordinaries shall give hearing to the diocesan commission on sacred art, and if need be, to others who are especially expert, as well as to the commissions referred to in art. 44, 45, and 46. Ordinaries must be very careful to see that sacred furnishings and valuable works of art are not disposed of or damaged, for they are the adornment of the house of God.

127. Bishops should have a special concern for artists, so as to imbue them with the spirit of sacred art and liturgy. This they may do in person or through competent priests who are gifted with a knowledge and love of art.

It is also recommended that schools or academies of sacred art to train artists be founded in those parts of the world where they seem useful.

All artists who, prompted by their talents, desire to serve God's glory in holy Church, should ever bear in mind that they are engaged in a kind of sacred imitation of God the Creator and are concerned with works intended to be used in Catholic worship, to uplift the faithful, and to foster their devotion and religious formation.

128. Along with the revision of the liturgical books, as laid down in art. 25, there is to be an early revision of the canons and ecclesiastical statutes regulating the supplying of material things involved in sacred worship. This applies in particular to the worthy and well-planned construction of places of worship, the design and construction of altars, the nobility, placement, and security of the eucharistic tabernacle, the practicality and dignity of the baptistry, the appropriate arrangement of sacred images and church decorations and appointments. Laws that seem less suited to the reformed liturgy are to be brought into harmony with it or else abolished; laws that are helpful are to be retained if already in use or introduced where they are lacking.

With art. 22 of this Constitution as the norm, the territorial bodies of bishops are empowered to make adaptations to the needs and customs of their different regions; this applies especially to the material and design of sacred furnishings and vestments.

129. During their philosophical and theological studies, clerics are to be taught about the history and development of sacred art and about the sound principles on which the production of its works must be grounded. In consequence they will be able to appreciate and preserve the Church's treasured monuments and be in a position to offer good advice to artists who are engaged in producing works of art.

130. It is fitting that the use of pontifical insignia be reserved to those ecclesiastical persons who have either episcopal rank or some definite jurisdiction.

Appendix
Declaration of the Second Vatican Ecumenical Council on Revision of the Calendar

131. The Second Vatican Ecumenical Council recognizes the importance of the wishes expressed by many on assigning the feast of Easter to a fixed Sunday and on an unchanging calendar and has considered the effects that could result from the introduction of a new calendar. Accordingly the Council issues the following declaration:

1. The Council is not opposed to the assignment of the feast of Easter to a particular Sunday of the Gregorian Calendar, provided those whom it may concern, especially other Christians who are not in communion with the Apostolic See, give their assent.

2. The Council likewise declares that it does not oppose measures designed to introduce a perpetual calendar into civil society.

Among the various systems being suggested to establish a perpetual calendar and to introduce it into civil life, only those systems are acceptable to the Church that retain and safeguard a seven-day week with Sunday and introduce no days outside the week, so that the present sequence of weeks is left intact, unless the most serious reasons arise. Concerning these the Apostolic See will make its own judgment.

The Fathers of the Council have given assent to all and to each part of the matters set forth in this Constitution. And together with the venerable Fathers, we, by the apostolic power given to us by Christ, approve, enact, and establish in the Holy Spirit each and all the decrees in this Constitution and command that what has been thus established in the Council be promulgated for the glory of God.

1. RomM, prayer over the gifts, Holy Thursday and 2d Sunday in Ordinary Time.

2. See Heb. 13:14.

3. See Eph. 2:21–22.

4. See Eph. 4:13.

5. See Is. 11:12.

6. See Jn. 11:52.

7. See Jn. 10:16.

Chapter I

1. See Is. 61:1; Lk. 4:18.

2. Ignatius of Antioch, *To the Ephesians* 7, 2.

3. See 1 Tm. 2:5.

4. *Sacramentarium Veronense* (ed. Mohlberg), n. 1265.

5. RomM, preface I of Easter.

6. RomM, prayer after the seventh reading, Easter Vigil.

7. See Mk. 16:15.

8. See Acts 26:18.

9. See Rom. 6:4, Eph. 2:6; Col. 3:1.

10. See Jn. 4:23.

11. See 1 Cor. 11:26.

12. Council of Trent, sess. 13, 11 Oct. 1551, *Decree on the Holy Eucharist,* chap. 5.

13. Council of Trent, sess. 22, 17 Sept. 1562, *Doctrine on the Holy Sacrifice of the Mass,* chap. 2.

14. See Augustine, *In Ioannis Evangelium Tractatus 6,* chap. 1, n. 7.

15. See Rv. 21:2; Col. 3:1; Heb. 8:2.

16. See Phil. 3:20; Col 3:4.

17. See Jn. 17:3; Lk. 24:47; Acts 2:38.

18. See Mt. 28:20.

19. RomM, prayer after communion, Easter Vigil.

20. RomM, opening prayer, mass for Monday of Easter Week.

21. See 2 Cor. 6:1.

22. See Mt. 6:6.

23. See 1 Thes. 5:17.

24. See 2 Cor. 4:10–11.

25. RomM, prayer over the gifts, Saturday after the 2d, 4th, and 6th Sundays of Easter.

26. Cyprian, *On the Unity of the Catholic Church 7;* see *Letter 66,* n. 8, 3.

27. See Council of Trent, sess. 22, 17 Sept. 1562, *Doctrine on the Holy Sacrifice of the Mass,* chap. 8.

28. See Ignatius of Antioch, *To the Magnesians,* 7; *To the Philadelphians,* 4; *To the Smyrnians,* 8.

Chapter II

1. See Augustine, *In Ioannis Evangelium Tractatus 36,* chap. 6, n. 13.

2. Liturgy of the Hours, antiphon for Canticle of Mary, evening prayer II, feast of Corpus Christi.

3. See Cyril of Alexandria, *Commentary on the Gospel of John,* book 11, chap. 11–12.

4. See 1 Tm. 2:1–2.

5. Council of Trent, sess. 21, *Doctrine on Communion under Both Species,* chap. 1–3.

Chapter III

1. Council of Trent, sess. 24, *Decree on Reform,* chap. 1. See also RomR, title 8, chap. 2, n. 6.

Chapter VI

1. See Eph. 5:19; Col. 3:16.

Restoration of Sacred Music

Motu Proprio *Tra le sollecitudini*
His Holiness Pope Pius X

November 22, 1903

Introduction

216. There is one pastoral care paramount not only for this Holy See—to which we have unworthily been raised by Divine Providence—but also for individual churches: maintaining and promoting the beauty of the house of God. Here the august mysteries of religion are celebrated, here the faithful gather to receive the grace of the sacraments, to assist at the Holy Sacrifice of the altar, to adore the most Blessed Sacrament and to be united at the Church's common prayer in her public and solemn liturgy.

217. Therefore, there must be nothing in this sacred building that might be a reasonable cause for disgust of scandal; above all, nothing directly offensive to the decorum and holiness of the sacred rites and thus unworthy of the house of prayer and the majesty of God.

218. We do not here propose to treat individually each of the abuses that may occur. Rather, we devote our attention today to one of the most common abuses, one most difficult to uproot. This must be condemned, even where everything else deserves the highest praise, where there is beauty and grandeur of building, splendor and exactness of ceremonies, full attendance of the clergy, gravity and piety of the officiating ministers. We speak of the abuse in singing and in sacred music. This may have resulted from the changeable and varied nature of the art itself, or from the successive alterations in taste and custom through the ages. It may also be due to the disastrous influence of secular and theatrical music on that of the Church, or to the pleasure excited by the music itself—a pleasure not easily contained within its proper limits. Lastly, it may be the result of the many prejudices on this subject which so easily begin and so obstinately remain, even among persons of piety and authority. Still the fact remains: there certainly is a continual tendency to deviate from the right norm of sacred music, a norm established in admitting this art to the service of public worship, expressed very clearly in the ecclesiastical canons, in the decrees of general and provincial councils, and in the repeated prescriptions of the Sacred Roman Congregations and of the Supreme Pontiffs, Our predecessors.

219. With deep satisfaction We recognize the great good that has already been done in recent years, not only in this Our own City, but also in many dioceses of Our country, and especially in certain other countries. There illustrious men, zealous for the liturgy, acting with the approval of the Holy See and under the direction of their bishops, have founded flourishing societies and thus, in nearly all their churches and chapels, have restored to sacred music that full honor which is its due. But this great gain is still far from being universal. Reflecting on Our own experience and considering the many complaints that have been addressed to Us from all parts of the world during the short time since it pleased God to raise Our humble person to the supreme dignity of the Roman Pontificate, We believe it is Our first duty to raise Our voice without delay in reproving and condemning, in the functions of public worship and ecclesiastical prayer, everything that does not agree with the norm We have indicated above.

220. Being moved with the most ardent desire to see the true Christian spirit flourish again in every way among all the faithful, the first thing to which We must turn our attention is the holiness and dignity of the temple. There Our people assemble for the purpose of acquiring the Christian spirit from its first and indispensable source, namely, active participation in the most sacred mysteries and in the public and solemn prayer of the Church. It is vain to hope for such copious blessings from Heaven if our worship of the Most High, rather than ascending with an odor of sweetness, again puts into our Lord's hands the scourges with which the unworthy profaners were once driven out of the temple by the Divine Redeemer.

221. Therefore, in order that no one may hereafter plead in excuse that he does not clearly understand his duty, in order that all possible uncertainty concerning the interpretation of laws already made may be removed, We consider it expedient to point out briefly the principles that govern the sacred music of public worship, and to present in one general survey the chief laws of the Church against the more common abuses in the matter. Now, therefore, of Our own initiative—*Motu propio*—and with certain knowledge, We publish this Our present *Instruction*. We decree with the fullness of Our apostolic authority that the force of law be given to this *Instruction* as to a *juridical code of sacred music,* and in this Our own handwriting, We impose upon all a strict observance of this law.

General Principles

222. Sacred music, because it is an integral part of the liturgy (a) participates in the same general purpose of this solemn liturgy, that is: the glory of God and the sanctification and edification of the faithful. It enhances the beauty and splendor of the ceremonies of the Church. Since its chief function is to clothe with suitable melody the liturgical text presented for the understanding of the faithful, its own proper end is to make the text more meaningful for them. Through this means they can more easily be moved to devotion and

better disposed to receive the fruits of grace coming from the celebration of the holy mysteries.

223. Sacred music must, therefore, possess in the highest degree the qualities which characterize the liturgy. In particular it must possess holiness and beauty of form: from these two qualities a third will spontaneously arise—universality (a).

Sacred music must be holy, and therefore exclude everything that is secular, both in itself and in its rendition.

It must be true art. In no other way can it affect the minds of the hearers in the manner which the Church intends in admitting into her liturgy the art of sound.

It must also be universal in this sense, that, although individual countries may admit into their ecclesiastical compositions proper forms native to each, still these forms must remain so subordinate to the general character of sacred music that no hearer of another nation might be disturbed thereby.

Kinds of Sacred Music

224. These qualities are found most perfectly in Gregorian Chant, which is the proper chant of the Roman Church—the only chant inherited from the ancient Fathers. Jealously guarding it these many centuries in her liturgical books, the Church directly proposes it to the faithful as her own music and prescribes it exclusively for some parts of her liturgy. Happily, recent studies have restored this chant to its original purity and integrity.

For these reasons Gregorian Chant has always been considered the supreme model of sacred music. Hence with every reason we lay down the following rule: "the more closely a Church composition approaches Gregorian Chant in movement, inspiration, and feeling, the more holy and liturgical it becomes; and the more it deviates from this supreme model, the less worthy it is of the temple" (a).

225. This traditional Gregorian Chant must be fully restored to the functions of divine worship. It must be accepted with certainty that the sacred liturgy loses nothing of its solemnity when the chant alone is used.

Gregorian Chant must be restored to the people so that they may again take a more active part in the sacred liturgy, as was the case in ancient times.

226. The qualities described above are also possessed in a very high degree by classical polyphony, especially by that of the Roman School, which reached its greatest perfection in the sixteenth century under Pierluigi da Palestrina, and subsequently continued to produce excellent musical and liturgical compositions. Classical polyphony accords very well with Gregorian Chant, that supreme model of all sacred music. Together with the chant, it deserves to be used in the more solemn functions of the Church, such as those of the Papal chapel. This music, too, should be restored especially in the greater basilicas, in cathedrals, and in the churches of seminaries and ecclesiastical institutions, where the means necessary for its performance are usually not lacking.

227. The Church has always recognized and encouraged all progress in the arts. Throughout the ages she has always admitted to her public worship whatever genius has discovered of the good and the beautiful, provided it be in keeping with liturgical law. Consequently, modern music is also admitted into the Church, for it too furnishes compositions of such excellence, sobriety, and dignity, that they are in no way unworthy of the liturgical functions.

Nevertheless, since modern music arose mainly for secular purposes, greater care must be taken with it. For those compositions in modern style which are admitted to the Church must contain nothing of a secular character; they should be free from all suggestions of theatrical motifs and should not resemble the movement of secular works in their external form.

228. Of modern music, that least suited to accompany divine worship is the theatrical style, so much in vogue during the last century, for instance, in Italy. This style is by nature most unlike Gregorian Chant and classical polyphony, and therefore least compatible with the fundamental laws of sacred music. The intrinsic structure, the rhythm, and the so-called conventionalism of this style do not fulfill the requirements of true liturgical music.

Liturgical Text

229. Latin is the language of the Roman Church. Therefore, any vernacular singing during solemn liturgical functions is forbidden. This holds even more especially for the proper and common parts of the Mass and the Office.

230. Since the texts to be sung and the order in which they are to be sung are already determined for every liturgical service, it is not lawful to change this order, or to substitute other texts selected at will, or to omit anything, either entirely or even in part, unless the rubrics allow some verses of the text to be taken by the organ while these verses are at the same time recited by the choir. It is allowed, according to the custom of the Roman Church, to sing a motet in honor of the Blessed Sacrament after the *Benedictus* in a Solemn Mass. A short motet with words approved by the Church also may be added after the prescribed Offertory of the Mass has been sung.

231. The liturgical text must be sung exactly as it is given in the books, without changing or transposing the words, without undue repetition, without distorting the syllables, and is always to be sung in a manner intelligible to the faithful.

External Form of Sacred Compositions

232. Each part of the Mass and the Office must keep, even in its music, that form and character which it has from ecclesiastical tradition and which is so

well expressed in Gregorian Chant. Therefore, an Introit, a Gradual, an Antiphon, a Psalm, a Hymn, a *Gloria in excelsis,* etc., will be composed each in its proper way.

Let these special rules be observed:

233. a) The *Kyrie, Gloria, Credo,* etc., of the Mass must preserve in the music the unity of composition proper to their text. They may not be made up of separate pieces, each forming a complete musical composition that could be taken out and replaced by another.

b) At Vespers the *Caeremoniale Episcoporum* must ordinarily be followed. This requires Gregorian Chant for the psalms, but allows figured music for the verses of the Gloria Patri and the hymn.

Nevertheless, on great feasts Gregorian Chant may alternate with the so-called *faux bourdons* or with verses likewise suitably composed.

Individual psalms may, at times, be sung entirely in figured music, provided the proper form of psalmody is preserved. This form is retained as long as the singers really appear to be chanting the verses alternately, either with new motifs or with motifs taken form Gregorian Chant or modeled on it. Psalms sung in the manner called *di concerto* are forever excluded and forbidden.

c) The hymns of the Church must also keep their traditional form. It is not lawful, for instance, to compose a *Tantum Ergo* so that the first stanza presents a *romanza* or and *adagio,* and then the *Genitori* an *allegro.*

d) The antiphons at Vespers should ordinarily be sung in their own Gregorian melody. If for any special reason they are sung to other music, they must never have either the form of a concert melody or the length of a motet or a cantata.

Singers

234. Some melodies are proper to the celebrant and to the sacred ministers at the altar; these must be sung in Gregorian Chant without any organ accompaniment. The rest of the liturgical chant belongs properly to the choir of clerics; for this reason, singers in church, even if they are laymen, really take the place of the ecclesiastical choir. Hence their music, at least for the greater part, must retain the character of choral music. Solos are not entirely excluded; but they must never so predominate in the liturgical service as to absorb the greater part of the liturgical text; rather they must be used merely for emphasis or melodic accentuation, and must be an integral part of the choral composition.

235. It follows from the same principle that the singers in church have a real liturgical office and that women, therefore, being incapable of such an office, cannot be admitted to form a part of the choir. If soprano and alto voices are desired, let them be supplied by boys, according to the ancient custom of the Church.

236. Finally, only men of known piety and integrity of life may be allowed to be members of the choir; men, who by their reverence and devotion during the service, show themselves worthy of the sacred duty they perform. It is also fitting that singers, while in choir, wear cassock and surplice; and if the choir be too much exposed to the gaze of the people, the singers should be hidden behind a grille.

Organ and Instruments

237. Although the proper music of the Church is purely vocal, the accompaniment of an organ is allowed. In some special cases, within due limits and with proper safeguards, other instruments may be used, but never without the special permission of the Ordinary, according to the prescriptions of the *Caeremoniale Episcoporum.*

238. Since the singing must always have the chief place, the organ and other instruments should merely sustain, never suppress it.

It is not lawful to introduce the singing with long preludes, or to interrupt it with intermezzos.

The sound of the organ in accompanying the chant, it preludes, interludes, and so on, must not only be governed by the character of the instrument, but must also share in all the qualities of sacred music which we have enumerated above.

239. Use of the piano is forbidden in the church, as is also the use of drums, kettledrums, cymbals, bells, and the like.

Bands are strictly forbidden to play in church; only for some special reason, and with the consent of the Ordinary, may a limited number of wind instruments be admitted. The composition and actual playing should be in a style dignified and entirely in keeping with that of the organ.

240. In processions outside the church, the Ordinary may give permission for a band, provided it does not play profane music. It is desired for such occasions that the band merely accompany some spiritual hymn sung either in Latin or in the vernacular by the choir or by the religious societies that take part in the procession.

Length of Sacred Music

241. It is not lawful to make the priest at the altar wait longer than the liturgical ceremonies warrant for the sake of either the singing or the instrumental music. According to ecclesiastical prescriptions, the Sanctus of the Mass must be completed before the elevation; therefore the celebrant should also have consideration for the singers. According to Gregorian tradition, the Gloria and the Credo ought to be relatively short.

242. As a general norm, to place the sacred ceremonies of the liturgy in a secondary role as a servant of the music is a very grave abuse that is to be wholly condemned. Rather, the music is simply a part of the liturgy.

Principal Means

243. That these instructions be exactly carried out, the Bishops, if they have not already done so, should establish in their dioceses special commissions of persons truly expert in sacred music. To them is entrusted the duty of watching over the music performed in their churches as the Bishop sees fit. The commissions should see to it that the music is not merely good in itself, but that it is also suited to the ability of the singers and is always well sung.

244. In seminaries and ecclesiastical institutions the traditional Gregorian Chant recommended above must be cultivated with all diligence and love. This is required by the Council of Trent. Superiors should wholeheartedly promote the chant and encourage their subjects in the singing of it. Wherever possible among clerics, let a *Scholae Cantorum* be established for sacred polyphony and good liturgical music.

245. In the usual studies of liturgy, moral theology, and canon law given to students of theology, let not those points that more directly touch the principles and laws of sacred music be omitted. Means should be sought to complete this teaching with some special instruction on the aesthetics of sacred art, lest clerics leave the seminary deficient in these ideas so necessary for a full ecclesiastical culture (a).

246. Care must be taken to restore the ancient *Scholae Cantorum* at least in the principal churches. This has been done with very good results in many places. Indeed, it would not be difficult for zealous priests to establish such *Scholae* even in smaller churches and in country parishes. Here would be a very easy means of gathering about themselves both children and adults, to the priests' profit and to the edification of the people.

247. Where they are already established, all higher schools of Church music should be sustained and increased in every way. As far as possible new ones should be founded. It is most important that the Church should herself provide instruction for her own choirmasters, organists, and singers, so that she may inspire them with the true principles of sacred art.

248. Lastly, We desire that all choirmasters, singers, and clerics, all superiors of seminaries, ecclesiastical institutions, and religious communities, all parish priests and rectors of churches, all canons of collegiate and cathedral churches, and most especially, the Ordinaries of all dioceses, zealously support

these wise reforms—so long desired and so unanimously hoped for—lest the very authority of the Church fall under contempt. For it is the Church which has repeatedly proposed these reforms and which now again promotes them.

222a *La musica sacra, come parte integrante della solenne Liturgia.*

223a *E precisamente la santità e la bontà delle forme, onde sorge spontaneo l'altro suo carattere, che è l'universalità.*

224a *Per tali motivi, il canto gregoriano fu sempre considerato come il supremo modello della musica sacra, potendosi stabilire con ogni ragione la sequente legge generale: tanto una composizione per chiesa è più sacra e liturgica, quanto più nell'andamento, nella ispirazione, e nel sapore si accosta alla melodia gregoriana, e tanto è meno degna del tempio, quanto più da quel supremo modello si riconosce difforme.*

245a *Nelle ordinarie lezioni di liturgia, di morale, di diritto canonico che si danno agli studenti di teologia non si tralasci di toccare quei punti che più particolarmente riguardano i principii e le leggi della musica sacra, e si cerchi di compierne la dottrina con qualche particolare istruzione circa l'estetica dell'arte sacra, affinché i chierici non escano dal seminario digiuni di tutte queste nozioni pur necessarie alla piena cultura ecclesiastica.*

Editor's Note: *This English translation of* Tra le sollecitudini *is from* Papal Teachings: The Liturgy, *selected and arranged by the Benedictine Monks of Solesmes, translated by the Daughters of St. Paul (Boston: Daughters of St. Paul © 1962). In order to preserve the exact nature of the work, we have included the original paragraph numbers from the Daughters of St. Paul edition as an aid to the citation of translator endnotes, which are referenced by a lower case (a) in the text.*

Mediator Dei

Encyclical of His Holiness Pope Pius XII
On the Sacred Liturgy

November 20, 1947

To the Venerable Brethren, the Patriarchs, Primates, Archbishops, Bishops and other Ordinaries in Peace and Communion with the Apostolic See.

Venerable Brethren, Health and Apostolic Benediction.

Mediator between God and men[1] and High Priest who has gone before us into heaven, Jesus the Son of God[2] quite clearly had one aim in view when He undertook the mission of mercy which was to endow mankind with the rich blessings of supernatural grace. Sin had disturbed the right relationship between man and his Creator; the Son of God would restore it. The children of Adam were wretched heirs to the infection of original sin; He would bring them back to their heavenly Father, the primal source and final destiny of all things. For this reason He was not content, while He dwelt with us on earth, merely to give notice that redemption had begun, and to proclaim the long-awaited Kingdom of God, but gave Himself besides in prayer and sacrifice to the task of saving souls, even to the point of offering Himself, as He hung from the cross, a Victim unspotted unto God, to purify our conscience of dead works, to serve the living God.[3] Thus happily were all men summoned back from the byways leading them down to ruin and disaster, to be set squarely once again upon the path that leads to God. Thanks to the shedding of the blood of the Immaculate Lamb, now each might set about the personal task of achieving his own sanctification, so rendering to God the glory due to Him.

2. But what is more, the divine Redeemer has so willed it that the priestly life begun with the supplication and sacrifice of His mortal body should continue without intermission down the ages in His Mystical Body which is the Church. That is why He established a visible priesthood to offer everywhere the clean oblation[4] which would enable men from East to West, freed from the shackles of sin, to offer God that unconstrained and voluntary homage which their conscience dictates.

3. In obedience, therefore, to her Founder's behest, the Church prolongs the priestly mission of Jesus Christ mainly by means of the sacred liturgy. She does this in the first place at the altar, where constantly the sacrifice of the cross is represented[5] and with a single difference in the manner of its offering, renewed.[6] She does it next by means of the sacraments, those special channels through which men are made partakers in the supernatural life. She does it,

finally, by offering to God, all Good and Great, the daily tribute of her prayer of praise. "What a spectacle for heaven and earth," observes Our predecessor of happy memory, Pius XI, "is not the Church at prayer! For centuries without interruption, form midnight to midnight, the divine psalmody of the inspired canticles is repeated on earth; there is no hour of the day that is not hallowed by its special liturgy; there is no state of human life that has not its part in the thanksgiving, praise, supplication and reparation of this common prayer of the Mystical Body of Christ which is His Church!"[7]

4. You are of course familiar with the fact, Venerable Brethren, that a remarkably widespread revival of scholarly interest in the sacred liturgy took place towards the end of the last century and has continued through the early years of this one. The movement owed its rise to commendable private initiative and more particularly to the zealous and persistent labor of several monasteries within the distinguished Order of Saint Benedict. Thus there developed in this field among many European nations, and in lands beyond the seas as well, a rivalry as welcome as it was productive of results. Indeed, the salutary fruits of this rivalry among the scholars were plain for all to see, both in the sphere of the sacred sciences, where the liturgical rites of the Western and Eastern Church were made the object of extensive research and profound study, and in the spiritual life of considerable numbers of individual Christians.

5. The majestic ceremonies of the sacrifice of the altar became better known, understood and appreciated. With more widespread and more frequent reception of the sacraments, with the beauty of the liturgical prayers more fully savored, the worship of the Eucharist came to be regarded for what it really is: the fountain-head of genuine Christian devotion. Bolder relief was given likewise to the fact that all the faithful make up a single and very compact body with Christ for its Head, and that the Christian community is in duty bound to participate in the liturgical rites according to their station.

6. You are surely well aware that this Apostolic See has always made careful provision for the schooling of the people committed to its charge in the correct spirit and practice of the liturgy; and that it has been no less careful to insist that the sacred rites should be performed with due external dignity. In this connection We ourselves, in the course of our traditional address to the Lenten preachers of this gracious city of Rome in 1943, urged them warmly to exhort their respective hearers to more faithful participation in the eucharistic sacrifice. Only a short while previously, with the design of rendering the prayers of the liturgy more correctly understood and their truth and unction more easy to perceive, We arranged to have the Book of Psalms, which forms such an important part of these prayers in the Catholic Church, translated again into Latin from their original text.[8]

7. But while We derive no little satisfaction from the wholesome results of the movement just described, duty obliges Us to give serious attention to this

"revival" as it is advocated in some quarters, and to take proper steps to preserve it at the outset from excess or outright perversion.

8. Indeed, though we are sorely grieved to note, on the one hand, that there are places where the spirit, understanding or practice of the sacred liturgy is defective, or all but inexistent, We observe with considerable anxiety and some misgiving, that elsewhere certain enthusiasts, over-eager in their search for novelty, are straying beyond the path of sound doctrine and prudence. Not seldom, in fact, they interlard their plans and hopes for a revival of the sacred liturgy with principles which compromise this holiest of causes in theory or practice, and sometimes even taint it with errors touching Catholic faith and ascetical doctrine.

9. Yet the integrity of faith and morals ought to be the special criterion of this sacred science, which must conform exactly to what the Church out of the abundance of her wisdom teaches and prescribes. It is, consequently, Our prerogative to commend and approve whatever is done properly, and to check or censure any aberration from the path of truth and rectitude.

10. Let not the apathetic or half-hearted imagine, however, that We agree with them when We reprove the erring and restrain the overbold. No more must the imprudent think that we are commending them when We correct the faults of those who are negligent and sluggish.

11. If in this encyclical letter We treat chiefly of the Latin liturgy, it is not because We esteem less highly the venerable liturgies of the Eastern Church, whose ancient and honorable ritual traditions are just as dear to Us. The reason lies rather in a special situation prevailing in the Western Church, of sufficient importance, it would seem, to require this exercise of Our authority.

12. With docile hearts, then, let all Christians hearken to the voice of their Common Father, who would have them, each and every one, intimately united with him as they approach the altar of God, professing the same faith, obedient to the same law, sharing in the same Sacrifice with a single intention and one sole desire. This is a duty imposed, of course, by the honor due to God. But the needs of our day and age demand it as well. After a long and cruel war which has rent whole peoples asunder with it rivalry and slaughter, men of good will are spending themselves in the effort to find the best possible way to restore peace to the world. It is, notwithstanding, Our belief that no plan or initiative can offer better prospect of success than that fervent religious spirit and zeal by which Christians must be formed and guided; in this way their common and whole-hearted acceptance of the same truth, along with their united obedience and loyalty to their appointed pastors, while rendering to God the worship due to Him, makes of them one brotherhood: "for we, being many, are one body: all that partake of one bread."⁹

13. It is unquestionably the fundamental duty of man to orientate his person and his life towards God. "For He it is to whom we must first be bound, as to an unfailing principle; to whom even our free choice must be directed as to an ultimate objective. It is He, too, whom we lose when carelessly we sin. It is He whom we must recover by our faith and trust."[10] But man turns properly to God when he acknowledges His Supreme majesty and supreme authority; when he accepts divinely revealed truths with a submissive mind; when he scrupulously obeys divine law, centering in God his every act and aspiration; when he accords, in short, due worship to the One True God by practicing the virtue of religion.

14. This duty is incumbent, first of all, on men as individuals. But it also binds the whole community of human beings, grouped together by mutual social ties: mankind, too, depends on the sovereign authority of God.

15. It should be noted, moreover, that men are bound by his obligation in a special way in virtue of the fact that God has raised them to the supernatural order.

16. Thus we observe that when God institutes the Old Law, He makes provision besides for sacred rites, and determines in exact detail the rules to be observed by His people in rendering Him the worship He ordains. To this end He established various kinds of sacrifice and designated the ceremonies with which they were to be offered to Him. His enactments on all matters relating to the Ark f the Covenant, the Temple and the holy days are minute and clear. He established a sacerdotal tribe with its high priest, selected and described the vestments with which the sacred ministers were to be clothed, and every function in any way pertaining to divine worship.[11] Yet this was nothing more that a faint foreshadowing[12] of the worship which the High Priest of the New Testament was to render to the Father in heaven.

17. No sooner, in fact, "is the Word made flesh"[13] than he shows Himself to the world vested with a priestly office, making to the Eternal Father an act of submission which will continue uninterruptedly as long as He lives: "When He cometh into the world he saith . . . 'behold I come . . . to do Thy Will.' "[14] This act He was to consummate admirably in the bloody Sacrifice of the Cross: "It is in this will we are sanctified by the oblation of the Body of Jesus Christ once."[15] He plans His active life among men with no other purpose in view. As a child He is presented to the Lord in the Temple. To the Temple He returns as a grown boy, and often afterwards to instruct the people and to pray. He fasts for forty days before beginning His public ministry. His counsel and example summon all to prayer, daily and at night as well. As Teacher of the truth He "enlighteneth every man"[16] to the end that mortals may duly acknowledge the immortal God, "not withdrawing unto perdition, but faithful to the saving of the soul"[17] As Shepherd He watches over His flock, leads it to life-giving pasture, lays down a law that none shall wander from His side, off the straight path He has pointed out, and that all shall lead holy lives imbued with His spirit and moved by His active aid. At the Last Supper He celebrates a new Pasch with solemn rite and ceremonial, and provides for its continuance through the divine institution of the Eucharist. On the morrow, lifted up between heaven and earth, He offers the saving sacrifice of His life, and pours forth, as it were, from His pierced Heart the sacraments destined to impart the treasures of redemption to the souls of men. All this He does with but a single aim: the glory of His Father and man's ever greater sanctification.

18. But it is His will, besides, that the worship He instituted and practiced during His life on earth shall continue ever afterwards without intermission. For he has not left mankind an orphan. He still offers us the support of His powerful, unfailing intercession, acting as our "advocate with the Father."[18] He aids us likewise through His Church where He is present indefectibly as the ages run their course: through the Church which He constituted "the pillar of truth"[19] and dispenser of grace, and which by His sacrifice on the cross, He founded, consecrated and confirmed forever.[20]

19. The Church has, therefore, in common with the Word Incarnate the aim, the obligation and the function of teaching all men the truth, of governing and directing them aright, of offering to God the pleasing and acceptable sacrifice; in this way the Church re-establishes between the Creator and His creatures that unity and harmony to which the Apostle of the Gentiles alludes in these words: "Now, therefore, you are no more strangers and foreigners; but you are fellow citizens with the saints and domestics of God, built upon the foundation of the apostles and prophets, Jesus Christ Himself being the chief corner-stone; in whom all the building, being framed together, groweth up into a holy temple in the Lord, in whom you also are built together in a habitation of God in the Spirit."[21] Thus the society founded by the divine Redeemer, whether in her doctrine and government, or in the sacrifice and sacraments instituted by Him, or finally, in the ministry, which He has confided to her charge with the outpouring of His prayer and the shedding of His blood, has no other goal or purpose than to increase ever in strength and unity.

20. This result is, in fact, achieved when Christ lives and thrives, as it were, in the hearts of men, and when men's hearts in turn are fashioned and expanded as though by Christ. This makes it possible for the sacred temple, where the Divine Majesty receives the acceptable worship which His law prescribes, to increase and prosper day by day in this land of exile of earth. Along with the Church, therefore, her Divine Founder is present at every liturgical function: Christ is present at the august sacrifice of the altar both in the person of His minister and above all under the eucharistic species. He is present in the sacraments, infusing into them the power which makes them ready instruments of sanctification. He is present, finally, in prayer of praise and petition we direct to God, as it is written: "Where there are two or three gathered together in My Name, there am I in the midst of them."[22] The sacred liturgy is, consequently, the public worship which our Redeemer as Head of the Church renders to the Father, as well as the worship which the community of the faithful renders to its Founder, and through Him to the heavenly Father. It is, in short, the worship rendered by the Mystical Body of Christ in the entirety of its Head and members.

21. Liturgical practice begins with the very founding of the Church. The first Christians, in fact, "were persevering in the doctrine of the apostles and in the communication of the breaking of bread and in prayers."[23] Whenever their pastors can summon a little group of the faithful together, they set up an altar on which they proceed to offer the sacrifice, and around which are ranged all the other rites appropriate for the saving of souls and for the honor due to God. Among these latter rites, the first place is reserved for the sacraments, namely, the seven principal founts of salvation. There follows the celebration of the divine praises in which the faithful also join, obeying the behest of the Apostle Paul, "In all wisdom, teaching and admonishing one another in psalms, hymns and spiritual canticles, singing in grace in your hearts to God."[24] Next comes the reading of the Law, the prophets, the gospel and the apostolic epistles; and last of all the homily or sermon in which the official head of the congregation recalls and explains the practical bearing of the commandments of the divine Master and the chief events of His life, combining instruction with appropriate exhortation and illustration of the benefit of all his listeners.

22. As circumstances and the needs of Christians warrant, public worship is organized, developed and enriched by new rites, ceremonies and regulations, always with the single end in view, "that we may use these external signs to keep us alert, learn from them what distance we have come along the road, and by them be heartened to go on further with more eager step; for the effect will be more precious the warmer the affection which precedes it."[25] Here then is a better and more suitable way to raise the heart to God. Thenceforth the priesthood of Jesus Christ is a living and continuous reality through all the ages to the end of time, since the liturgy is nothing more nor less than the exercise of this priestly function. Like her divine Head, the Church is forever present in the midst of her children. She aids and exhorts them to holiness, so that they may one day return to the Father in heaven clothed in that beauteous raiment of the supernatural. To all who are born to life on earth she gives a second, supernatural kind of birth. She arms them with the Holy Spirit for the struggle against the implacable enemy. She gathers all Christians about her altars, inviting and urging them repeatedly to take part in the celebration of the Mass, feeding them with the Bread of angels to make them ever stronger. She purifies and consoles the hearts that sin has wounded and soiled. Solemnly she consecrates those whom God has called to the priestly ministry. She fortifies with new gifts of grace the chaste nuptials of those who are destined to found and bring up a Christian family. When at last she has

soothed and refreshed the closing hours of this earthly life by holy Viaticum and extreme unction, with the utmost affection she accompanies the mortal remains of her children to the grave, lays them reverently to rest, and confides them to the protection of the cross, against the day when they will triumph over death and rise again. She has a further solemn blessing and invocation for those of her children who dedicate themselves to the service of God in the life of religious perfection. Finally, she extends to the souls in purgatory, who implore her intercession and her prayers, the helping hand which may lead them happily at last to eternal blessedness in heaven.

23. The worship rendered by the Church to God must be, in its entirety, interior a swell as exterior. It is exterior because the nature of man as a composite of body and soul requires it to be so. Likewise, because divine Providence has disposed that "while we recognize God visibly, we may be drawn by Him to love of things unseen."[26] Every impulse of the human heart, besides, expresses itself naturally through the senses; and the worship of God, being the concern not merely of individuals but of the whole community of mankind, must therefore be social as well. This obviously it cannot be unless religious activity is also organized and manifested outwardly. Exterior worship, finally, reveals and emphasizes the unity of the Mystical Body, feeds new fuel to its holy zeal, fortifies its energy, intensifies its action day by day: "for although the ceremonies themselves can claim no perfection or sanctity in their own right, they are, nevertheless, the outward acts of religion, designed to rouse the heart, like signals of a sort, to veneration of the sacred realities, and to raise the mind to meditation on the supernatural. They serve to foster piety, to kindle the flame of charity, to increase our faith and deepen our devotion. They provide instruction for simple folk, decoration for divine worship, continuity of religious practice. They make it possible to tell genuine Christians from their false or heretical counterparts."[27]

24. But the chief element of divine worship must be interior. For we must always live in Christ and give ourselves to Him completely, so that in Him, with Him and through Him the heavenly Father may be duly glorified. The sacred liturgy requires, however, that both of these elements be intimately linked with each another. This recommendation the liturgy itself is careful to repeat, as often as it prescribes an exterior act of worship. Thus we are urged, when there is question of fasting, for example, "to give interior effect to our outward observance."[28] Otherwise religion clearly amounts to mere formalism, without meaning and without content. You recall, Venerable Brethren, how the divine Master expels from the sacred temple, as unworthily to worship there, people who pretend to honor God with nothing but neat and well turned phrases, like actors in a theater, and think themselves perfectly capable of working out their eternal salvation without plucking their inveterate vices form their hearts.[29] It is, therefore, the keen desire of the Church that all of the faithful kneel at the feet of the Redeemer to tell Him how much they venerate and love Him. She wants them present in crowds—like the children whose joyous cries accompanied His entry into Jerusalem—to sing their hymns and chant their song of praise and thanksgiving to Him who is King of Kings and Source of every blessing. She would have them move their lips in prayer, sometimes in petition, sometimes in joy and gratitude, and in this way experience His merciful aid and power like the apostles at the lakeside of Tiberias, or abandon themselves totally, like Peter on Mount Tabor, to mystic union with the eternal God in contemplation.

25. It is an error, consequently, and a mistake to think of the sacred liturgy as merely the outward or visible part of divine worship or as an ornamental ceremonial. No less erroneous is the notion that it consists solely in a list of laws and prescriptions according to which the ecclesiastical hierarchy orders the sacred rites to be performed.

26. It should be clear to all, then, that God cannot be honored worthily unless the mind and heart turn to Him in quest of the perfect life, and that the worship rendered to God by the Church in union with her divine Head is the most efficacious means of achieving sanctity.

27. This efficacy, where there is question of the eucharistic sacrifice and the sacraments, derives first of all and principally from the act itself *(ex opere operato)*. But if one considers the part which the Immaculate Spouse of Jesus Christ takes in the action, embellishing the sacrifice and sacraments with prayer and sacred ceremonies, or if one refers to the "sacramentals" and the other rites instituted by the hierarchy of the Church, then its effectiveness is due rather to the action of the church *(ex opere operantis Ecclesiae)*, inasmuch as she is holy and acts always in closest union with her Head.

28. In this connection, Venerable Brethren, We desire to direct your attention to certain recent theories touching a so-called "objective" piety. While these theories attempt, it is true, to throw light on the mystery of the Mystical Body, on the effective reality of sanctifying grace, on the action of God in the sacraments and in the Mass, it is nonetheless apparent that they tend to belittle, or pass over in silence, what they call "subjective," or "personal" piety.

29. It is an unquestionable fact that the work of our redemption is continued, and that its fruits are imparted to us, during the celebration of the liturgy, notable in the august sacrifice of the altar. Christ acts each day to save us, in the sacraments and in His holy sacrifice. By means of them He is constantly atoning for the sins of mankind, constantly consecrating it to God. Sacraments and sacrifice do, then, possess that "objective" power to make us really and personally sharers in the divine life of Jesus Christ. Not from any ability of our own, but by the power of God, are they endowed with the capacity to unite the piety of members with that of the head, and to make this, in a sense, the action of the whole community. From these profound considerations some are led to conclude that all Christian piety must be centered in the mystery

of the Mystical Body of Christ, with no regard for what is "personal" or "subjective," as they would have it. As a result they feel that all other religious exercises not directly connected with the sacred liturgy, and performed outside public worship, should be omitted.

30. But though the principles set forth above are excellent, it must be plain to everyone that the conclusions drawn from them respecting two sorts of piety are false, insidious and quite pernicious.

31. Very truly, the sacraments and the sacrifice of the altar, being Christ's own actions, must be held to be capable in themselves of conveying and dispensing grace from the divine Head to the members of the Mystical Body. But if they are to produce their proper effect, it is absolutely necessary that our hearts be properly disposed to receive them. Hence the warning of Paul the Apostle with reference to holy communion, "But let a man first prove himself; and then let him eat of this bread and drink of the chalice."[30] This explains why the Church in a brief and significant phrase calls the various acts of mortification, especially those practiced during the season of Lent, "the Christian army's defenses."[31] They represent, in fact, the personal effort and activity of members who desire, as grace urges and aids them, to join forces with their Captain—"that we may discover . . . in our Captain," to borrow St. Augustine's words, "the fountain of grace itself."[32] But observe that these members are alive, endowed and equipped with an intelligence and will of their own. It follows that they are strictly required to put their own lips to the fountain, imbibe and absorb for themselves the life-giving water, and rid themselves personally of anything that might hinder its nutritive effect in their souls. Emphatically, therefore, the work of redemption, which in itself is independent of our will, requires a serious interior effort on our part if we are to achieve eternal salvation.

32. If the private and interior devotion of individuals were to neglect the august sacrifice of the altar and the sacraments, and to withdraw them from the stream of vital energy that flows from Head to members, it would indeed be sterile, and deserve to be condemned. But when devotional exercises, and pious practices in general, not strictly connected with the sacred liturgy, confine themselves to merely human acts, with the express purpose of directing these latter to the Father in heaven, of rousing people to repentance and holy fear of God, of weaning them from the seductions of the world and its vice, and leading them back to the difficult path of perfection, then certainly such practices are not only highly praiseworthy but absolutely indispensable, because they expose the dangers threatening the spiritual life; because they promote the acquisition of virtue; and because they increase the fervor and generosity with which we are bound to dedicate all that we are and all that we have to the service of Jesus Christ. Genuine and real piety, which the Angelic Doctor calls "devotion," and which is the principal act of the virtue of religion—that act which correctly relates and fitly directs men to God; and by which they freely and spontaneously give themselves to the worship of God in its fullest

sense[33]—piety of this authentic sort needs meditation on the supernatural
realities and spiritual exercises, if it is to be nurtured, stimulated and sustained,
and if it is to prompt us to lead a more perfect life. For the Christian religion,
practiced as it should be, demands that the will especially be consecrated to
God and exert its influence on all the other spiritual faculties. But every act of
the will presupposes an act of the intelligence, and before one can express the
desire and the intention of offering oneself in sacrifice to the eternal Godhead,
a knowledge of the facts and truths which make religion a duty is altogether
necessary. One must first know, for instance, man's last end and the supremacy
of the Divine Majesty; after that, our common duty of submission to our
Creator; and finally, the inexhaustible treasures of love with which God yearns
to enrich us, as well as the necessity of supernatural grace for the achievement
of our destiny, and that special path marked out for us by divine Providence
in virtue of the fact that we have been united, one and all, like members of a
body, to Jesus Christ the Head. But further, since our hearts, disturbed as they
are at times by the lower appetites, do not always respond to motives of love,
it is also extremely helpful to let consideration and contemplation of the justice of God provoke us on occasion to salutary fear, and guide us thence to
Christian humility, repentance and amendment.

33. But it will not do to possess these facts and truths after the fashion of an
abstract memory lesson or lifeless commentary. They must lead to practical
results. They must impel us to subject our senses and their faculties to reason,
as illuminated by the Catholic faith. They must help to cleanse and purify the
heart, uniting it to Christ more intimately every day, growing ever more to
His likeness, and drawing from Him the divine inspiration and strength of
which it stands in need. They must serve as increasingly effective incentives
to action: urging men to produce good fruit, to perform their individual duties
faithfully, to give themselves eagerly to the regular practice of their religion
and the energetic exercise of virtue. "You are Christ's, and Christ is God's."[34]
Let everything, therefore, have its proper place and arrangement; let everything
be "theocentric," so to speak, if we really wish to direct everything to the
glory of God through the life and power which flow from the divine Head
into our hearts: "Having therefore, brethren, a confidence in the entering into
the holies by the blood of Christ, a new and living way which He both dedicated for us through the veil, that is to say, His flesh, and a high priest over
the house of God; let us draw near with a true heart, in fullness of faith, having our hearts sprinkled from an evil conscience and our bodies washed with
clean water, let us hold fast the confession of our hope without wavering . . .
and let us consider one another, to provoke unto charity and to good works."[35]

34. Here is the source of the harmony and equilibrium which prevails among
the members of the Mystical Body of Jesus Christ. When the Church teaches
us our Catholic faith and exhorts us to obey the commandments of Christ,
she is paving a way for her priestly, sanctifying action in its highest sense; she

disposes us likewise for more serious meditation on the life of the divine Redeemer and guides us to profounder knowledge of the mysteries of faith where we may draw the supernatural sustenance, strength and vitality that enable us to progress safely, through Christ, towards a more perfect life. Not only through her ministers but with the help of the faithful individually, who have imbibed in this fashion the spirit of Christ, the Church endeavors to permeate with this same spirit the life and labors of men—their private and family life, their social, even economic and political life—that all who are called God's children may reach more readily the end He has proposed for them.

35. Such action on the part of individual Christians, then, along with the ascetic effort promoting them to purify their hearts, actually stimulates in the faithful those energies which enable them to participate in the august sacrifice of the altar with better dispositions. They now can receive the sacraments with more abundant fruit, and come from the celebration of the sacred rites more eager, more firmly resolved to pray and deny themselves like Christians, to answer the inspirations and invitation of divine grace and to imitate daily more closely the virtues of our Redeemer. And all of this not simply for their own advantage, but for that of the whole Church, where whatever good is accomplished proceeds from the power of her Head and redounds to the advancement of all her members.

36. In the spiritual life, consequently, there can be no opposition between the action of God, who pours forth His grace into men's hearts so that the work of the redemption may always abide, and the tireless collaboration of man, who must not render vain the gift of God.[36] No more can the efficacy of the external administration of the sacraments, which comes from the rite itself *(ex opere operato),* be opposed to the meritorious action of their ministers of recipients, which we call the agent's action *(opus operantis).* Similarly, no conflict exists between public prayer and prayers in private, between morality and contemplation, between the ascetical life and devotion to the liturgy. Finally, there is no opposition between the jurisdiction and teaching office of the ecclesiastical hierarchy, and the specifically priestly power exercised in the sacred ministry.

37. Considering their special designation to perform the liturgical functions of the holy sacrifice and divine office, the Church has serious reason for prescribing that the ministers she assigns to the service of the sanctuary and members of religious institutes betake themselves at stated times to mental prayer, to examination of conscience, and to various other spiritual exercises.[37] Unquestionably, liturgical prayer, being the public supplication of the illustrious Spouse of Jesus Christ, is superior in excellence to private prayers. But this superior worth does not at all imply contrast or incompatibility between these two kinds of prayer. For both merge harmoniously in the single spirit which animates them, "Christ is all and in all."[38] Both tend to the same objective: until Christ be formed in us.[39]

38. For a better and more accurate understanding of the sacred liturgy another of its characteristic features, no less important, needs to be considered.

39. The Church is a society, and as such requires an authority and hierarchy of her own. Though it is true that all the members of the Mystical Body partake of the same blessings and pursue the same objective, they do not all enjoy the same powers, nor are they all qualified to perform the same acts. The divine Redeemer has willed, as a matter of fact, that His Kingdom should be built and solidly supported, as it were, on a holy order, which resembles in some sort the heavenly hierarchy.

40. Only to the apostles, and thenceforth to those on whom their successors have imposed hands, is granted the power of the priesthood, in virtue of which they represent the person of Jesus Christ before their people, acting at the same time as representatives of their people before God. This priesthood is not transmitted by heredity or human descent. It does not emanate from the Christian community. It is not a delegation from the people. Prior to acting as representative of the community before the throne of God, the priest is the ambassador of the divine Redeemer. He is God's vice-gerent in the midst of his flock precisely because Jesus Christ is Head of that body of which Christians are the members. The power entrusted to him, therefore, bears no natural resemblance to anything human. It is entirely supernatural. It comes form God. "As the Father hath sent me, I also send you[40] . . . he that heareth you heareth me[41] . . . go ye into the whole world and preach the gospel to every creature; he that believeth and is baptized shall be saved."[42]

41. That is why the visible, external priesthood of Jesus Christ is not handed down indiscriminately to all members of the Church in general, but is conferred on designated men, through what may be called the spiritual generation of holy orders.

42. This latter, one of the seven sacraments, not only imparts the grace appropriate to the clerical function and state of life, but imparts an indelible "character" besides, indicating the sacred ministers' conformity to Jesus Christ the Priest and qualifying them to perform those official acts of religion by which men are sanctified and God is duly glorified in keeping with the divine laws and regulations.

43. In the same way, actually that baptism is the distinctive mark of all Christians, and serves to differentiate them from those who have not been cleansed in this purifying stream and consequently are not members of Christ, the sacrament of holy orders sets the priest apart from the rest of the faithful who have not received this consecration. For they alone, in answer to an inward supernatural call, have entered the august ministry, where they are assigned to service in the sanctuary and become, as it were, the instruments God uses to communicate supernatural life from on high to the Mystical Body of Jesus Christ. Add to this, as We have noted above, the fact that they alone have been marked with the indelible sign "conforming" them to Christ the Priest, and that their hands alone have been consecrated "in order that whatever they bless may be blessed, whatever they consecrate may become sacred and holy, in the name of our Lord Jesus Christ."[43] Let all, then, who would live in Christ flock to their priests. By them they will be supplied with the comforts and food of the spiritual life. From them they will procure the medicine of salvation assuring their cure and happy recovery from the fatal sickness of their sins. The priest, finally, will bless their homes, consecrate their families and help them, as they breathe their last, across the threshold of eternal happiness.

44. Since, therefore, it is the priest chiefly who performs the sacred liturgy in the name of the Church, its organization, regulation and details cannot but be subject to Church authority. This conclusion, based on the nature of Christian worship itself, is further confirmed by the testimony of history.

45. Additional proof of this indefeasible right of the ecclesiastical hierarchy lies in the circumstances that the sacred liturgy is intimately bound up with doctrinal propositions which the Church proposes to be perfectly true and certain, and must as a consequence conform to the decrees respecting Catholic faith issued by the supreme teaching authority of the Church with a view to safeguarding the integrity of the religion revealed by God.

46. On this subject We judge it Our duty to rectify an attitude with which you are doubtless familiar, Venerable Brethren. We refer to the error and fallacious reasoning of those who have claimed that the sacred liturgy is a kind of proving ground for the truths to be held of faith, meaning by this that the Church is obliged to declare such a doctrine sound when it is found to have produced fruits of piety and sanctity through the sacred rites of the liturgy, and to reject it otherwise. Hence the epigram, *"Lex orandi, lex credendi"*—the law for prayer is the law for faith.

47. But this is not what the Church teaches and enjoins. The worship she offers to God, all good and great, is a continuous profession of Catholic faith and a continuous exercise of hope and charity, as Augustine puts it tersely. "God is to be worshipped," he says, "by faith, hope and charity."[44] In the sacred liturgy we profess the Catholic faith explicitly and openly, not only by the celebration of the mysteries, and by offering the holy sacrifice and administering the sacraments, but also by saying or singing the credo of Symbol of the faith—it is indeed the sign and badge, as it were, of the Christian—along with other texts, and likewise by the reading of holy scripture, written under the inspiration of the Holy Ghost. The entire liturgy, therefore, has the Catholic faith for its content, inasmuch as it bears public witness to the faith of the Church.

48. For this reason, whenever there was question of defining a truth revealed by God, the Sovereign Pontiff and the Councils in their recourse to the "theological sources," as they are called, have not seldom drawn many an argument from this sacred science of the liturgy. For an example in point, Our predecessor of immortal memory, Pius IX, so argued when he proclaimed the Immaculate Conception of the Virgin Mary. Similarly during the discussion of a doubtful or controversial truth, the Church and the Holy Fathers have not failed to look to the age-old and age-honored sacred rites for enlightenment. Hence the well-known and venerable maxim, *"Legem credendi lex statuat supplicandi"*—let the rule for prayer determine the rule of belief.[45] The sacred liturgy, consequently, does not decide or determine independently and of itself what is of Catholic faith. More properly, since the liturgy is also a profession of eternal truths, and subject, as such, to the supreme teaching authority of the Church, it can supply proofs and testimony, quite clearly, of no little value, towards the determination of a particular point of Christian doctrine. But if one desires to differentiate and describe the relationship between faith and the sacred liturgy in absolute and general terms, it is perfectly correct to say, *"Lex credendi legem statuat supplicandi"*—let the rule of belief determine the rule of prayer. The same holds true for the other theological virtues also, *"In . . . fide, spe, caritate continuato desiderio semper oramus"*—we pray always, with constant yearning in faith, hope and charity.[46]

49. From time immemorial the ecclesiastical hierarchy has exercised this right in matters liturgical. It has organized and regulated divine worship, enriching it constantly with new splendor and beauty, to the glory of God and the spiritual profit of Christians. What is more, it has not been slow—keeping the substance of the Mass and sacraments carefully intact—to modify what it deemed not altogether fitting, and to add what appeared more likely to increase the honor paid to Jesus Christ and the august Trinity, and to instruct and stimulate the Christian people to greater advantage.[47]

50. The sacred liturgy does, in fact, include divine as well as human elements. The former, instituted as they have been by God, cannot be changed an any way by men. But the human components admit of various modifications, as the needs of the age, circumstance and the good of souls may require, and as the ecclesiastical hierarchy, under guidance of the Holy Spirit, may have authorized. This will explain the marvelous variety of Eastern and Western rites. Here is the reason for the gradual addition, through successive development, of particular religious customs and practices of piety only faintly discernible in earlier times. Hence likewise it happens from time to time that certain devotions long since forgotten are revived and practiced anew. All these developments attest the abiding life of the immaculate Spouse of Jesus Christ through these many centuries. They are the sacred language she uses, as the ages run their course, to profess to her divine Spouse her own faith along with that of the nations committed to her charge, and her own unfailing love. They furnish proof, besides, of the wisdom of the teaching method she employs to arouse and nourish constantly the "Christian instinct."

51. Several causes, really have been instrumental in the progress and development of the sacred liturgy during the long and glorious life of the Church.

52. Thus, for example, as Catholic doctrine on the Incarnate Word of God, the eucharistic sacrament and sacrifice, and Mary the Virgin Mother of God came to be determined with greater certitude and clarity, new ritual forms were introduced through which the acts of the liturgy proceeded to reproduce this brighter light issuing from the decrees of the teaching authority of the Church, and to reflect it, in a sense so that it might reach the minds and hearts of Christ's people more readily.

53. The subsequent advances in ecclesiastical discipline for the administering of the sacraments, that of penance for example; the institution and later suppression of the catechumenate; and again, the practice of eucharistic communion under a single species, adopted in the Latin Church; these developments were assuredly responsible in no little measure for the modification of the ancient ritual in the course of time, and for the gradual introduction of new rites considered more in accord with prevailing discipline in these matters.

54. Just as notable a contribution to this progressive transformation was made by devotional trends and practices not directly related to the sacred liturgy, which began to appear, by God's wonderful design, in later periods, and grew to be so popular. We may instance the spread and ever mounting ardor of devotion to the Blessed Eucharist, devotion to the most bitter passion of our Redeemer, devotion to the most Sacred Heart of Jesus, to the Virgin Mother of God and to her most chaste spouse.

55. Other manifestations of piety have also played their circumstantial part in this same liturgical development. Among them may be cited the public pilgrimages to the tombs of the martyrs prompted by motives of devotion, the special periods of fasting instituted for the same reason, and lastly, in this gracious city of Rome, the penitential recitation of the litanies during the "station" processions, in which even the Sovereign Pontiff frequently joined.

56. It is likewise easy to understand that the progress of the fine arts, those of architecture, painting and music above all, has exerted considerable influence on the choice and disposition of the various external features of the sacred liturgy.

57. The Church has further used her right of control over liturgical observance to protect the purity of divine worship against abuse from dangerous and imprudent innovations introduced by private individuals and particular churches. Thus it came about—during the 16th century, when usages and customs of this sort had become increasingly prevalent and exaggerated, and when private initiative in matters liturgical threatened to compromise the integrity of faith and devotion, to the great advantage of heretics and further spread of their errors—that in the year 1588, Our predecessor Sixtus V of immortal memory established the Sacred Congregation of Rites, charged with the defense of the legitimate rites of the Church and with the prohibition of any spurious innovation.[48] This body fulfills even today the official function of supervision and legislation with regard to all matters touching the sacred liturgy.[49]

58. It follows from this that the Sovereign Pontiff alone enjoys the right to recognize and establish any practice touching the worship of God, to introduce and approve new rites, as also to modify those he judges to require modification.[50] Bishops, for their part, have the right and duty carefully to watch over the exact observance of the prescriptions of the sacred canons respecting divine worship.[51] Private individuals, therefore, even though they be clerics, may not be left to decide for themselves in these holy and venerable matters, involving as they do the religious life of Christian society along with the exercise of the priesthood of Jesus Christ and worship of God; concerned as they are with the honor due to the Blessed Trinity, the Word Incarnate and His august mother and the other saints, and with the salvation of souls as well. For the same reason no private person has any authority to regulate external practices of this kind, which are intimately bound up with Church discipline and with the order, unity and concord of the Mystical Body and frequently even with the integrity of Catholic faith itself.

59. The Church is without question a living organism, and as an organism, in respect of the sacred liturgy also, she grows, matures, develops, adapts and accommodates herself to temporal needs and circumstances, provided only that the integrity of her doctrine be safeguarded. This notwithstanding, the temerity and daring of those who introduce novel liturgical practices, or call for the revival of obsolete rites out of harmony with prevailing laws and rubrics, deserve severe reproof. It has pained Us grievously to note, Venerable Brethren, that such innovations are actually being introduced, not merely in minor details but in matters of major importance as well. We instance, in point of fact, those who make use of the vernacular in the celebration of the august eucharistic sacrifice; those who transfer certain feast-days—which have been appointed and established after mature deliberation—to other dates; those, finally, who delete from the prayerbooks approved for public use the sacred texts of the Old Testament, deeming them little suited and inopportune for modern times.

60. The use of the Latin language, customary in a considerable portion of the Church, is a manifest and beautiful sign of unity, as well as an effective antidote for any corruption of doctrinal truth. In spite of this, the use of the mother tongue in connection with several of the rites may be of much advantage to the people. But the Apostolic See alone is empowered to grant this permission. It is forbidden, therefore, to take any action whatever of this nature without having requested and obtained such consent, since the sacred liturgy, as We have said, is entirely subject to the discretion and approval of the Holy See.

61. The same reasoning holds in the case of some persons who are bent on the restoration of all the ancient rites and ceremonies indiscriminately. The liturgy of the early ages is most certainly worthy of all veneration. But ancient usage must not be esteemed more suitable and proper, either in its own right or in its significance for later times and new situations, on the simple ground that it carries the savor and aroma of antiquity. The more recent liturgical rites likewise deserve reverence and respect. They, too, owe their inspiration to the Holy Spirit, who assists the Church in every age even to the consummation of the world.[52] They are equally the resources used by the majestic Spouse of Jesus Christ to promote and procure the sanctity of man.

62. Assuredly it is a wise and most laudable thing to return in spirit and affection to the sources of the sacred liturgy. For research in this field of study, by tracing it back to its origins, contributes valuable assistance towards a more thorough and careful investigation of the significance of feast-days, and of the meaning of the texts and sacred ceremonies employed on their occasion. But it is neither wise nor laudable to reduce everything to antiquity by every possible device. Thus, to cite some instances, one would be straying from the straight path were he to wish the altar restored to its primitive tableform; were he to want black excluded as a color for the liturgical vestments; were he to forbid the use of sacred images and statues in Churches; were he to order the crucifix so designed that the divine Redeemer's body shows no trace of His cruel sufferings; and lastly were he to disdain and reject polyphonic music or singing in parts, even where it conforms to regulations issued by the Holy See.

63. Clearly no sincere Catholic can refuse to accept the formulation of Christian doctrine more recently elaborated and proclaimed as dogmas by the Church, under the inspiration and guidance of the Holy Spirit with abundant fruit for souls, because it pleases him to hark back to the old formulas. No more can any Catholic in his right senses repudiate existing legislation of the Church to revert to prescriptions based on the earliest sources of canon law. Just as obviously unwise and mistaken is the zeal of one who in matters liturgical would go back to the rites and usage of antiquity, discarding the new patterns introduced by disposition of divine Providence to meet the changes of circumstances and situation.

64. This way of acting bids fair to revive the exaggerated and senseless antiquarianism to which the illegal Council of Pistoia gave rise. It likewise attempts to reinstate a series of errors which were responsible for the calling of that meeting as well as for those resulting from it, with grievous harm to souls, and which the Church, the ever watchful guardian of the "deposit of faith" committed to her charge by her divine Founder, had every right and reason to condemn.[53] For perverse designs and ventures of this sort tend to

paralyze and weaken that process of sanctification by which the sacred liturgy directs the sons of adoption to their Heavenly Father of their souls' salvation.

65. In every measure taken, then, let proper contact with the ecclesiastical hierarchy be maintained. Let no one arrogate to himself the right to make regulations and impose them on others at will. Only the Sovereign Pontiff, as the successor of Saint Peter, charged by the divine Redeemer with the feeding of His entire flock,[54] and with him, in obedience to the Apostolic See, the bishops "whom the Holy Ghost has placed . . . to rule the Church of God,"[55] have the right and the duty to govern the Christian people. Consequently, Venerable Brethren, whenever you assert your authority—even on occasion with wholesome severity—you are not merely acquitting yourselves of your duty; you are defending the very will of the Founder of the Church.

66. The mystery of the most Holy Eucharist which Christ, the High Priest instituted, and which He commands to be continually renewed in the Church by His ministers, is the culmination and center, as it were, of the Christian religion. We consider it opportune in speaking about the crowning act of the sacred liturgy, to delay for a little while and call your attention, Venerable Brethren, to this most important subject.

67. Christ the Lord, "Eternal Priest according to the order of Melchisedech,"[56] "loving His own who were of the world,"[57] "at the last supper, on the night He was betrayed, wishing to leave His beloved Spouse, the Church, a visible sacrifice such as the nature of men requires, that would re-present the bloody sacrifice offered once on the cross, and perpetuate its memory to the end of time, and whose salutary virtue might be applied in remitting those sins which we daily commit, . . . offered His body and blood under the species of bread and wine to God the Father, and under the same species allowed the apostles, whom he at that time constituted the priests of the New Testament, to partake thereof; commanding them and their successors in the priesthood to make the same offering."[58]

68. The august sacrifice of the altar, then, is no mere empty commemoration of the passion and death of Jesus Christ, but a true and proper act of sacrifice, whereby the High Priest by an unbloody immolation offers Himself a most acceptable victim to the Eternal Father, as He did upon the cross. "It is one and the same victim; the same person now offers it by the ministry of His priests, who then offered Himself on the cross, the manner of offering alone being different."[59]

69. The priest is the same, Jesus Christ, whose sacred Person His minister represents. Now the minister, by reason of the sacerdotal consecration which he has received, is made like to the High Priest and possesses the power of performing actions in virtue of Christ's very person.[60] Wherefore in his priestly activity he in a certain manner "lends his tongue, and gives his hand" to Christ.[61]

70. Likewise the victim is the same, namely, our divine Redeemer in His human nature with His true body and blood. The manner, however, in which Christ is offered is different. On the cross He completely offered Himself and all His sufferings to God, and the immolation of the victim was brought about by the bloody death, which He underwent of His free will. But on the altar, by reason of the glorified state of His human nature, "death shall have no more dominion over Him,"[62] and so the shedding of His blood is impossible; still, according to the plan of divine wisdom, the sacrifice of our Redeemer is shown forth in an admirable manner by external signs which are the symbols of His death. For by the "transubstantiation" of bread into the body of Christ and of wine into His blood, His body and blood are both really present: now the eucharistic species under which He is present symbolize the actual separation of His body and blood. Thus the commemorative representation of His death, which actually took place on Calvary, is repeated in every sacrifice of the altar, seeing that Jesus Christ is symbolically shown by separate symbols to be in a state of victimhood.

71. Moreover, the appointed ends are the same. The first of these is to give glory to the Heavenly Father. From His birth to His death Jesus Christ burned with zeal for the divine glory; and the offering of His blood upon the cross rose to heaven in an odor of sweetness. To perpetuate this praise, the members of the Mystical Body are united with their divine Head in the eucharistic sacrifice, and with Him, together with the Angels and Archangels, they sing immortal praise to God[63] and give all honor and glory to the Father Almighty.[64]

72. The second end is duly to give thanks to God. Only the divine Redeemer, as the eternal Father's most beloved son whose immense love He knew, could offer Him a worthy return of gratitude. This was His intention and desire at the Last Supper when He "gave thanks."[65] He did not cease to do so when hanging upon the cross, nor does He fail to do so in the august sacrifice of the altar, which is an act of thanksgiving or a "eucharistic" act; since this "is truly meet and just, right and availing unto salvation."[66]

73. The third end proposed is that of expiation, propitiation and reconciliation. Certainly, no one was better fitted to make satisfaction to Almighty God for all the sins of men than was Christ. Therefore, He desired to be immolated upon the cross "as a propitiation for our sins, not for ours only but also for those of the whole world"[67] and likewise He daily offers Himself upon our altars for our redemption, that we may be rescued from eternal damnation and admitted into the company of the elect. This He does, not for us only who are in this mortal life, but also "for all who rest in Christ, who have gone before us with the sign of faith and repose in the sleep of peace";[68] for whether we live, or whether we die "still we are not separated from the one and only Christ."[69]

74. The fourth end, finally, is that of impetration. Man, being the prodigal son, has made bad use of and dissipated the goods which he received from his heavenly Father. Accordingly, he has been reduced to the utmost poverty and to extreme degradation. However, Christ on the cross "offering prayers and supplications with a loud cry and tears, has been heard for His reverence."[70] Likewise upon the altar He is our mediator with God in the same efficacious manner, so that we may be filled with every blessing and grace.

75. It is easy, therefore, to understand why the holy Council of Trent lays down that by means of the eucharistic sacrifice the saving virtue of the cross is imparted to us for the remission of the sins we daily commit.[71]

76. Now the Apostle of the Gentiles proclaims the copious plentitude and the perfection of the sacrifice of the cross, when he says that Christ by one oblation has perfected for ever them that are sanctified.[72] For the merits of this sacrifice, since they are altogether boundless and immeasurable, know no limits; for they are meant for all men of every time and place. This follows from the fact that in this sacrifice the God-Man is the priest and victim; that His immolation was entirely perfect, as was His obedience to the will of His eternal Father; and also that He suffered death as the Head of the human race: "See how we were bought: Christ hangs upon the cross, see at what a price He makes His purchase . . . He sheds His blood, He buys with His blood, He buys with the blood of the Spotless Lamb, He buys with the blood of God's only Son. He who buys is Christ; the price is His blood; the possession bought is the world."[73]

77. This purchase, however, does not immediately have its full effect; since Christ, after redeeming the world at the lavish cost of His own blood, still must come into complete possession of the souls of men. Wherefore, that the redemption and salvation of each person and of future generations unto the end of time may be effectively accomplished, and be acceptable to God, it is necessary that men should individually come into vital contact with the sacrifice of the cross, so that the merits, which flow from it, should be imparted to them. In a certain sense it can be said that on Calvary Christ built a font of purification and salvation which He filled with the blood He shed; but if men do not bathe in it and there wash away the stains of their iniquities, they can never be purified and saved.

78. The cooperation of the faithful is required so that sinners may be individually purified in the blood of the Lamb. For though, speaking generally, Christ reconciled by His painful death the whole human race with the Father, He wished that all should approach and be drawn to His cross, especially by means of the sacraments and the eucharistic sacrifice, to obtain the salutary fruits produced by Him upon it. Through this active and individual participation, the members of the Mystical Body not only become daily more like to their divine Head, but the life flowing from the Head is imparted to the

members, so that we can each repeat the words of St. Paul, "With Christ I am nailed to the cross: I live, now not I, but Christ liveth in me."[74] We have already explained sufficiently and of set purpose on another occasion, that Jesus Christ "when dying on the cross, bestowed upon His Church, as a completely gratuitous gift, the immense treasure of the redemption. But when it is a question of distributing this treasure, He not only commits the work of sanctification to His Immaculate Spouse, but also wishes that, to a certain extent, sanctity should derive from her activity."[75]

79. The august sacrifice of the altar is, as it were, the supreme instrument whereby the merits won by the divine Redeemer upon the cross are distributed to the faithful: "as often as this commemorative sacrifice is offered, there is wrought the work of our Redemption."[76] This, however, so far from lessening the dignity of the actual sacrifice on Calvary, rather proclaims and renders more manifest its greatness and its necessity, as the Council of Trent declares.[77] Its daily immolation reminds us that there is no salvation except in the cross of our Lord Jesus Christ[78] and that God Himself wishes that there should be a continuation of this sacrifice "from the rising of the sun till the going down thereof,"[79] so that there may be no cessation of the hymn of praise and thanksgiving which man owes to God, seeing that he required His help continually and has need of the blood of the Redeemer to remit sin which challenges God's justice.

80. It is, therefore, desirable, Venerable Brethren, that all the faithful should be aware that to participate in the eucharistic sacrifice is their chief duty and supreme dignity, and that not in an inert and negligent fashion, giving way to distractions and day-dreaming, but with such earnestness and concentration that they may be united as closely as possible with the High Priest, according to the Apostle, "Let this mind be in you which was also in Christ Jesus."[80] And together with Him and through Him let them make their oblation, and in union with Him let them offer up themselves.

81. It is quite true that Christ is a priest; but He is a priest not for Himself but for us, when in the name of the whole human race He offers our prayers and religious homage to the eternal Father; He is also a victim and for us since He substitutes Himself for sinful man. Now the exhortation of the Apostle, "Let this mind be in you which was also in Christ Jesus," requires that all Christians should possess, as far as is humanly possible, the same dispositions as those which the divine Redeemer had when He offered Himself in sacrifice: that is to say, they should in a humble attitude of mind, pay adoration, honor, praise and thanksgiving to the supreme majesty of God. Moreover, it means that they must assume to some extent the character of a victim, that they deny themselves as the Gospel commands, that freely and of their own accord they do penance and that each detests and satisfies for his sins. It means, in a word, that we must all undergo with Christ a mystical death on the cross so that we can apply to ourselves the words of St. Paul, "With Christ I am nailed to the cross."[81]

82. The fact, however, that the faithful participate in the eucharistic sacrifice does not mean that they also are endowed with priestly power. It is very necessary that you make this quite clear to your flocks.

83. For there are today, Venerable Brethren, those who, approximating to errors long since condemned[82] teach that in the New Testament by the word "priesthood" is meant only that priesthood which applies to all who have been baptized; and hold that the command by which Christ gave power to His apostles at the Last Supper to do what He Himself had done, applies directly to the entire Christian Church, and that thence, and thence only, arises the hierarchical priesthood. Hence they assert that the people are possessed of a true priestly power, while the priest only acts in virtue of an office committed to him by the community. Wherefore, they look on the eucharistic sacrifice as a "concelebration," in the literal meaning of that term, and consider it more fitting that priests should "concelebrate" with the people present than that they should offer the sacrifice privately when the people are absent.

84. It is superfluous to explain how captious errors of this sort completely contradict the truths which we have just stated above, when treating of the place of the priest in the Mystical Body of Jesus Christ. But we deem it necessary to recall that the priest acts for the people only because he represents Jesus Christ, who is Head of all His members and offers Himself in their stead. Hence, he goes to the altar as the minister of Christ, inferior to Christ but superior to the people.[83] The people, on the other hand, since they in no sense represent the divine Redeemer and are not mediator between themselves and God, can in no way possess the sacerdotal power.

85. All this has the certitude of faith. However, it must also be said that the faithful do offer the divine Victim, though in a different sense.

86. This has already been stated in the clearest terms by some of Our predecessors and some Doctors of the Church. "Not only," says Innocent III of immortal memory, "do the priests offer the sacrifice, but also all the faithful: for what the priest does personally by virtue of his ministry, the faithful do collectively by virtue of their intention."[84] We are happy to recall one of St. Robert Bellarmine's many statements on this subject. "The sacrifice," he says, "is principally offered in the person of Christ. Thus the oblation that follows the consecration is a sort of attestation that the whole Church consents in the oblation made by Christ, and offers it along with Him."[85]

87. Moreover, the rites and prayers of the eucharistic sacrifice signify and show no less clearly that the oblation of the Victim is made by the priests in company with the people. For not only does the sacred minister, after the oblation of the bread and wine when he turns to the people, say the significant

prayer: "Pray brethren, that my sacrifice and yours may be acceptable to God the Father Almighty";[86] but also the prayers by which the divine Victim is offered to God are generally expressed in the plural number: and in these it is indicated more than once that the people also participate in this august sacrifice inasmuch as they offer the same. The following words, for example, are used: "For whom we offer, or who offer up to Thee . . . We therefore beseech thee, O Lord, to be appeased and to receive this offering of our bounded duty, as also of thy whole household . . . We thy servants, as also thy whole people . . . do offer unto thy most excellent majesty, of thine own gifts bestowed upon us, a pure victim, a holy victim, a spotless victim."[87]

88. Nor is it to be wondered at, that the faithful should be raised to this dignity. By the waters of baptism, as by common right, Christians are made members of the Mystical Body of Christ the Priest, and by the "character" which is imprinted on their souls, they are appointed to give worship to God. Thus they participate, according to their condition, in the priesthood of Christ.

89. In every age of the Church's history, the mind of man, enlightened by faith, has aimed at the greatest possible knowledge of things divine. It is fitting, then, that the Christian people should also desire to know in what sense they are said in the canon of the Mass to offer up the sacrifice. To satisfy such a pious desire, then, We shall here explain the matter briefly and concisely.

90. First of all the more extrinsic explanations are these: it frequently happens that the faithful assisting at Mass join their prayers alternately with those of the priest, and sometimes—a more frequent occurrence in ancient times— they offer to the ministers at the altar bread and wine to be changed into the body and blood of Christ, and, finally, by their alms they get the priest to offer the divine Victim for their intentions.

91. But there is also a more profound reason why all Christians, especially those who are present at Mass, are said to offer the sacrifice.

92. In this most important subject it is necessary, in order to avoid giving rise to a dangerous error, that we define the exact meaning of the word "offer." The unbloody immolation at the words of consecration, when Christ is made present upon the altar in the state of a victim, is performed by the priest and by him alone, as the representative of Christ and not as the representative of the faithful. But it is because the priest places the divine Victim upon the altar that he offers it to God the Father as an oblation for the glory of the Blessed Trinity and for the good of the whole Church. Now the faithful participate in the oblation, understood in this limited sense, after their own fashion and in a twofold manner, namely, because they not only offer the sacrifice by the hands of the priest, but also, to a certain extent, in union with him. It is by reason of this participation that the offering made by the people is also included in liturgical worship.

93. Now it is clear that the faithful offer the sacrifice by the hands of the priest from the fact that the minister at the altar, in offering a sacrifice in the name of all His members, represents Christ, the Head of the Mystical Body. Hence the whole Church can rightly be said to offer up the victim through Christ. But the conclusion that the people offer the sacrifice with the priest himself is not based on the fact that, being members of the Church no less than the priest himself, they perform a visible liturgical rite; for this is the privilege only of the minister who has been divinely appointed to this office: rather it is based on the fact that the people unite their hearts in praise, impetration, expiation and thanksgiving with prayers or intention of the priest, even of the High Priest himself, so that in the one and same offering of the victim and according to a visible sacerdotal rite, they may be presented to God the Father. It is obviously necessary that the external sacrificial rite should, of its very nature, signify the internal worship of the heart. Now the sacrifice of the New Law signifies that supreme worship by which the principal Offerer himself, who is Christ, and, in union with Him and through Him, all the members of the Mystical Body pay God the honor and reverence that are due to Him.

94. We are very pleased to learn that this teaching, thanks to a more intense study of the liturgy on the part of many, especially in recent years, has been given full recognition. We must, however, deeply deplore certain exaggerations and over-statements which are not in agreement with the true teaching of the Church.

95. Some in fact disapprove altogether of those Masses which are offered privately and without any congregation, on the ground that they are a departure from the ancient way of offering the sacrifice; moreover, there are some who assert that priests cannot offer Mass at different altars at the same time, because, by doing so, they separate the community of the faithful and imperil its unity; while some go so far as to hold that the people must confirm and ratify the sacrifice if it is to have its proper force and value.

96. They are mistaken in appealing in this matter to the social character of the eucharistic sacrifice, for as often as a priest repeats what the divine Redeemer did at the Last Supper, the sacrifice is really completed. Moreover, this sacrifice, necessarily and of its very nature, has always and everywhere the character of a public and social act, inasmuch as he who offers it acts in the name of Christ and of the faithful, whose Head is the divine Redeemer, and he offers it to God for the holy Catholic Church, and for the living and the dead.[88] This is undoubtedly so, whether the faithful are present— as we desire and commend them to be in great numbers and with devotion— or are not present, since it is in no [way] required that the people ratify what the sacred minister has done.

97. Still, though it is clear from what We have said that the Mass is offered in the name of Christ and of the Church and that it is not robbed of its social effects though it be celebrated by a priest without a server, nonetheless, on account of the dignity of such an august mystery, it is our earnest desire—as Mother Church has always commanded—that no priest should say Mass unless a server is at hand to answer the prayers, as canon 813 prescribes.

98. In order that the oblation by which the faithful offer the divine Victim in this sacrifice to the heavenly Father may have its full effect, it is necessary that the people add something else, namely, the offering of themselves as a victim.

99. This offering in fact is not confined merely to the liturgical sacrifice. For the Prince of the Apostles wishes us, as living stones built upon Christ, the cornerstone, to be able as "a holy priesthood, to offer up spiritual sacrifices, acceptable to God by Jesus Christ."[89] St. Paul the Apostle addresses the following words of exhortation to Christians, without distinction of time, "I beseech you therefore, . . . that you present your bodies, a living sacrifice, holy, pleasing unto God, your reasonable service."[90] But at that time especially when the faithful take part in the liturgical service with such piety and recollection that it can truly be said of them: "whose faith and devotion is known to Thee,"[91] it is then, with the High Priest and through Him they offer themselves as a spiritual sacrifice, that each one's faith ought to become more ready to work through charity, his piety more real and fervent, and each one should consecrate himself to the furthering of the divine glory, desiring to become as like as possible to Christ in His most grievous sufferings.

100. This we are also taught by those exhortations which the Bishop, in the Church's name, addresses to priests on the day of their ordination, "Understand what you do, imitate what you handle, and since you celebrate the mystery of the Lord's death, take good care to mortify your members with their vices and concupiscences."[92] In almost the same manner the sacred books of the liturgy advise Christians who come to Mass to participate in the sacrifice: "At this . . . altar let innocence be in honor, let pride be sacrificed, anger slain, impurity and every evil desire laid low, let the sacrifice of chastity be offered in place of doves and instead of the young pigeons the sacrifice of innocence."[93] While we stand before the altar, then, it is our duty so to transform our hearts, that every trace of sin may be completely blotted out, while whatever promotes supernatural life through Christ may be zealously fostered and strengthened even to the extent that, in union with the immaculate Victim, we become a victim acceptable to the eternal Father.

101. The prescriptions in fact of the sacred liturgy aim, by every means at their disposal, at helping the Church to bring about this most holy purpose in the most suitable manner possible. This is the object not only of readings, homilies and other sermons given by priests, as also the whole cycle of mysteries which are proposed for our commemoration in the course of the year, but it is also the purpose of vestments, of sacred rites and their external splendor. All these things aim at "enhancing the majesty of this great Sacrifice, and raising the minds of the faithful by means of these visible signs of religion and piety, to the contemplation of the sublime truths contained in this sacrifice."[94]

102. All the elements of the liturgy, then, would have us reproduce in our hearts the likeness of the divine Redeemer through the mystery of the cross, according to the words of the Apostle of the Gentiles, "With Christ I am nailed to the cross. I live, now not I, but Christ liveth in me."[95] Thus we become a victim, as it were, along with Christ to increase the glory of the eternal Father.

103. Let this, then, be the intention and aspiration of the faithful, when they offer up the divine Victim in the Mass. For if, as St. Augustine writes, our mystery is enacted on the Lord's table, that is Christ our Lord Himself,[96] who is the Head and symbol of that union through which we are the body of Christ[97] and members of His Body;[98] if St. Robert Bellarmine teaches, according to the mind of the Doctor of Hippo, that in the sacrifice of the altar there is signified the general sacrifice by which the whole Mystical Body of Christ, that is, all the city of redeemed, is offered up to God through Christ, the High Priest:[99] nothing can be conceived more just or fitting than that all of us in union with our Head, who suffered for our sake, should also sacrifice ourselves to the eternal Father. For in the sacrament of the altar, as the same St. Augustine has it, the Church is made to see that in what she offers she herself is offered.[100]

104. Let the faithful, therefore, consider to what a high dignity they are raised by the sacrament of baptism. They should not think it enough to participate in the eucharistic sacrifice with that general intention which befits members of Christ and children of the Church, but let them further, in keeping with the spirit of the sacred liturgy, be most closely united with the High Priest and His earthly minister, at the time the consecration of the divine Victim is enacted, and at that time especially when those solemn words are pronounced, "By Him and with Him and in Him is to Thee, God the Father almighty, in the unity of the Holy Ghost, all honor and glory for ever and ever";[101] to these words in fact the people answer, "Amen." Nor should Christians forget to offer themselves, their cares, their sorrows, their distress and their necessities in union with their divine Savior upon the cross.

105. Therefore, they are to be praised who, with the idea of getting the Christian people to take part more easily and more fruitfully in the Mass, strive to make them familiar with the "Roman Missal," so that the faithful, united with the priest, may pray together in the very words and sentiments of the Church. They also are to be commended who strive to make the liturgy even in an external way a sacred act in which all who are present may share. This can be done in more than one way, when, for instance, the whole

congregation, in accordance with the rules of the liturgy, either answer the priest in an orderly and fitting manner, or sing hymns suitable to the different parts of the Mass, or do both, or finally in high Masses when they answer the prayers of the minister of Jesus Christ and also sing the liturgical chant.

106. These methods of participation in the Mass are to be approved and recommended when they are in complete agreement with the precepts of the Church and the rubrics of the liturgy. Their chief aim is to foster and promote the people's piety and intimate union what Christ and His visible minister and to arouse those internal sentiments and dispositions which should make our hearts become like to that of the High Priest of the New Testament. However, though they show also in an outward manner that the very nature of the sacrifice, as offered by the Mediator between God and men,[102] must be regarded as the act of the whole Mystical Body of Christ, still they are by no means necessary to constitute it a public act or to give it a social character. And besides, a "dialogue" Mass of this kind cannot replace the high Mass, which, as a matter of fact, though it should be offered with only the sacred ministers present, possesses its own special dignity due to the impressive character of its ritual and the magnificence of its ceremonies. The splendor and grandeur of a high Mass, however, are very much increased if, as the Church desires, the people are present in great numbers and with devotion.

107. It is to be observed, also, that they have strayed from the path of truth and right reason who, led away by false opinions, make so much of these accidentals as to presume to assert that without them the Mass cannot fulfill its appointed end.

108. Many of the faithful are unable to use the Roman Missal even though it is written in the vernacular; nor are all capable of understanding correctly the liturgical rites and formulas. So varied and diverse are men's talents and characters that it is impossible for all to be moved and attracted to the same extent by community prayers, hymns and liturgical services. Moreover, the needs and inclinations of all are not the same, nor are they always constant in the same individual. Who, then, would say, on account of such a prejudice, that all these Christians cannot participate in the Mass nor share its fruits? On the contrary, they can adopt some other method which proves easier for certain people; for instance, they can lovingly meditate on the mysteries of Jesus Christ or perform other exercises of piety or recite prayers which, though they differ from the sacred rites, are still essentially in harmony with them.

109. Wherefore We exhort you, Venerable Brethren, that each in his diocese or ecclesiastical jurisdiction supervise and regulate the manner and method in which the people take part in the liturgy, according to the rubrics of the missal and in keeping with the injunctions which the Sacred Congregation of Rites and the Code of canon law have published. Let everything be done with due order and dignity, and let no one, not even a priest, make use of the sacred edifices according to his whim to try out experiments. It is also Our wish that in each diocese an advisory committee to promote the liturgical apostolate should be established, similar to that which cares for sacred music and art, so that with your watchful guidance everything may be carefully carried out in accordance with the prescriptions of the Apostolic See.

110. In religious communities let all those regulations be accurately observed which are laid down in their respective constitutions, nor let any innovations be made which the superiors of these communities have not previously approved.

111. But however much variety and disparity there may be in the exterior manner and circumstances in which the Christian laity participate in the Mass and other liturgical functions, constant and earnest effort must be made to unite the congregation in spirit as much as possible with the divine Redeemer, so that their lives may be daily enriched with more abundant sanctity, and greater glory be given to the heavenly Father.

112. The august sacrifice of the altar is concluded with communion or the partaking of the divine feast. But, as all know, the integrity of the sacrifice only requires that the priest partake of the heavenly food. Although it is most desirable that the people should also approach the holy table, this is not required for the integrity of the sacrifice.

113. We wish in this matter to repeat the remarks which Our predecessor Benedict XIV makes with regard to the definitions of the Council of Trent: "First We must state that none of the faithful can hold that private Masses, in which the priest alone receives holy communion, are therefore unlawful and do not fulfill the idea of the true, perfect and complete unbloody sacrifice instituted by Christ our Lord. For the faithful know quite well, or at least can easily be taught, that the Council of Trent, supported by the doctrine which the uninterrupted tradition of the Church has preserved, condemned the new and false opinion of Luther as opposed to this tradition."[103] "If anyone shall say that Masses in which the priest only receives communion, are unlawful, and therefore should be abolished, let him be anathema."[104]

114. They, therefore, err from the path of truth who do not want to have Masses celebrated unless the faithful communicate; and those are still more in error who, in holding that it is altogether necessary for the faithful to receive holy communion as well as the priest, put forward the captious argument that here there is question not of a sacrifice merely, but of a sacrifice and a supper of brotherly union, and consider the general communion of all present as the culminating point of the whole celebration.

115. Now it cannot be over-emphasized that the eucharistic sacrifice of its very nature is the unbloody immolation of the divine Victim, which is made manifest in a mystical manner by the separation of the sacred species and by

their oblation to the eternal Father. Holy communion pertains to the integrity of the Mass and to the partaking of the august sacrament; but while it is obligatory for the priest who says the Mass, it is only something earnestly recommended to the faithful.

116. The Church, as the teacher of truth, strives by every means in her power to safeguard the integrity of the Catholic faith, and like a mother solicitous for the welfare of her children, she exhorts them most earnestly to partake fervently and frequently of the richest treasure of our religion.

117. She wishes in the first place that Christians—especially when they cannot easily receive holy communion should do so at least by desire, so that with renewed faith, reverence, humility and complete trust in the goodness of the divine Redeemer, they may be united to Him in the spirit of the most ardent charity.

118. But the desire of Mother Church does not stop here. For since by feasting upon the bread of angles we can by a "sacramental" communion, as we have already said, also become partakers of the sacrifice, she repeats the invitation to all her children individually, "Take and eat . . . Do this in memory of Me"[105] so that "we may continually experience within us the fruit of our redemption"[106] in a more efficacious manner. For this reason the Council of Trent, reechoing, as it were, the invitation of Christ and His immaculate Spouse, has earnestly exhorted "the faithful when they attend Mass to communicate not only by a spiritual communion but also by a sacramental one, so that they may obtain more abundant fruit from this most holy sacrifice."[107] Moreover, our predecessor of immortal memory, Benedict XIV, wishing to emphasize and throw fuller light upon the truth that the faithful by receiving the Holy Eucharist become partakers of the divine sacrifice itself, praises the devotion of those who, when attending Mass, not only elicit a desire to receive holy communion but also want to be nourished by hosts consecrated during the Mass, even though, as he himself states, they really and truly take part in the sacrifice should they receive a host which has been duly consecrated at a previous Mass. He writes as follows: "And although in addition to those to whom the celebrant gives a portion of the Victim he himself has offered in the Mass, they also participate in the same sacrifice to whom a priest distributes the Blessed Sacrament that has been reserved; however, the Church has not for this reason ever forbidden, nor does she now forbid, a celebrant to satisfy the piety and just request of those who, when present at Mass, want to become partakers of the same sacrifice, because they likewise offer it after their own manner, nay more, she approves of it and desires that it should not be omitted and would reprehend those priests through whose fault and negligence this participation would be denied to the faithful."[108]

119. May God grant that all accept these invitations of the Church freely and with spontaneity. May he grant that they participate even every day, if possible, in the divine sacrifice, not only in a spiritual manner, but also by reception of the august sacrament, receiving the body of Jesus Christ which has been offered for all to the eternal Father. Arouse Venerable Brethren, in the hearts of those committed to your care, a great and insatiable hunger for Jesus Christ. Under your guidance let the children and youth crowd to the altar rails to offer themselves, their innocence and their works of zeal to the divine Redeemer. Let husbands and wives approach the holy table so that nourished on this food they may learn to make the children entrusted to them conformed to the mind and heart of Jesus Christ.

120. Let the workers be invited to partake of this sustaining and never failing nourishment that it may renew their strength and obtain for their labors an everlasting recompense in heaven; in a word, invite all men of whatever class and compel them to come in;[109] since this is the bread of life which all require. The Church of Jesus Christ needs no other bread than this to satisfy fully our souls' wants and desires, and to unite us in the most intimate union with Jesus Christ, to make us "one body,"[110] to get us to live together as brothers who, breaking the same bread, sit down to the same heavenly table, to partake of the elixir of immortality.[111]

121. Now it is very fitting, as the liturgy otherwise lays down, that the people receive holy communion after the priest has partaken of the divine repast upon the altar; and, as we have written above, they should be commended who, when present at Mass, receive hosts consecrated at the same Mass, so that it is actually verified, "that as many of us, as, at this altar, shall partake of and receive the most holy body and blood of thy Son, may be filled with every heavenly blessing and grace."[112]

122. Still sometimes there may be a reason, and that not infrequently, why holy communion should be distributed before or after Mass and even immediately after the priest receives the sacred species—and even though hosts consecrated at a previous Mass should be used. In these circumstances—as we have stated above—the people duly take part in the eucharistic sacrifice and not seldom they can in this way more conveniently receive holy communion. Still, though the Church with the kind heart of a mother strives to meet the spiritual needs of her children, they, for their part, should not readily neglect the directions of the liturgy and, as often as there is no reasonable difficulty, should aim that all their actions at the altar manifest more clearly the living unity of the Mystical Body.

123. When the Mass, which is subject to special rules of the liturgy, is over, the person who has received holy communion is not thereby freed from his duty of thanksgiving; rather, it is most becoming that, when the Mass is finished, the person who has received the Eucharist should recollect himself, and in intimate union with the divine Master hold loving and fruitful converse with Him. Hence they have departed from the straight way of truth,

who, adhering to the letter rather than the sense, assert and teach that, when Mass has ended, no such thanksgiving should be added, not only because the Mass is itself a thanksgiving, but also because this pertains to a private and personal act of piety and not to the good of the community.

124. But, on the contrary, the very nature of the sacrament demands that its reception should produce rich fruits of Christian sanctity. Admittedly the congregation has been officially dismissed, but each individual, since he is united with Christ, should not interrupt the hymn of praise in his own soul, "always returning thanks for all in the name of our Lord Jesus Christ to God the Father."[113] The sacred liturgy of the Mass also exhorts us to do this when it bids us pray in these words, "Grant, we beseech thee, that we may always continue to offer thanks[114] . . . and may never cease from praising thee."[115] Wherefore, if there is no time when we must not offer God thanks, and if we must never cease from praising Him, who would dare to reprehend or find fault with the Church, because she advises her priests[116] and faithful to converse with the divine Redeemer for at least a short while after holy communion, and inserts in her liturgical books, fitting prayers, enriched with indulgences, by which the sacred ministers may make suitable preparation before Mass and holy communion or may return thanks afterwards? So far is the sacred liturgy from restricting the interior devotion of individual Christians, that it actually fosters and promotes it so that they may be rendered like to Jesus Christ and through Him be brought to the heavenly Father; wherefore this same discipline of the liturgy demands that whoever has partaken of the sacrifice of the altar should return fitting thanks to God. For it is the good pleasure of the divine Redeemer to hearken to us when we pray, to converse with us intimately and to offer us a refuge in His loving Heart.

125. Moreover, such personal colloquies are very necessary that we may all enjoy more fully the supernatural treasures that are contained in the Eucharist and according to our means, share them with others, so that Christ our Lord may exert the greatest possible influence on the souls of all.

126. Why then, Venerable Brethren, should we not approve of those who, when they receive holy communion, remain on in closest familiarity with their divine Redeemer even after the congregation has been officially dismissed, and that not only for the consolation of conversing with Him, but also to render Him due thanks and praise and especially to ask help to defend their souls against anything that may lessen the efficacy of the sacrament and to do everything in their power to cooperate with the action of Christ who is so intimately present. We exhort them to do so in a special manner by carrying out their resolutions, by exercising the Christian virtues, as also by applying to their own necessities the riches they have received with royal Liberality. The author of that golden book The Imitation of Christ certainly speaks in accordance with the letter and the spirit of the liturgy, when he gives the following advice to the person who approaches the altar, "Remain on in secret and take

delight in you God; for He is yours whom the whole world cannot take away from you."[117]

127. Therefore, let us all enter into closest union with Christ and strive to lose ourselves, as it were, in His most holy soul and so be united to Him that we may have a share in those acts with which He adores the Blessed Trinity with a homage that is most acceptable, and by which He offers to the eternal Father supreme praise and thanks which find an harmonious echo throughout the heavens and the earth, according to the words of the prophet, "All ye works of the Lord, bless the Lord."[118] Finally, in union with these sentiments of Christ, let us ask for heavenly aid at that moment in which it is supremely fitting to pray for and obtain help in His name.[119] For it is especially in virtue of these sentiments that we offer and immolate ourselves as a victim, saying, "make of us thy eternal offering."[120]

128. The divine Redeemer is ever repeating His pressing invitation, "Abide in Me."[121] Now by the sacrament of the Eucharist, Christ remains in us and we in Him, and just as Christ, remaining in us, lives and works, so should we remain in Christ and live and work through Him.

129. The Eucharistic Food contains, as all are aware, "truly, really and substantially the Body and Blood together with soul and divinity of our Lord Jesus Christ."[122] It is no wonder, then, that the Church, even from the beginning, adored the body of Christ under the appearance of bread; this is evident from the very rites of the august sacrifice, which prescribe that the sacred ministers should adore the most holy sacrament by genuflecting or by profoundly bowing their heads.

130. The Sacred Councils teach that it is the Church's tradition right from the beginning, to worship "with the same adoration the Word Incarnate as well as His own flesh,"[123] and St. Augustine asserts that, "No one eats that flesh, without first adoring it," while he adds that "not only do we not commit a sin by adoring it, but that we do sin by not adoring it."[124]

131. It is on this doctrinal basis that the cult of adoring the Eucharist was founded and gradually developed as something distinct from the sacrifice of the Mass. The reservation of the sacred species for the sick and those in danger of death introduced the praiseworthy custom of adoring the blessed Sacrament which is reserved in our churches. This practice of adoration, in fact, is based on strong and solid reasons. For the Eucharist is at once a sacrifice and a sacrament; but it differs from the other sacraments in this that it not only produces grace, but contains in a permanent manner the Author of grace Himself. When, therefore, the Church bids us adore Christ hidden behind the eucharistic veils and pray to Him for spiritual and temporal favors, of which we ever stand in need, she manifests living faith in her divine Spouse who is present beneath these veils, she professes her gratitude to Him and she enjoys the intimacy of His friendship.

132. Now, the Church in the course of centuries has introduced various forms of this worship which are ever increasing in beauty and helpfulness: as, for example, visits of devotion to the tabernacles, even every day; benediction of the Blessed Sacrament; solemn processions, especially at the time of Eucharistic Congress, which pass through cities and villages; and adoration of the Blessed Sacrament publicly exposed. Sometimes these public acts of adoration are of short duration. Sometimes they last for one, several and even for forty hours. In certain places they continue in turn in different churches throughout the year, while elsewhere adoration is perpetual day and night, under the care of religious communities, and the faithful quite often take part in them.

133. These exercises of piety have brought a wonderful increase in faith and supernatural life to the Church militant upon earth and they are reechoed to a certain extent by the Church triumphant in heaven which sings continually a hymn of praise to God and to the Lamb "who was slain."[125] Wherefore, the Church not merely approves these pious practices, which in the course of centuries have spread everywhere throughout the world, but makes them her own, as it were, and by her authority commends them.[126] They spring from the inspiration of the liturgy and if they are performed with due propriety and with faith and piety, as the liturgical rules of the Church require, they are undoubtedly of the very greatest assistance in living the life of the liturgy.

134. Nor is it to be admitted that by this Eucharistic cult men falsely confound the historical Christ, as they say, who once lived on earth, with the Christ who is present in the august Sacrament of the altar, and who reigns glorious and triumphant in heaven and bestows supernatural favors. On the contrary, it can be claimed that by this devotion the faithful bear witness to and solemnly avow the faith of the Church that the Word of God is identical with the Son of the Virgin Mary, who suffered on the cross, who is present in a hidden manner in the Eucharist and who reigns upon His heavenly throne. Thus, St. John Chrysostom states: "When you see It [the Body of Christ] exposed, say to yourself: Thanks to this body, I am no longer dust and ashes, I am no more a captive but a freeman: hence I hope to obtain heaven and the good things that are there in store for me, eternal life, the heritage of the angles, companionship with Christ; death has not destroyed this body which was pierced by nails and scourged, . . . this is that body which was once covered with blood, pierced by a lance, from which issued saving fountains upon the world, one of blood and the other of water. . . . This body He gave to us to keep and eat, as a mark of His intense love."[127]

135. That practice in a special manner is to be highly praised according to which many exercises of piety, customary among the faithful, and with benediction of the blessed sacrament. For excellent and of great benefit is that custom which makes the priest raise aloft the Bread of Angels before congregations with heads bowed down in adoration, and forming with It the sign of the cross implores the heavenly Father to deign to look upon His Son who for love of us was nailed to the cross, and for His sake and through Him who willed to be our Redeemer and our brother, be pleased to shower down heavenly favors upon those whom the immaculate blood of the Lamb has redeemed.[128]

136. Strive then, Venerable Brethren, with your customary devoted care so the churches, which the faith and piety of Christian peoples have built in the course of centuries for the purpose of singing a perpetual hymn of glory to God almighty and of providing a worthy abode for our Redeemer concealed beneath the eucharistic species, may be entirely at the disposal of greater numbers of the faithful who, called to the feet of their Savior, hearken to His most consoling invitation, "Come to Me all you who labor and are heavily burdened, and I will refresh you."[129] Let your churches be the house of God where all who enter to implore blessings rejoice in obtaining whatever they ask[130] and find there heavenly consolation.

137. Only thus can it be brought about that the whole human family settling their differences may find peace, and united in mind and heart may sing this song of hope and charity, "Good Pastor, truly bread—Jesus have mercy on us— feed us, protect us—bestow on us the vision of all good things in the land of living."[131]

138. The ideal of Christian life is that each one be united to God in the closest and most intimate manner. For this reason, the worship that the Church renders to God, and which is based especially on the eucharistic sacrifice and the use of the sacraments, is directed and arranged in such a way that it embraces by means of the divine office, the hours of the day, the weeks and the whole cycle of the year, and reaches all the aspects and phases of human life.

139. Since the divine Master commanded "that we ought always to pray and not to faint,"[132] the Church faithfully fulfills this injunction and never ceases to pray: she urges us in the words of the Apostle of the Gentiles, "by him Jesus let us offer the sacrifice of praise always to God."[133]

140. Public and common prayer offered to God by all at the same time was customary in antiquity only on certain days and at certain times. Indeed, people prayed to God not only in groups but in private houses and occasion- ally with neighbors and friends. But soon in different parts of the Christian world the practice arose of setting aside special times for praying, as for example, the last hour of the day when evening set in and the lamps were lighted; or the first, heralded, when the night was coming to an end, by the crowing of the cock and the rising of the morning star. Other times of the day, as being more suitable for prayer are indicated in Sacred Scripture, in Hebrew customs or in keeping with the practice of every-day life. According to the acts of the Apostles, the disciples of Jesus Christ all came together to pray at the third hour, when they were all filled with the Holy Ghost;[134] and before eating, the Prince of the Apostles went up to the higher parts of the

house to pray, about the sixth hour;[135] Peter and John "went up into the Temple at the ninth hour of prayer"[136] and at "midnight Paul and Silas praying . . . praised God."[137]

141. Thanks to the work of the monks and those who practice asceticism, these various prayers in the course of time become ever more perfected and by the authority of the Church are gradually incorporated into the sacred liturgy.

142. The divine office is the prayer of the Mystical Body of Jesus Christ, offered to God in the name and on behalf of all Christians, when recited by priests and other ministers of the Church and by religious who are deputed by the Church for this.

143. The character and value of the divine office may be gathered from the words recommended by the Church to be said before starting the prayers of the office, namely, that they be said "worthily, with attention and devotion."

144. By assuming human nature, the Divine Word introduced into this earthly exile a hymn which is sung in heaven for all eternity. He unites to Himself the whole human race and with it sings this hymn to the praise of God. As we must humbly recognize that "we know not what we should pray for, as we ought, the Spirit Himself asketh for us with unspeakable groanings."[138] Moreover, through His Spirit in us, Christ entreats the Father, "God could not give a greater gift to men. . . . Jesus prays for us, as our Priest; He prays in us as our Head; we pray to Him as our God; . . . we recognize in Him our voice and His voice in us; . . . He is prayed to as God, He prays under the appearance of a servant; in heaven He is Creator; here, created though not changed, He assumes a created nature which is to be changed and makes us with Him one complete man, head and body."[139]

145. To this lofty dignity of the Church's prayer, there should correspond earnest devotion in our souls. For when in prayer the voice repeats those hymns written under the inspiration of the Holy Ghost and extols God's infinite perfections, it is necessary that the interior sentiment of our souls should accompany the voice so as to make those sentiments our own in which we are elevated to heaven, adoring and giving due praise and thanks to the Blessed Trinity; "so let us chant in choir that mind and voice may accord together."[140] It is not merely a question of recitation or of singing which, however perfect according to norms of music and the sacred rites, only reaches the ear, but it is especially a question of the ascent of the mind and heart to God so that, united with Christ, we may completely dedicate ourselves and all our actions to Him.

146. On this depends in no small way the efficacy of our prayers. These prayers in fact, when they are not addressed directly to the Word made man, conclude with the phrase "though Jesus Christ our Lord." As our Mediator with God, He shows to the heavenly Father His glorified wounds, "always living to make intercessions for us."[141]

147. The Psalms, as all know, form the chief part of the divine office. They encompass the full round of the day and sanctify it. Cassiodorus speaks beautifully about the Psalms as distributed in his day throughout the divine office: "With the celebration of matins they bring a blessing on the coming day, they set aside for us the first hour and consecrate the third hour of the day, they gladden the sixth hour with the breaking of bread, at the ninth they terminate our fast, they bring the evening to a close and at nightfall they shield our minds from darkness."[142]

148. The Psalms recall to mind the truths revealed by God to the chosen people, which were at one time frightening and at another filled with wonderful tenderness; they keep repeating and fostering the hope of the promised Liberator which in ancient times was kept alive with song, either around the hearth or in the stately temple; they show forth in splendid light the prophesied glory of Jesus Christ: first, His supreme and eternal power, then His lowly coming to this terrestrial exile, His kingly dignity and priestly power and, finally, His beneficent labors, and the shedding of His blood for our redemption. In a similar way they express the joy, the bitterness, the hope and fear of our hearts and our desire of loving God and hoping in Him alone, and our mystic ascent to divine tabernacles.

149. "The psalm is . . . a blessing for the people, it is the praise of God, the tribute of the nation, the common language and acclamation of all, it is the voice of the Church, the harmonious confession of faith, signifying deep attachment to authority; it is the joy of freedom, the expression of happiness, an echo of bliss."[143]

150. In an earlier age, these canonical prayers were attended by many of the faithful. But this gradually ceased, and, as We have already said, their recitation at present is the duty only of the clergy and of religious. The laity have no obligation in this matter. Still, it is greatly to be desired that they participate in reciting or chanting vespers sung in their own parish on feast days. We earnestly exhort you, Venerable Brethren, to see that this pious practice is kept up, and that wherever it has ceased you restore it if possible. This, without doubt, will produce salutary results when vespers are conducted in a worthy and fitting manner and with such helps as foster the piety of the faithful. Let the public and private observance of the feasts of the Church, which are in a special way dedicated and consecrated to God, be kept inviolable; and especially the Lord's day which the Apostles, under the guidance of the Holy Ghost, substituted for the Sabbath. Now, if the order was given to the Jews: "Six days shall you do work; in the seventh day is the Sabbath, the rest holy to the Lord. Every one that shall do any work on this day, shall die";[144] how will these Christians not fear spiritual death who perform servile

work on feast-days, and whose rest on these days is not devoted to religion and piety but given over to the allurements of the world? Sundays and holy-days, then, must be made holy by divine worship, which gives homage to God and heavenly food to the soul. Although the Church only commands the faithful to abstain from servile work and attend Mass and does not make it obligatory to attend evening devotions, still she desires this and recommends it repeatedly. Moreover, the needs of each one demand it, seeing that all are bound to win the favor of God if they are to obtain His benefit. Our soul is filled with the greatest grief when We see how the Christian people of today profane the afternoon of feast days; public places of amusement and public games are frequented in great numbers while the churches are not as full as they should be. All should come to our churches and there be taught the truth of the Catholic faith, sing the praises of God, be enriched with benediction of the blessed sacrament given by the priest and be strengthened with help from heaven against the adversities of this life. Let all try to learn those prayers which are recited at vespers and fill their souls with their meaning. When deeply penetrated by these prayers, they will experience what St. Augustine said about himself: "How much did I weep during hymns and verses, greatly moved at the sweet singing of thy Church. Their sound would penetrate my ears and their truth melt my heart, sentiments of piety would well up, tears would flow and that was good for me."[145]

151. Throughout the entire year, the Mass and the divine office center especially around the person of Jesus Christ. This arrangement is so suitably disposed that our Savior dominates the scene in the mysteries of His humilia-tion, of His redemption and triumph.

152. While the sacred liturgy calls to mind the mysteries of Jesus Christ, it strives to make all believers take their part in them so that the divine Head of the mystical Body may live in all the members with the fullness of His holiness. Let the souls of Christians be like altars on each one of which a dif-ferent phase of the sacrifice, offered by the High priest, comes to life again, as it were: pains and tears which wipe away and expiate sin; supplication to God which pierces heaven; dedication and even immolation of oneself made promptly, generously and earnestly; and, finally, that intimate union by which we commit ourselves and all we have to God, in whom we find our rest. "The perfection of religion is to imitate whom you adore."[146]

153. By these suitable ways and methods in which the liturgy at stated times proposes the life of Jesus Christ for our meditation, the Church gives us examples to imitate, points out treasures of sanctity for us to make our own, since it is fitting that the mind believes what the lips sing, and that what the mind believes should be practiced in public and private life.

154. In the period of Advent, for instance, the Church arouses in us the consciousness of the sins we have had the misfortune to commit, and urges

us, by restraining our desires and practicing voluntary mortification of the body, to recollect ourselves in meditation, and experience a longing desire to return to God who alone can free us by His grace from the stain of sin and from its evil consequences.

155. With the coming of the birthday of the Redeemer, she would bring us to the cave of Bethlehem and there teach that we must be born again and undergo a complete reformation; that will only happen when we are intimately and vitally united to the Word of God made man and participate in His divine nature, to which we have been elevated.

156. At the solemnity of the Epiphany, in putting before us the call of the Gentiles to the Christian faith, she wishes us daily to give thanks to the Lord for such a blessing; she wishes us to seek with lively faith the living and true God, to penetrate deeply and religiously the things of heaven, to love silence and meditation in order to perceive and grasp more easily heavenly gifts.

157. During the days of Septuagesima and Lent, our Holy Mother the Church over and over again strives to make each of us seriously consider our misery, so that we may be urged to a practical emendation of our lives, detest our sins heartily and expiate them by prayer and penance. For constant prayer and penance done for past sins obtain for us divine help, without which every work of ours is useless and unavailing.

158. In Holy Week, when the most bitter sufferings of Jesus Christ are put before us by the liturgy, the Church invites us to come to Calvary and follow in the blood-stained footsteps of the divine Redeemer, to carry the cross willingly with Him, to reproduce in our own hearts His spirit of expiation and atonement, and to die together with Him.

159. At the Paschal season, which commemorates the triumph of Christ, our souls are filled with deep interior joy: we, accordingly, should also consider that we must rise, in union with the Redeemer, from our cold and slothful life to one of greater fervor and holiness by giving ourselves completely and generously to God, and by forgetting this wretched world in order to aspire only to the things of heaven: "If you be risen with Christ, seek the things that are above . . . mind the things that are above."[147]

160. Finally, during the time of Pentecost, the Church by her precept and practice urges us to be more docile to the action of the Holy Spirit who wishes us to be on fire with divine love so that we may daily strive to advance more in virtue and thus become holy as Christ our Lord and His Father are holy.

161. Thus, the liturgical year should be considered as a splendid hymn of praise offered to the heavenly Father by the Christian family through Jesus, their perpetual Mediator. Nevertheless, it requires a diligent and well ordered study on our part to be able to know and praise our Redeemer ever more and more. It requires a serious effort and constant practice to imitate His

mysteries, to enter willingly upon His path of sorrow and thus finally share His glory and eternal happiness.

162. From what We have already explained, Venerable Brethren, it is perfectly clear how much modern writers are wanting in the genuine and true liturgical spirit who, deceived by the illusion of a higher mysticism, dare to assert that attention should be paid not to the historic Christ but to a "pneumatic" or glorified Christ. They do not hesitate to assert that a change has taken place in the piety of the faithful by dethroning, as it were, Christ from His position; since they say that the glorified Christ, who liveth and reigneth forever and sitteth at the right hand of the Father, has been overshadowed and in His place has been substituted that Christ who lived on earth. For this reason, some have gone so far as to want to remove from the churches images of the divine Redeemer suffering on the cross.

163. But these false statements are completely opposed to the solid doctrine handed down by tradition. "You believe in Christ born in the flesh," says St. Augustine, "and you will come to Christ begotten of God."[148] In the sacred liturgy, the whole Christ is proposed to us in all the circumstances of His life, as the Word of the eternal Father, as born of the Virgin Mother of God, as He who teaches us truth, heals the sick, consoles the afflicted, who endures suffering and who dies; finally, as He who rose triumphantly from the dead and who, reigning in the glory of heaven, sends us the Holy Paraclete and who abides in His Church forever; "Jesus Christ, yesterday and today, and the same forever."[149] Besides, the liturgy shows us Christ not only as a model to be imitated but as a master to whom we should listen readily, a Shepherd whom we should follow, Author of our salvation, the Source of our holiness and the Head of the Mystical Body whose members we are, living by His very life.

164. Since His bitter sufferings constitute the principal mystery of our redemption, it is only fitting that the Catholic faith should give it the greatest prominence. This mystery is the very center of divine worship since the Mass represents and renews it every day and since all the sacraments are most closely united with the cross.[150]

165. Hence, the liturgical year, devotedly fostered and accompanied by the Church, is not a cold and lifeless representation of the events of the past, or a simple and bare record of a former age. It is rather Christ Himself who is ever living in His Church. Here He continues that journey of immense mercy which He lovingly began in His mortal life, going about doing good,[151] with the design of bringing men to know His mysteries and in a way live by them. These mysteries are ever present and active not in a vague and uncertain way as some modern writers hold, but in the way that Catholic doctrine teaches us. According to the Doctors of the Church, they are shining examples of Christian perfection, as well as sources of divine grace, due to the merit and prayers of Christ; they still influence us because each mystery brings its own special grace for our salvation. Moreover, our holy Mother the Church, while proposing for our contemplation the mysteries of our Redeemer, asks in her prayers for those gifts which would give her children the greatest possible share in the spirit of these mysteries through the merits of Christ. By means of His inspiration and help and through the cooperation of our wills we can receive from Him living vitality as branches do from the tree and members from the head; thus slowly and laboriously we can transform ourselves "unto the measure of the age of the fullness of Christ."[152]

166. In the course of the liturgical year, besides the mysteries of Jesus Christ, the feasts of the saints are celebrated. Even though these feasts are of a lower and subordinate order, the Church always strives to put before the faithful examples of sanctity in order to move them to cultivate in themselves the virtues of the divine Redeemer.

167. We should imitate the virtues of the saints just as they imitated Christ, for in their virtues there shines forth under different aspects the splendor of Jesus Christ. Among some of these saints the zeal of the apostolate stood out, in others courage prevailed even to the shedding of blood, constant vigilance marked others out as they kept watch for the divine Redeemer, while in others the virginal purity of soul was resplendent and their modesty revealed the beauty of Christian humility; there burned in all of them the fire of charity towards God and their neighbor. The sacred liturgy puts all these gems of sanctity before us so that we may consider them for our salvation, and "rejoicing at their merits, we may be inflamed by their example."[153] It is necessary, then, to practice "in simplicity innocence, in charity concord, in humility modesty, diligence in government, readiness in helping those who labor, mercy in serving the poor, in defending truth, constancy, in the strict maintenance of discipline justice, so that nothing may be wanting in us of the virtues which have been proposed for our imitation. These are the footprints left by the saints in their journey homeward, that guided by them we might follow them into glory."[154] In order that we may be helped by our senses, also, the Church wishes that images of the saints be displayed in our churches, always, however, with the same intention "that we imitate the virtues of those whose images we venerate."[155]

168. But there is another reason why the Christian people should honor the saints in heaven, namely, to implore their help and "that we be aided by the pleadings of those whose praise is our delight."[156] Hence, it is easy to understand why the sacred liturgy provides us with many different prayers to invoke the intercession of the saints.

169. Among the saints in heaven the Virgin Mary Mother of God is venerated in a special way. Because of the mission she received from God, her life is most closely linked with the mysteries of Jesus Christ, and there is no one

who has followed in the footsteps of the Incarnate Word more closely and with more merit than she: and no one has more grace and power over the most Sacred Heart of the Son of God and through Him with the Heavenly Father. Holier than the Cherubim and Seraphim, she enjoys unquestionably greater glory than all the other saints, for she is "full of grace,"[157] she is the Mother of God, who happily gave birth to the Redeemer for us. Since she is therefore, "Mother of mercy, our life, our sweetness and our hope," let us all cry to her "mourning and weeping in this vale of tears,"[158] and confidently place ourselves and all we have under her patronage. She became our Mother also when the divine Redeemer offered the sacrifice of Himself; and hence by this title also, we are her children. She teaches us all the virtues; she gives us her Son and with Him all the help we need, for God "wished us to have everything through Mary."[159]

170. Throughout this liturgical journey which begins anew for us each year under the sanctifying action of the Church, and strengthened by the help and example of the saints, especially of the Immaculate Virgin Mary, "let us draw near with a true heart, in fullness of faith having our hearts sprinkled from an evil conscience, and our bodies washed with clean water,"[160] let us draw near to the "High Priest"[161] that with Him we may share His life and sentiments and by Him penetrate "even within the veil,"[162] and there honor the heavenly Father for ever and ever.

171. Such is the nature and the object of the sacred liturgy: it treats of the Mass, the sacraments, the divine office; it aims at uniting our souls with Christ and sanctifying them through the divine Redeemer in order that Christ be honored and, through Him and in Him, the most Holy Trinity, Glory be to the Father and to the Son and to the Holy Ghost.

172. In order that the errors and inaccuracies, mentioned above, may be more easily removed from the Church, and that the faithful following safer norms may be able to use more fruitfully the liturgical apostolate, We have deemed it opportune, Venerable Brethren, to add some practical applications of the doctrine which We have explained.

173. When dealing with genuine and solid piety We stated that there could be no real opposition between the sacred liturgy and other religious practices, provided they be kept within legitimate bounds and performed for a legitimate purpose. In fact, there are certain exercises of piety which the Church recommends very much to clergy and religious.

174. It is Our wish also that the faithful, as well, should take part in these practices. The chief of these are: meditation on spiritual things, diligent examination of conscience, enclosed retreats, visits to the blessed sacrament, and those special prayers in honor of the Blessed Virgin Mary among which the rosary, as all know, has pride of place.[163]

175. From these multiple forms of piety, the inspiration and action of the Holy Spirit cannot be absent. Their purpose is, in various ways, to attract and direct our souls to God, purifying them from their sins, encouraging them to practice virtue and, finally, stimulating them to advance along the path of sincere piety by accustoming them to meditate on the eternal truths and disposing them better to contemplate the mysteries of the human and divine natures of Christ. Besides, since they develop a deeper spiritual life of the faithful, they prepare them to take part in sacred public functions with greater fruit, and they lessen the danger of liturgical prayers becoming an empty ritualism.

176. In keeping with your pastoral solitude, Venerable Brethren, do not cease to recommend and encourage these exercises of piety from which the faithful, entrusted to your care, cannot but derive salutary fruit. Above all, do not allow—as some do, who are deceived under the pretext of restoring the liturgy or who idly claim that only liturgical rites are of any real value and dignity— that churches be closed during the hours not appointed for public functions, as has already happened in some places: where the adoration of the august sacrament and visits to our Lord in the tabernacles are neglected; where confession of devotions is discouraged; and devotion to the Virgin Mother of God, a sign of "predestination" according to the opinion of holy men, is so neglected, especially among the young, as to fade away and gradually vanish. Such conduct most harmful to Christian piety is like poisonous fruit, growing on the infected branches of a healthy tree, which must be cut off so that the life-giving sap of the tree may bring forth only the best fruit.

177. Since the opinions expressed by some about frequent confession are completely foreign to the spirit of Christ and His Immaculate Spouse and are also most dangerous to the spiritual life, let Us call to mind what with sorrow We wrote about this point in the encyclical on the Mystical Body. We urgently insist once more that what We expounded in very serious words be proposed by you for the serious consideration and dutiful obedience of your flock, especially to students for the priesthood and young clergy.

178. Take special care that as many as possible, not only of the clergy but of the laity and especially those in religious organizations and in the ranks of Catholic Action, take part in monthly days of recollection and in retreats of longer duration made with a view to growing in virtue. As We have previously stated, such spiritual exercises are most useful and even necessary to instill into souls solid virtue, and to strengthen them in sanctity so as to be able to derive from the sacred liturgy more efficacious and abundant benefits.

179. As regards the different methods employed in these exercises, it is perfectly clear to all that in the Church on earth, no less in the Church in heaven, there are many mansions,[164] and that asceticism cannot be the monopoly of anyone. It is the same spirit who breatheth where He will,[165] and who with differing gifts and in different ways enlightens and guides souls to sanctity.

Let their freedom and the supernatural action of the Holy Spirit be so sacrosanct that no one presume to disturb or stifle them for any reason whatsoever.

180. However, it is well known that the spiritual exercise according to the method and norms of St. Ignatius have been fully approved and earnestly recommended by Our predecessors on account of their admirable efficacy. We, too, for the same reason have approved and commended them and willingly do We repeat this now.

181. Any inspiration to follow and practice extraordinary exercises of piety must most certainly come from the Father of Lights, from whom every good and perfect gift descends;[166] and, of course, the criterion of this will be the effectiveness of these exercises in making the divine cult loved and spread daily ever more widely, and in making the faithful approach the sacraments with more longing desire, and in obtaining for all things holy due respect and honor. If on the contrary, they are an obstacle to principles and norms of divine worship, or if they oppose or hinder them, one must surely conclude that they are not in keeping with prudence and enlightened zeal.

182. There are, besides, other exercises of piety which, although not strictly belonging to the sacred liturgy, are, nevertheless, of special import and dignity, and may be considered in a certain way to be an addition to the liturgical cult; they have been approved and praised over and over again by the Apostolic See and by the bishops. Among these are the prayers usually said during the month of May in honor of the Blessed Virgin Mother of God, or during the month of June to the most Sacred Heart of Jesus: also novenas and triduums, stations of the cross and other similar practices.

183. These devotions make us partakers in a salutary manner of the liturgical cult, because they urge the faithful to go frequently to the sacrament of penance, to attend Mass and receive communion with devotion, and, as well, encourage them to meditate on the mysteries of our redemption and imitate the example of the saints.

184. Hence, he would do something very wrong and dangerous who would dare to take on himself to reform all these exercises of piety and reduce them completely to the methods and norms of liturgical rites. However, it is necessary that the spirit of the sacred liturgy and its directives should exercise such a salutary influence on them that nothing improper be introduced nor anything unworthy of the dignity of the house of God or detrimental to the sacred functions or opposed to solid piety.

185. Take care then, Venerable Brethren, that this true and solid piety increases daily and more under your guidance and bears more abundant fruit. Above all, do not cease to inculcate into the minds of all that progress in the Christian life does not consist in the multiplicity and variety of prayers and exercises of piety, but rather in their helpfulness towards spiritual progress of the faithful and constant growth of the Church universal. For the eternal Father "chose us in Him [Christ] before the foundation of the world that we should be holy and unspotted in His sight."[167] All our prayers, then, and all our religious practices should aim at directing our spiritual energies towards attaining this most noble and lofty end.

186. We earnestly exhort you, Venerable Brethren, that after errors and falsehoods have been removed, and anything that is contrary to truth or moderation has been condemned, you promote a deeper knowledge among the people of the sacred liturgy so that they more readily and easily follow the sacred rites and take part in them with true Christian dispositions.

187. First of all, you must strive that with due reverence and faith all obey the decrees of the Council of Trent, of the Roman Pontiffs, and the Sacred Congregation of Rites, and what the liturgical books ordain concerning external public worship.

188. Three characteristics of which Our predecessor Pius X spoke should adorn all liturgical services: sacredness, which abhors any profane influence; nobility, which true and genuine arts should serve and foster; and universality, which, while safeguarding local and legitimate custom, reveals the catholic unity of the Church.[168]

189. We desire to commend and urge the adornment of churches and altars. Let each one feel moved by the inspired word, "the zeal of thy house hath eaten me up";[169] and strive as much as in him lies that everything in the church, including vestments and liturgical furnishings, even though not rich or lavish, be perfectly clean and appropriate, since all is consecrated to the Divine Majesty. If we have previously disapproved of the error of those who would wish to outlaw images from churches on the plea of reviving an ancient tradition, We now deem it Our duty to censure the inconsiderate zeal of those who propose for veneration in the Churches and on the altars, without any just reason, a multitude of sacred images and statues, and also those who display unauthorized relics, those who emphasize special and insignificant practices, neglecting essential and necessary things. They thus bring religion into derision and lessen the dignity of worship.

190. Let us recall, as well, the decree about "not introducing new forms of worship and devotion."[170] We commend the exact observance of this decree to your vigilance.

191. As regards music, let the clear and guiding norms of the Apostolic See be scrupulously observed. Gregorian chant, which the Roman Church considers her own as handed down from antiquity and kept under her close tutelage, is proposed to the faithful as belonging to them also. In certain parts of the liturgy the Church definitely prescribes it;[171] it makes the celebration of the sacred mysteries not only more dignified and solemn but helps very

much to increase the faith and devotion of the congregation. For this reason, Our predecessors of immortal memory, Pius X and Pius XI, decree—and We are happy to confirm with Our authority the norms laid down by them— that in seminaries and religious institutes, Gregorian chant be diligently and zealously promoted, and moreover that the old Scholae Cantorum be restored, at least in the principal churches. This has already been done with happy results in not a few places.[172]

192. Besides, "so that the faithful take a more active part in divine worship, let Gregorian chant be restored to popular use in the parts proper to the people. Indeed it is very necessary that the faithful attend the sacred cere-monies not as if they were outsiders or mute onlookers, but let them fully appreciate the beauty of the liturgy and take part in the sacred ceremonies, alternating their voices with the priest and the choir, according to the pre-scribed norms. If, please God, this is done, it will not happen that the congre-gation hardly ever or only in a low murmur answer the prayers in Latin or in the vernacular."[173] A congregation that is devoutly present at the sacrifice, in which our Savior together with His children redeemed with His sacred blood sings the nuptial hymn of His immense love, cannot keep silent, for "song befits the lover"[174] and, as the ancient saying has it, "he who sings well prays twice." Thus the Church militant, faithful as well as clergy, joins in the hymns of the Church triumphant and with the choirs of angels, and, all together, sing a wondrous and eternal hymn of praise to the most Holy Trinity in keeping with words of the preface, "with whom our voices, too, thou wouldst bid to be admitted."[175]

193. It cannot be said that modern music and singing should be entirely excluded from Catholic worship. For, if they are not profane nor unbecoming to the sacredness of the place and function, and do not spring from a desire of achieving extraordinary and unusual effects, then our churches must admit them since they can contribute in no small way to the splendor of the sacred ceremonies, can lift the mind to higher things and foster true devotion of soul.

194. We also exhort you, Venerable Brethren, to promote with care congre-gational singing, and to see to its accurate execution with all due dignity, since it easily stirs up and arouses the faith and piety of large gatherings of the faithful. Let the full harmonious singing of our people rise to heaven like the bursting of a thunderous sea[176] and let them testify by the melody of their song to the unity of their hearts and minds[177], as becomes brothers and the children of the same Father.

195. What We have said about music applies to the other fine arts, especially to architecture, sculpture and painting. Recent works of art which lend themselves to the materials of modern composition, should not be universally despised and rejected through prejudice. Modern art should be given free

scope in the due and reverent service of the church and the sacred rites, provided that they preserve a correct balance between styles tending neither to extreme realism nor to excessive "symbolism," and that the needs of the Christian community are taken into consideration rather than the particular taste or talent of the individual artist. Thus modern art will be able to join its voice to that wonderful choir of praise to which have contributed, in honor of the Catholic faith, the greatest artists throughout the centuries. Nevertheless, in keeping with the duty of Our office, We cannot help deploring and condemning those works of art, recently introduced by some, which seem to be a distortion and perversion of true art and which at times openly shock Christian taste, modesty and devotion, and shamefully offend the true religious sense. These must be entirely excluded and banished from our churches, like "anything else that is not in keeping with the sanctity of the place."[178]

196. Keeping in mind, Venerable Brethren, pontifical norms and decrees, take great care to enlighten and direct the minds and hearts of the artists to whom is given the task today of restoring or rebuilding the many churches which have been ruined or completely destroyed by war. Let them be capable and willing to draw their inspiration from religion to express what is suitable and more in keeping with the requirements of worship. Thus the human arts will shine forth with a wondrous heavenly splendor, and contribute greatly to human civilization, to the salvation of souls and the glory of God. The fine arts are really in conformity with religion when "as noblest handmaids they are at the service of divine worship."[179]

197. But there is something else of even greater importance, Venerable Brethren, which We commend to your apostolic zeal, in a very special manner. Whatever pertains to the external worship has assuredly its importance; however, the most pressing duty of Christians is to live the liturgical life, and increase and cherish its supernatural spirit.

198. Readily provide the young clerical student with facilities to understand the sacred ceremonies, to appreciate their majesty and beauty and to learn the rubrics with care, just as you do when he is trained in ascetics, in dogma and in a canon law and pastoral theology. This should not be done merely for cultural reasons and to fit the student to perform religious rites in the future, correctly and with due dignity, but especially to lead him into closest union with Christ, the Priest, so that he may become a holy minister of sanctity.

199. Try in every way, with the means and helps that your prudence deems best, that the clergy and people become one in mind and heart, and that the Christian people take such an active part in the liturgy that it becomes a truly sacred action of due worship to the eternal Lord in which the priest, chiefly responsible for the souls of his parish, and the ordinary faithful are united together.

200. To attain this purpose, it will greatly help to select carefully good and upright young boys from all classes of citizens who will come generously and spontaneously to serve at the altar with careful zeal and exactness. Parents of higher social standing and culture should greatly esteem this office for their children. If these youths, under the watchful guidance of the priests, are properly trained and encouraged to fulfill the task committed to them punctually, reverently and constantly, then from their number will readily come fresh candidates for the priesthood. The clergy will not then complain—as, alas, sometimes happens even in Catholic places—that in the celebration of the august sacrifice they find no one to answer or serve them.

201. Above all, try with your constant zeal to have all the faithful attend the eucharistic sacrifice from which they may obtain abundant and salutary fruit; and carefully instruct them in all the legitimate ways we have described above so that they may devoutly participate in it. The Mass is the chief act of divine worship; it should also be the source and center of Christian piety. Never think that you have satisfied your apostolic zeal until you see your faithful approach in great numbers the celestial banquet which is a sacrament of devotion, a sign of unity and a bond of love.[180]

202. By means of suitable sermons and particularly by periodic conferences and lectures, by special study weeks and the like, teach the Christian people carefully about the treasures of piety contained in the sacred liturgy so that they may be able to profit more abundantly by these supernatural gifts. In this matter, those who are active in the ranks of Catholic Action will certainly be a help to you, since they are ever at the service of the hierarchy in the work of promoting the kingdom of Jesus Christ.

203. But in all these matters, it is essential that you watch vigilantly lest the enemy come into the field of the Lord and sow cockle among the wheat;[181] in other words, do not let your flocks be deceived by the subtle and dangerous errors of false mysticism or quietism—as you know We have already condemned these errors;[182] also do not let a certain dangerous "humanism" lead them astray, nor let there be introduced a false doctrine destroying the notion of Catholic faith, nor finally an exaggerated zeal for antiquity in matters liturgical. Watch with like diligence lest the false teaching of those be propagated who wrongly think and teach that the glorified human nature of Christ really and continually dwells in the "just" by His presence and that one and numerically the same grace, as they say, unites Christ with the members of His Mystical Body.

204. Never be discouraged by the difficulties that arise, and never let your pastoral zeal grow cold. "Blow the trumpet in Sion, . . . call an assembly, gather together the people, sanctify the Church, assemble the ancients, gather together the little ones, and them that suck at the breasts,"[183] and use every help to get the faithful everywhere to fill the churches and crowd around the altars so that they may be restored by the graces of the sacraments and joined as living members to their divine Head, and with Him and through Him celebrate together the august sacrifice that gives due tribute of praise to the Eternal Father.

205. These, Venerable Brethren, are the subjects We desired to write to you about. We are moved to write that your children, who are also Ours, may more fully understand and appreciate the most precious treasures which are contained in the sacred liturgy: namely, the eucharistic sacrifice, representing and renewing the sacrifice of the cross, the sacraments which are the streams of divine grace and of divine life, and the hymn of praise, which heaven and earth daily offer to God.

206. We cherish the hope that these Our exhortations will not only arouse the sluggish and recalcitrant to a deeper and more correct study of the liturgy, but also instill into their daily lives its supernatural spirit according to the words of the Apostle, "extinguish not the spirit."[184]

207. To those whom an excessive zeal occasionally led to say and do certain things which saddened Us and which We could not approve, we repeat the warning of St. Paul, "But prove all things, hold fast that which is good."[185] Let Us paternally warn them to imitate in their thoughts and actions the Christian doctrine which is in harmony with the precepts of the immaculate Spouse of Jesus Christ, the mother of saints.

208. Let Us remind all that they must generously and faithfully obey their holy pastors who possess the right and duty of regulating the whole life, especially the spiritual life, of the Church. "Obey your prelates and be subject to them. For they watch as being to render an account of your souls; that they may do this with joy and not with grief."[186]

209. May God, whom we worship, and who is "not the God of dissension but of peace,"[187] graciously grant to us all that during our earthly exile we may with one mind and one heart participate in the sacred liturgy which is, as it were, a preparation and a token of that heavenly liturgy in which we hope one day to sing together with the most glorious Mother of God and our most loving Mother, "To Him that sitteth on the throne, and to the Lamb, benediction and honor, and glory and power for ever and ever."[188]

210. In this joyous hope, We most lovingly impart to each and every one of you, Venerable Brethren, and to the flocks confided to your care, as a pledge of divine gifts and as a witness of Our special love, the apostolic benediction.

211. Given at Castel Gandolfo, near Rome, on the 20th day of November in the year 1947, the 9th of Our Pontificate.

---

1. 1 Tim. 2:5.

2. Cf. Heb. 4:14.

3. Cf. Heb. 9:14.

4. Cf. Mal. 1:11.

5. Cf. Council of Trent, sess. 22, c. 1.

6. Cf. ibid., c. 2.

7. Encyclical Letter *Caritate Christi*, May 3, 1932.

8. Cf. Apostolic Letter (Motu Proprio) *In cotidianis precibus*, March 24, 1945.

9. 1 Cor. 10:17.

10. Saint Thomas, *Summa Theologica*, IIa IIae, q. 81, art. 1.

11. Cf. Book of Leviticus.

12. Cf. Heb. 10:1.

13. John, 1:14.

14. Heb. 10:5–7.

15. Ibid. 10:10.

16. John, 1:9.

17. Heb. 10:39.

18. Cf. 1 John, 2:1.

19. Cf. 1 Tim. 3:15.

20. Cf. Boniface IX, *Ab origine mundi*, October 7, 1391; Callistus III, *Summus Pontifex*, January 1, 1456; Pius II, *Triumphans Pastor*, April 22, 1459; Innocent XI, *Triumphans Pastor*, October 3, 1678.

21. Eph. 2:19–22.

22. Matt. 18:20.

23. Acts, 2:42.

24. Col. 3:16.

25. Saint Augustine, Epist. 130, *ad Probam*, 18.

26. Roman Missal, Preface for Christmas.

27. Giovanni Cardinal Bona, *De divina psalmodia*, c. 19, par. 3, 1.

28. Roman Missal, Secret for Thursday after the Second Sunday of Lent.

29. Cf. Mark, 7:6 and Isaiah, 29:13.

30. 1 Cor. 11:28.

31. Roman Missal, Ash Wednesday; Prayer after the imposition of ashes.

32. *De praedestinatione sanctorum,* 31.

33. Cf. Saint Thomas, *Summa Theologica,* IIa IIae, q. 82, art. 1.

34. Cf. 1 Cor. 3:23.

35. Heb. 10:19–24.

36. Cf. 2 Cor. 6:1.

37. Cf. Code of Canon Law, can. 125, 126, 565, 571, 595, 1367.

38. Col. 3:11.

39. Cf. Gal. 4:19.

40. John, 20:21.

41. Luke, 10:16.

42. Mark, 16:15–16.

43. Roman Pontifical, Ordination of a priest: anointing of hands.

44. Enchiridion, c. 3.

45. *De gratia Dei "Indiculus."*

46. Saint Augustine, Epist. 130, *ad Probam,* 18.

47. Cf. *Constitution Divini cultus,* December 20, 1928.

48. *Constitution Immensa,* January 22, 1588.

49. Code of Canon Law, can. 253.

50. Cf. Code of Canon Law, can. 1257.

51. Cf. Code of Canon Law, can. 1261.

52. Cf. Matt. 28:20.

53. Cf. Pius VI, *Constitution Auctorem fidei,* August 28, 1794, nn. 31–34, 39, 62, 66, 69–74.

54. Cf. John, 21:15–17.

55. Acts, 20:28.

56. Ps. 109:4.

57. John, 13:1.

58. Council of Trent, sess. 22, c. 1.

59. Ibid., c. 2.

60. Cf. Saint Thomas, *Summa Theologica,* IIIa, q. 22, art. 4.

61. Saint John Chrysostom, In Joann. Hom., 86:4.

62. Rom. 6:9.

63. Cf. Roman Missal, Preface.

64. Cf. Ibid., Canon.

65. Mark, 14:23.

66. Roman Missal, Preface.

67. 1 John, 2:2.

68. Roman Missal, Canon of the Mass.

69. Saint Augustine, *De Trinit.,* Book XIII, c. 19.

70. Heb. 5:7.

71. Cf. sess. 22, c. 1.

72. Cf. Heb. 10:14.

73. Saint Augustine, Enarr. in Ps. 147, n. 16.

74. Gal. 2:19-20.

75. Encyclical Letter *Mystici Corporis,* June 29, 1943.

76. Roman Missal, Secret of the Ninth Sunday after Pentecost.

77. Cf. sess. 22, c. 2. and can. 4.

78. Cf. Gal. 6:14.

79. Mal. 1:11.

80. Phil. 2:5.

81. Gal. 2:19.

82. Cf. Council of Trent, sess. 23. c. 4.

83. Cf. Saint Robert Bellarmine, *De Missa,* 2, c. 4.

84. *De Sacro Altaris Mysterio,* 3:6.

85. *De Missa,* 1, c. 27.

86. Roman Missal, Canon of the Mass.

87. Ibid., Canon of the Mass.

88. Roman Missal, Canon of the Mass.

89. 1 Peter, 2:5.

90. Rom. 12:1.

91. Roman Missal, Canon of the Mass.

92. Roman Pontifical, Ordination of a priest.

93. Ibid., Consecration of an altar, Preface.

94. Cf. Council of Trent, sess. 22, c. 5.

95. Gal. 2:19–20.

96. Cf. Serm. 272.

97. Cf. 1 Cor. 12:7.

98. Cf. Eph. 5:30.

99. Cf. Saint Robert Bellarmine, *De Missa,* 2, c. 8.

100. Cf. *De Civitate Dei,* Book 10, c. 6.

101. Roman Missal, Canon of the Mass.

102. Cf. 1 Tim. 2:5.

103. Encyclical Letter *Certiores effecti,* November 13, 1742, par. 1.

104. Council of Trent, sess. 22, can. 8.

105. 1 Cor. 11:24.

106. Roman Missal, Collect for Feast of Corpus Christi.

107. Sess. 22, c. 6.

108. Encyclical Letter *Certiores effecti,* par. 3.

109. Cf. Luke, 14:23.

110. 1 Cor. 10:17.

111. Cf. Saint Ignatius Martyr, Ad Eph 20.

112. Roman Missal, Canon of the Mass.

113. Eph. 5:20.

114. Roman Missal, Postcommunion for Sunday within the Octave of Ascension.

115. Ibid., Postcommunion for First Sunday after Pentecost.

116. Code of Canon Law, can. 810.

117. Book IV, c. 12.

118. Dan. 3:57.

119. Cf. John 16:3.

120. Roman Missal, Secret for Mass of the Most Blessed Trinity.

121. John, 15:4.

122. Council of Trent, sess. 13, can. 1.

123. Second Council of Constantinople, *Anath, de trib. Capit.*, can. 9; compare Council of Ephesus, Anath. Cyril, can 8. Cf. Council of Trent, sess. 13, can. 6; Pius VI *Constitution Auctorem fidei*, n. 61.

124. Cf. *Enarr. in Ps.* 98:9.

125. Apoc. 5:12, cp. 7:10.

126. Cf. Council of Trent, sess. 13, c. 5 and can. 6.

127. In 1 ad Cor., 24:4.

128. Cf. 1 Peter, 1:19.

129. Matt. 11:28.

130. Cf. Roman Missal, Collect for Mass for the Dedication of a Church.

131. Roman Missal, Sequence Lauda Sion in Mass for Feast of Corpus Christi.

132. Luke, 18:1.

133. Heb. 13:15.

134. Cf. Acts, 2:1-15.

135. Ibid., 10:9.

136. Ibid., 3:1.

137. Ibid., 16:25.

138. Rom. 8:26.

139. Saint Augustine, *Enarr. in Ps.* 85, n. 1.

140. Saint Benedict, *Regula Monachorum*, c. 19.

141. Heb. 7:25.

142. *Explicatio in Psalterium,* Preface. Text as found in Migne, Parres Larini, 70:10. But some are of the opinion that part of this passage should not be attributed to Cassiodorus.

143. Saint Ambrose, *Enarr in Ps.* 1, n. 9.

144. Exod. 31:15.

145. Confessions, Book 9, c. 6.

146. Saint Augustine, De Civitate Dei, Book 8, c. 17.

147. Col. 3:1–2.

148. Saint Augustine, *Enarr. in Ps.* 123, n. 2.

149. Heb. 13:8.

150. Saint Thomas, Summa Theologica, IIIa, q. 49 and q. 62, art. 5.

151. Cf. Acts, 10:38.

152. Eph. 4:13.

153. Roman Missal, Collect for Third Mass of Several Martyrs outside Paschaltide.

154. Saint Bede the Venerable, *Hom. subd.* 70 for Feast of All Saints.

155. Roman Missal, Collect for Mass of Saint John Damascene.

156. Saint Bernard, Sermon 2 for Feast of All Saints.

157. Luke, 1:28.

158. *"Salve Regina."*

159. Saint Bernard, *In Nativ.* B.M.V., 7.

160. Heb. 10:22.

161. Ibid., 10:1.

162. Ibid., 6:19.

163. Cf. Code of Canon Law, Can. 125.

164. Cf. John, 14:2.

165. John, 3:8.

166. Cf. James, 1:17.

167. Eph. 1:4.

168. Cf. Apostolic Letter (Motu Proprio) *Tra le sollecitudini,* November 22, 1903.

169. Ps. 68:9; John, 2:17.

170. Supreme Sacred Congregation of the Holy Office, Decree of May 26, 1937.

171. Cf. Pius X, Apostolic Letter (Motu Proprio) *Tra le sollecitudini.*

172. Cf. Pius X, loc. cit.; Pius XI, *Constitution Divini cultus,* 2, 5.

173. Pius XI, *Constitution Divini cultus,* 9.

174. Saint Augustine, Serm. 336, n. 1.

175. Roman Missal, Preface.

176. Saint Ambrose, *Hexameron,* 3:5, 23.

177. Cf. Acts, 4:32.

178. Code of Canon Law, can. 1178.

179. Pius XI, Constitution *Divini cultus.*

180. Cf. Saint Augustine, Tract. 26 in John 13.

181. Cf. Matt. 13:24–25.

182. Encyclical letter *Mystici Corporis.*

183. Joel, 2:15–16.

184. 1 Thess. 5:19.

185. Ibid., 5:21.

186. Heb. 13:7.

187. 1 Cor. 14:33.

188. Apoc. 5:13.

About the Liturgical Institute

The Liturgical Institute, founded in 2000 by His Eminence Francis Cardinal George of Chicago, offers a variety of options for education in liturgical studies. A unified, rites-based core curriculum constitutes the foundation of the program, providing integrated and balanced studies toward the advancement of the renewal promoted by the Second Vatican Council. The musical, artistic, and architectural dimensions of worship are given particular emphasis in the curriculum. Institute students are encouraged to participate in its "liturgical heart" of daily Mass and Morning and Evening Prayer. The academic program of the institute serves a diverse, international student population—laity, religious, and clergy—who are preparing for service in parishes, dioceses, and religious communities. Personalized mentoring is provided in view of each student's ministerial and professional goals.

The institute is housed on the campus of the University of St. Mary of the Lake/Mundelein Seminary, which offers the largest priestly formation program in the United States and is the center of the permanent diaconate and lay ministry training programs of the Archdiocese of Chicago. In addition, the university has the distinction of being the first chartered institution of higher learning in Chicago (1844), and one of only seven pontifical faculties in North America.

For more information about the Liturgical Institute and its programs, contact usml.edu/liturgicalinstitute; phone: 847-837-4542; e-mail: dmcnamara@usml.edu.

Msgr. Reynold Hillenbrand
1904-1979

Monsignor Reynold Hillenbrand, ordained a priest
by Cardinal George Mundelein in 1929, was Rector
of St. Mary of the Lake Seminary from 1936 to 1944.

He was a leading figure in the liturgical and social
action movement in the United States during the
1930s and worked to promote active, intelligent,
and informed participation in the Church's liturgy.

He believed that a reconstruction of society would
occur as a result of the renewal of the Christian
spirit, whose source and center is the liturgy.

Hillenbrand taught that, since the ultimate purpose
of Catholic action is to Christianize society, the
renewal of the liturgy must undoubtedly play the
key role in achieving this goal.

Hillenbrand Books strives to reflect the spirit of
Monsignor Reynold Hillenbrand's pioneering work
by making available innovative and scholarly
resources that advance the liturgical and sacramental
life of the Church.